Me Time Monday

The Weekly Wellness Plan
to Find Balance and Joy for a Busy Life

First Edition

This book is written as a source of information only. The information contained in this book should by no means be considered a substitute for the advice, decisions, or judgment of the reader's financial, legal, medical or other professional advice.

All efforts have been made to ensure the accuracy of the information contained in this book as of the date published. The author and the publisher expressly disclaim responsibility for any adverse effects arising from the use or application of the information contained herein.

All brand or other names are trademarks, service marks or registered trademarks of their respective parties.

Library of Congress Cataloging-in-Publication Data
Snelling, Sherri

Me Time Monday – The Weekly Wellness Plan to Find Balance and Joy for a Busy Life – 1st ed.

Copyright © 2023 Sherri Snelling.

All rights reserved. No part of this book may be used or reproduced by any means, graphic, electronic, or mechanical, including photocopying, recording, taping or by any information storage retrieval system without the written permission of the author except in the case of brief quotations embodied in critical articles and reviews.

Because of the dynamic nature of the Internet, any web addresses or links contained in this book may have changed since publication and may no longer be valid. The views expressed in this work are solely those of the author and do not necessarily reflect the views of the publisher, and the publisher hereby disclaims any responsibility for them.

ISBN: 979-8-9886372-0-2 (hc)
ISBN: 979-8-9886372-1-9 (e)

Library of Congress Control Number: 2023912184

rev. date: 07/31/2023

LUCKENBOOTH PRESS

The Weekly Wellness Plan
to Find Balance and Joy for a Busy Life

Me Time Monday

Sherri Snelling

LUCKENBOOTH PRESS

Also by Sherri Snelling

*A Cast of Caregivers – Celebrity Stories
to Help You Prepare to Care*

To my Mom who taught me to be happy
and curious and kind.
To my Grandma Ruth who loved to laugh
and was a great writer who inspired me.
To Brent who always has my back and is
my shelter in the storm.
To my family and many dear friends who help make
my life wonderful.

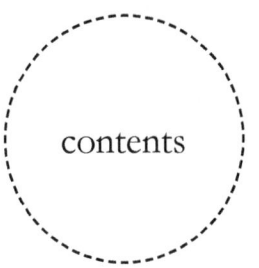

contents

introduction ix

PART 1
THE CAREGIVER WELLNESS JOURNEY

chapter 1	The Seven A's of Caregiving.. 4
chapter 2	Caregiving Redefined 7
chapter 3	Avoiding the Pot Holes: How Wellness Got Hijacked and Over-Hyped.. 13
chapter 4	The Alchemy of Wellness: The BioPsychoSocial Model.. 23
chapter 5	Neuro-Happiness: Nature and Sensemaking 30
chapter 6	Wellness Begins In the Womb.. 37
chapter 7	The Stress Effect on Caregiver Wellness 40

PART 2
ME TIME MONDAY

chapter 8	7 Days & 7 Ways to Find Balance and Joy for a Busy Life 48
	Step 1: Me = Ikigai.. 55
	Step 2: Time = Microflows (Baby Steps) 60
	Step 3: Monday = Science of Sustainable Wellness 72

PART 3
7 ELEMENTS OF WELLNESS

PHYSICAL

chapter 9	Night Shift: Body Goes to Sleep, Brain Goes to Work 86
chapter 10	Dietary Diversity: Rainbow + Sunshine Diet 100
chapter 11	Nature's Cleanse 117
chapter 12	The Matthew Effect of Health.. 120

EMOTIONAL

chapter 13	From FOMO to Flow to JOMO... 128
chapter 14	Happiness is both a Right and a Choice............................ 134

chapter 15	Good Vibrations: Emotional & Mental Health Energy ..145
chapter 16	The Four Hormones Against the Apocalypse 155
chapter 17	Pajama Class Revolt: Positivity and Personality.............. 157
chapter 18	How to Crack the Anxiety Code 166

SOCIAL

chapter 19	Social Convoys: Secret Sauce for Longevity......................172
chapter 20	Healing Power of Hugs 178
chapter 21	Laughter Can Treat Loneliness 184
chapter 22	Becoming Ruth: Find Your Tribe.. 189

INTELLECTUAL

chapter 23	Cross-Train Your Brain 198
chapter 24	Through the Looking Glass: Daydreams Build Resilience 215
chapter 25	Life-Work Balance: New Social Contracts at Work......... 221

ENVIRONMENTAL

chapter 26	Biophilic Design: Your Brain on Nature........................... 240
chapter 27	Color Psychology and Well Home Design....................... 264
chapter 28	Digital Detox Dynamic Duo: Hygge and Niksen............ 275

FINANCIAL

chapter 29	Healthspan and Wealthspan Financial Planning............. 282
chapter 30	From Peter Pan Housing to Forever Homes 293
chapter 31	The Escape Plan: How to Take a Wellcation.................... 297

SPIRITUAL

chapter 32	Gratitude and the God Code 308
chapter 33	Soul Food: Musical Menus, Sonic Seasoning and A Dash of SOC 318
chapter 34	Dragonflies and Post Traumatic Growth 331
chapter 35	Caregiver Walkabout: Finding Awe and Awesomeness.. 339

CONCLUSION:
ME TIME MONDAY FOR A WONDERFUL LIFE

Your Me Time Monday Survey... 348

acknowledgements 361
illustrations.. 363
notes 366
index 392
about the author 399

Author's Note

Readers of this book may interpret my comments as contrarian to and critical of the medical establishment. I have deep respect for the clinician-scientists with whom I have had the privilege of working and I would turn to experts if faced with serious health issues. However, the solutions embodied in wellness practices make too strong an argument to ignore. Traditional medicine is not the only answer. I leave the pursuit of health and wellness to the reader and hope I have provided some additional insights for your journey.

I have also shared some stories from my employer-sponsored and other organizational workshops. The names of individuals have been changed to shield their privacy but their stories are real.

Disclaimer

The information presented in this book is the author's opinion and does not constitute any health or medical advice. The content of this book is for informational purposes only and is not intended to diagnose, treat, cure, or prevent any condition or disease.

Please seek advice from your healthcare provider for your personal health concerns prior to taking healthcare advice from this book.

introduction

Do you feel that your life may be out of balance? Are you too tied to tech, drained by doomscrolling, overwhelmed and burned out from life's responsibilities and feeling inadequate when faced with all the wellness and self-care messages out there? If you answered "yes" you are in the right place. I wrote this book because I have felt my life was out of balance and what I have learned I am sharing with you. I will help you find joy again because the science and practical tips behind Me Time Monday work.

We have faced a lot of challenges these last few years: a deadly pandemic, polarizing politics, an increase in social tensions and a decrease in economic stability. Our lives have been transformed and we are now refocusing the lens on what is important. With so much turmoil we are seeking those things that soothe the soul: meaning and joy.

For the last 20 years I have provided online education through employers and other organizations to help family caregivers practice self-care. My approach is heuristic – I present the science, share engaging stories, tips and insights but let you create the action plan that works best for you. Each family caregiver has a unique situation and that makes the plan for self-care and wellness unique as well – there is no one-size-fits-all. As a gerontologist, I analyze the life course choices – from birth to death – to study what makes some people live longer, healthier and happier. Me Time Monday may have begun as a program for family caregivers but its principles can be used by anyone at any age or life stage.

How Me Time Monday Can Help

Ten years ago, when I wrote my first book, *A Cast of Caregivers – Celebrity Stories to Help You Prepare to Care*, one chapter was devoted to a concept I called Me Time Monday. It was about self-care and wellness and how to think about balance in life – concepts that are ubiquitous today but woefully overlooked back then. I became a champion for caregiver wellness and collaborated with a nonprofit organization, The Monday Campaigns, to support its new Caregiver Monday initiative and serve as their ambassador and consultant.

The idea of caregiver wellness and the psychology behind healthy behavioral change is important as we look at how to make healthspans and wellspans equal lifespans. As you will read, gerontology is the examination of the life course viewed within a BioPsychoSocial (BPS) framework. The alchemy of balance in these three essential areas of life is what intrigued me about gerontology and it captured all the themes I was examining: healthy body, happy mind, socially connected soul. I was especially fascinated by neuroscience and how the brain still taps into its ancient human origin from millions of years ago. And I wanted to help you understand the critical role nature plays in bringing your life into balance and soothing your body and brain.

Going back to my first book, the purpose was to help family caregivers understand the journey they might be taking. I included stories of high-profile caregivers to engage the reader, provided the roadmap of what to expect on the journey and reminded readers to take a break and just enjoy the ride as much as possible.

My mission with this second book is to continue the journey focused on self-care and wellness. I am taking the Me Time Monday chapter from my last book and not just telling you what helps but *why* it helps and *how to* do it easily. And along the way I will show you how to save time and money while feeling better about your life.

Your Wellness Journey

Most people think of wellness as a new diet or exercise routine, maybe with a little meditation thrown in. As you read this book, the "wellness diet" is not about eating or nutrition (at least not entirely). It is actually a diet as Hippocrates defined the term which is the healing art behind a lifestyle seeking well-being and joy. Wellness is now seen everywhere but not everything you hear or read will help your well-being. Me Time Monday is more about the personal happiness you create not what wellness products are promoting.

The paradox of many wellness plans is they make you feel like you are failing if you are not perfect. They also focus on problem-solving instead of strength-building. We are going to ditch all the noise pollution around cleanses, creams and snake oil solutions and instead take a fun but fact-filled road trip on this journey of self-care. You will see the Me Time Monday program looks at wellness as a lifelong *pursuit* not *perfection*.

One of my favorite journeys is cruising Highway 1 in California up the coast from Orange County to the serene beauty of Big Sur and the Carmel Valley area. This coastal ride through Santa Barbara, having wine at Nepenthe, watching the sunset while walking in the sand smelling the sea salt air on Pfeiffer Beach – to me this is heaven on earth. This book is also a journey for me to show the science and stories of wellness behind the Me Time Monday program. I am not one of those experts who says "do what I do." If something works for me I want to tell my friends. Through my research I have found some secrets for the balancing act of life that I want to share to help spark ideas for a plan that works for you.

Let's start this wellness road trip because it is time for renewal, relaxing, reminiscing and rewarding ourselves. Despite the setbacks, lockdowns, mandates, protests and problems, you get to reinvent your life starting right now.

Sherri Snelling
Newport Coast
August 8, 2023

PART ONE

THE CAREGIVER WELLNESS JOURNEY

The Caregiver Wellness Journey

We often characterize aging as something that just happens after age 50, 60 or 70 but in fact if you are ages five, 21 or 37 you are aging. Reading that sentence you became 10 seconds older. Please do not panic.

I always shake my head when I see "anti-aging" products that proliferate beauty and nutritional supplement advertising. Sorry folks you cannot reverse or prevent aging. However, you can manage the effects of aging and in some ways prevent disease and disability. You can also find happiness, satisfaction, wisdom and other positive facts of life that only come with age (worth more than the $500 anti-aging facial cream).

A byproduct of an aging America is the creation of family caregivers who often neglect their own self-care needs when caring for loved ones – whether it is a child, a spouse, a parent or grandparent. One study showed some caregivers have more stress, lowered immunity and higher levels of depression than the general public and over time this can take years off your life. This is where gerontologists focus our efforts. Our nirvana is to have healthspan and wellspan equal lifespan.[1]

To achieve these goals you have to rethink how you look at aging. A loved one may get 20-30 bonus years of life but not all those years will be spent in good health. This means anticipating your caregiving role.

It is hard to maintain a lifestyle infused with wellness practices when caregiving happens. The self-focus of wellness often gets dropped or ignored. But if you adopt wellness routines and habits even *before* becoming a caregiver, it is already embedded in your daily life. It starts by realizing you are a caregiver right now regardless of your other relationships because you are caring for yourself. When you master self-care, it becomes easier to add and adapt other caregiving responsibilities into your schedule. Wellness becomes your cornerstone between caring for yourself and caring for your loved one. Changing your perceptions on aging and caregiving from fear to fearless is what this book is all about.

---

[1] Healthspan is years spent free of disease or disability, wellspan is years spent in optimal well-being despite health status, lifespan relates to how many years you will live.

The Seven A's of Caregiving

What will this book teach you that all the other self-help, wellness, caregiving books have not? I will help you look at your life holistically – not just in the trendy, New Age sense but in a thoughtful, comprehensive way. I will cover 7 Elements of Wellness: Physical, Emotional, Social, Intellectual, Environmental, Financial and Spiritual and how each one contributes to your holistic well-being. You cannot achieve wellness without balance in these seven areas. You will also learn how to embrace these seven elements of wellness while still juggling the responsibilities and time deficiencies of being a family caregiver. And, you will find happiness while caregiving. This is not an oxymoron. Some caregivers find silver linings on their own while caring for others. But Me Time Monday will help you achieve joy throughout life.

As you will find throughout this book, the numeral seven (7) has powerful significance in your wellness pursuit. In addition, as a gerontologist I wanted you to learn from the evidence-backed science what really works versus what is just a fad so I put on my research hat to validate the wellness data. And as a storyteller, I wanted to engage you with interesting stories that I hope sparks your ideation for a personalized self-care wellness plan.

Instead of giving you a list of things to do, I will give you thoughtful lessons from history, wellness hacks that have worked for others and in the last chapter, Me Time Monday for a Wonderful Life, I will give you a list of questions to help shape your personal wellness plan.

Part of the success of the Me Time Monday program is how to embrace what I call the seven "A's" to create a personalized wellness plan:

ACCEPT – If you are in a caregiving role, your time flexibility has changed. But rather than abandoning self-care completely, you need to accept that while it may at first appear you have no time for self-care, that notion has to be replaced with "How do I find 5-7 minutes for me today?" Acceptance is the bridge to wellness.

ADAPT – As a caregiver you are already adapting. You have a disrupted schedule, new problems to solve, more time dealing with both the physical and emotional needs of your loved one as well as your own emotions about having a loved one who needs more care. Plato famously said, "Our need will be the creator." This later became the idiom, "Necessity is the mother of invention." This book will help you be creative in finding small ways to find your Me Time Monday.

ACT – Being able to accept the limits on your self-care needs without abandoning them all together means you have to put your adaptive plan into action.

ASK – Sometimes an action plan may mean asking others for help. This helps you turn *time poverty* into *time affluence*. Whether it is grocery shopping, the car wash, picking up medications for a loved one – wherever you can recapture time is how to think about your action plan for self-care. While a spouse, friend or Instacart app does your grocery shopping, you just found 30-60 minutes to focus on you.

ASSESS – If it was a bad week and self-care evaporated, do not beat yourself up. There is always another Monday in the calendar to restart the pursuit of wellness. Assess what derailed you and look forward to finding another shot at wellness next week. Monday will become your friend because it is there week after week to encourage your efforts and guide your progress.

ABANDON – You want to have moments when you live life with abandon and throw off the constraints that hold you back from joy and laughter. You also want to ensure you DO NOT abandon your self-care plan. What you will abandon is anxiety, depression and stress.

APPLAUD – When you become a caregiver, you do not get a lot of accolades and "thank-yous." This means you have to thank yourself. Finding little rewards and feel-good moments where you understand that despite someone upsetting your equilibrium you were able to get life back into balance – these are reasons to applaud yourself for the gifts you give to your loved one and to yourself.

chapter 2

Caregiving Redefined

In 2021, a family living in Scotland made headlines as an illustration of how we are living longer. Mary Marshall, who at age 86, had recently become a great-great-great grandmother to two-week-old, Nyla Ferguson, was confirmed by the Guinness Book of World Records as being the only living grandmother in the United Kingdom with six generations of her immediate family living at the same time. Only four years old when World War II began, Mary went on to have eight children and today boasts 90 grandchildren of various generations.

But Mary's family is one generation shy of the all-time world record for most living generations, an honor that goes to Augusta Bunge Pagel. Before Augusta passed away at age 109 in 1989, she was a four-time great grandmother with seven generations living at the same time – the only family to claim this worldwide at that time. If you are trying to wrap your head around how old everyone is to have seven generations living: Augusta Bunge Pagel (aged 109), followed by her daughter Ella Sabin (aged 89), her granddaughter Anna Wendlandt (aged 70), her great-granddaughter Betty Wolter (aged 52), her great-great granddaughter Debra Bollig (aged 33) and her great-great-great-granddaughter Lori Bollig (aged 15) and her great-great-great-great-grandson Christopher (one month).

This type of news would have been unimaginable even a few decades ago as most grandparents died when their grandchildren were young or not yet born. But with people worldwide living longer, grandparents who have relationships with adult grandchildren and even great-grandchildren are becoming more the norm. Longevity has created 3 million grandparents who are caregivers to grandchildren and 3 million children under age 18 who are currently caregivers to a parent or grandparent.

Figure 1: 6-generation family: Mary Marshall (86) to 3x great granddaughter, Nyla

Figure 2: Augusta Pagel (age 109, seated in middle) headed the only recorded family having seven generations alive at the same time in 1989.

Today with multiple generations living at the same time, the philosophy of seven generational stewardship and your connection to the past and future is part of the discovery of Me Time. You cannot create a Me Time plan without knowing who "Me" is and what is important to you. What anchors you to the past and lets you soar into the future? Those are the elements of this book I think you will find enlightening and empowering.

Throughout this book you will see how the number seven is innately important to your personalized wellness plan. In Native American tribes, mostly ascribed to the Iroquois nation, there are powerful obligatory principles around the concept of seven generation planning. Many define this as the impact of decisions today to affect seven generations into the future, roughly 150 years from now, and the state of the environment in which we live. But there is a personal side to the Seventh Generation Principle.[2]

With life expectancy creating a lot of the news headlines these days it is important to look at the differences between life expectancy and lifespan potential. Life expectancy is the average age for all Americans despite genetics or health status. Lifespan potential is more about your personal health and lifestyle to determine how long you may live. In 1996, U.S. researchers postulated that many Americans could reach age 120 and 1 in 20 women currently age 63 will reach age 100. Another study conducted in the United Kingdom found 50% of the 10-year-olds in 2020 would have a life expectancy of 104 but an average lifespan potential of living to 125 – 20 years more than what is predicted for boomers.

The decade of 2030 – 2040 will be transformative for America. By 2034 we will have more people over age 65 than under age 18 for the first time in our nation's history. In fact, the 65-and-older population is

---

[2] You will learn more about oral histories and family ancestry in the Spiritual Wellness chapters.

projected to nearly double in size in coming decades, from 49 million in 2016 to 95 million people in 2060. The number of people 85 years and older is expected to reach 19 million by 2060 – nearly triple the number today. And yes, the centenarian club, also known as the "old, old," has ramped up from 32,000 in 1980 living to age 100+ to almost tripling in 2020 to 92,000 and then growing six-fold to about 600,000 by 2060.[3]

It is not hard to understand why more family members will take on the role of caregiver for older loved ones. Ten years ago, when I wrote my first book, most people defined the word "caregiver" as a professional in health care, someone who was trained to provide hands-on health care. Most family caregivers did not identify with the term, they were simply adult daughters and sons, wives, husbands or partners, siblings and friends who stepped into the essential role of caregiver when a loved one needed more help.

Today, most people still do not self-identify as caregivers. However, since the demographics of family caregiving have changed – for instance we know 24% of millennials are caregivers for parents or grandparents – so too has the definition of caregiver. Using the term caregiver for child care, elder care or spousal care is now the norm. A TV commercial even identified pet owners as their pet's caregiver.

You may be wondering what this has to do with your wellness and self-care needs? The reality is providing care or receiving care is a constant throughout our lives. I have taken what former First Lady Rosalynn Carter said more than 40 years ago when she defined "caregiver" as a role we will all play at some point in life. I have reframed Mrs. Carter's message on how to look at caregiving throughout your life and I call it The Gen

---

[3] From 2005-2010, I led annual research studies into centenarians and their secrets for living longer called "The 100@100 Survey." Most of the centenarian's advice was to focus on happy things in life and "never let the old person in."

C Continuum. Gen C[4] refers to Generation Caregiver and Continuum recognizes that caregiving is a constant, something that remains a fixed state and unchanging. Today, we have five generations in caregiving roles – from teenagers caring for parents to 70-year-olds caring for 90-year-old parents and everyone in between those ages.

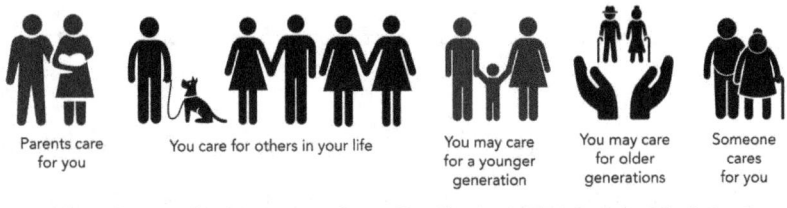

THE GEN C CONTINUUM

You practice self-care throughout life

Figure 3: The Gen C Continuum: Caregiving is a constant throughout our lives

It is not about age or stages in your life. Caregiving can happen anywhere to anyone at any time. It is a constant: You begin life being cared for and end life being cared for – in between you care for others depending on the choices and relationships you make across your life. Looking at psychographics (behaviors, attitudes and needs) instead of demographics (age, race, gender) means the Gen C Continuum reveals a life role almost everyone will experience during their lifespan.

You may notice the largest and most important icon in this graphic is self-care – the caregiving you give yourself. The practice of self-care

---

[4] Brian Solis, a digital analyst, author and futurist, first coined "Gen C" to define a group of people by their psychographic digital behavior. I also use the term as a psychographic representation of the caregiving spectrum regardless of age or stage of life.

is of ancient origins and is inherently tied to wellness and well-being. It may be the most important caregiving role you play: caring for yourself. Maintaining balance even while caregiving makes you a better caregiver.

As you will discover in this book, the road to wellness is paved with values found through ikigai (Me), the ability to build flow and consistency and focus your choices through microflow baby steps and habit-stacking (Time) using a seven-day reset and reward routine to stay on the right track and not get off course (Monday).

Since I am using a car and road trip analogy, this Car Council press release is a perfect metaphor for family caregivers and your wellness journey:

> If your vehicle sits idle for too long, the battery could die, the tires can develop flat spots and the engine oil may start to deteriorate. Just a short solo drive once a week and a little car care will keep your car running efficiently and safely. When starting your car weekly, let it run for at least five minutes. If the vehicle is started in a garage, make sure the garage door is open and there is plenty of ventilation.

Do not sit idle (practice self-care). Every day take 5-7 minutes to run the engine and check the gauges (Me Time Monday). Make sure you can see outside for good ventilation (being in nature, fresh air). If you veer off track or wind up parking for a while, eventually you will get back on track. Me Time Monday will help you continue the wellness journey.

chapter 3

Avoiding the Pot Holes: How Wellness Got Hijacked and Over-Hyped

On any long journey, you encounter potholes and delays that can disrupt your smooth wellness ride. As you will read, wellness and holistic health practices are not a new trend. Creating a holistic approach to your physical, psychological and social health has been an essential part of many ancient cultures. Yet over the years wellness has encountered some detours.

Despite today's obsession with Soul Cycle[5], cold-pressed juice bars, meditation apps, yoga – ashtanga, hot, goat, chair – and Goop's vagina eggs and vampire repellent spray (more on this later), wellness is actually rooted in ancient traditions that have consistently been hijacked by consumerism and cultish-led marketing practitioners. Snake oil anyone?

Today we have corporate wellness in the workplace, wellness tourism including wellness cruises and wellness resorts, pet wellness programs, wellness fitness centers, financial wellness check-ups, wellness mattresses

---

[5] You will read in the Social Wellness section how the founders of Soul Cycle have evolved their wellness plan from physical fitness to social fitness with Peoplehood.

and pillows, wellness aisles in grocery stores, wellness restaurants and now in Europe but coming to America soon: wellness shower gel and wellness tuna fish. There does not seem to be anything being sold or promoted these days that does not have a wellness connection. In the first few months of 2023, the hashtag #wellness had been used in more than 61 million Instagram posts and had 8.5 billion views on TikTok. Some of these industries and organizations are authentic and dedicated to holistic wellness practices and design while others are just posers trying to cash in on the latest trend. To decide what is real and what is ridiculous we have to go back to the origins of wellness.

In the beginning, wellness had pure ambitions. Around 3,000 BC Ayurveda became what many consider the first original health care system and wellness practice originating in India. Begun as oral history but eventually recorded as sacred Hindu texts, Ayurveda created the concept of harmony between the body, mind, and spirit similar to what gerontologists study in biopsychosocial balance.

Around the same timeframe (3,000 – 2,000 BC), the Chinese created health practices based on Taosim and Buddhism. Known as Traditional Chinese Medicine (TCM) it incorporates holistic health practices of acupuncture, herbal medicine, qi gong and tai chi. TCM is also interrelated with feng shui, a practice of arranging our environments and what is within them to optimize health and good fortune.

Not to be outdone, two ancient Greeks also offered philosophies of wellness and a balanced life. Aristotle (384 – 322 BC) promoted a new understanding of health as dynamic equilibrium between internal and external environments and guided Greek physicians to look at physical and social environments as well as at human behavior. But it was the physician,

Hippocrates (460 – 370 BC), who wrote about the balance of environmental elements (wind, air, water, food, temperature, land) and individual lifestyle choices (diet, alcohol, work, sex, family and leisure). He defined wellness not just as the absence of disease but rather the existence of quality of life. His philosophy was in the absence of physical activity you become anxious; in the absence of social family life, you become angry; in the absence of passion and purpose, you become depressed; without the correct food, you become weak; without personal achievement, you have no meaning in your life. And the Greeks understood this meant you would become ill and die sooner.

Hippocrates conceptualized the biopsychosocial wellness framework and personal responsibility for health with aphorisms such as, "Walking is man's best medicine," "Let food be thy medicine and medicine by thy food," and, "All disease begins in the gut."[6] If he were living today, Hippocrates would be the Kim Kardashian social media influencer of healthy aging.

The ancient Romans added their innovation in 50 BC with a template for our modern hygiene practices creating a sophisticated public health care system including aqueducts, sewers, toilets and public baths. The mission was to improve drainage of pooling water in the cities but the supplemental benefit helped improve sanitation and prevent the spread of germs and disease. The public baths became the precursor to modern spa culture and the importance of water in wellness plans.[7]

Flash forward to the 1790s when homeopathy made its debut with the help of German physician, Samuel Christian Hahnemann. The good doctor used natural substances from plants, minerals and animals to personalize prescriptions for a patient's body type, health history and symptoms.

---

[6] Hippocrates was prescient of modern dictates about gut microbiome as the key to inflammation, obesity, Type 2 diabetes and other chronic health issues.

[7] You will learn more about blue wellness in Environmental Wellness.

Homeopathy became a growing industry well into the 19th century where it represented one-sixth of all medical practitioners. However, as the medical profession flexed its dominance over health, homeopaths were shunned into semi-obscurity in the early 20th century.

In the early 1900s the Hopkins Circle consisted of several men from medicine, education and theology who came together to create a gold standard for medical education. The result was the Flexner Report that established the effective pedagogical theory that students learned by doing and solving real-world problems not from rote memorization of literature. The report also eliminated one-third of low-rate medical schools that closed in the wake of the report. Detractors of the report cautioned it was a Faustian bargain where patient-centered care and holistic health – what some call "functional medicine" – were sacrificed at the altar of medical education and research. As one critic, Edmund Pelegrino, claimed, "[The Flexner Report] puts patients in the service of science rather than science in the service of patients."

Eventually the critics were proved right given the atrocious Tuskegee syphilis experiments that began in 1932, the disgraceful Henrietta Lacks tissue culture scandal in the 1950s and in 2022 the outrage over Alzheimer's researchers who doctored images to secure funding for their hypothesis that beta amyloid is the cause for dementia.

Before World War II, we were mostly reactionary to health issues whereas in the middle of the last century, we began to focus on preventive measures rather than simply relying on treatment of chronic diseases such as cancer, diabetes, heart disease and Alzheimer's. In our modern world you want to conquer these diseases not be defeated by them and this means taking proactive, early measures.

Today, a return to wellness and social determinants of health (SDoH) are dawning. In 2019 the Centers for Medicare and Medicaid (CMS) began adding social activities that were tied to better health outcomes as covered benefits under Medicare Advantage plans affecting 22-28 million older adults. In the United Kingdom, the psychosocial tie to wellness is being given more attention as Britain's National Health Service (NHS) has an aggressive plan to embrace social prescribing with a goal to have 1 million patients referred for social-prescriptions by 2024, with many of these being "green social prescriptions" tied to being in nature.

2.5 million - 40,000 BC

Ancient origin of humans live on African savanna (1-3 million BC)

Neanderthals extinct, Homo sapiens survive as hunter-gatherers-explorers (40,000 BC)

3000 - 1 BC

Ayurveda (3,000-1,500 BC)

Traditional Chinese Medicine (2,000-1,500 BC)

Hippocrates – Holistic Health (490 BC)

Romans – Public baths (50 BC)

1600 - 1799

Avicenna – Healing Colortherapy (980 AD)

Hannah Woolley English healer, author (1668)

Homeopathy (1790)

1800 - 1920

New York City Central Park (1858)

Hydrotherapy (1860s)

Edwin Babbitt - Chromatherapy (1870s)

1900 - 1999

J.P. Müller "My System" (1904)

Elie Metchnikoff creates biopsychosocial (BPS) framework (1904)

Flexner Report (1910)

Dr. "Monkey Gland" (1920s)

Organic food movement (1940s)

Jack LaLanne TV Show – (1951-1985)

Dr. Halbert Dunn "Higher Level Wellness" (1959)

National Institute on Aging (1974)

Dr. John Travis - 1st Wellness Center (1970s)

James Birren becomes first Dean of first gerontology school at USC (1976)

National Wellness Institute founded (1977)

Jane Fonda Workout (1980s)

Research in neuroplasticity accelerates (1980s)

2000 - Present Modern Wellness Era

Workplace Wellness – Healthy People 2000 (1990-Present)

1st Chief Wellness Officer – Dr. Michael Roizen Cleveland Clinic (2004)

Gwyneth Paltrow creates Goop (2008)

Global Wellness Institute founded (2014)

Global Wellness Economy $4.5 Trillion (2022)

Figure 4: The Wellness Historical Timeline

The Monkey Gland Affair

When it comes to the annals of cautionary wellness trends and weird health treatments, Serge Abrahamovitch Voronoff, known as the "monkey gland man" in the 1920s, takes top billing.

Born in Russia and trained as a surgeon in France, Voronoff became fascinated with the connection between male castration and longevity when he was running a medical clinic in Egypt. He observed older animals appeared reinvigorated after he performed more than 500 testicle transplantations on goats, sheep and bulls, by removing gonads from the younger animals and placing the organs in the older bovines.

He returned to Europe to bring this fountain of youth discovery to older men. However, since younger males were not willing to give up the family jewels, Voronoff turned to monkeys as the donors. Older men were enthusiastic for a cure to treat erectile dysfunction, but they were not jumping up and down to swap their goodies for monkey balls. Voronoff overcame this hurdle by grafting the monkey skin onto the men's scrotums while still promising longer life, improved vision and libido, decreased fatigue and even offering a cure for schizophrenia.

Millionaires worldwide raced to France for this miracle cure and their wives quickly followed suit demanding a female version of the operation. Voronoff obliged with ovary transplants. The word-of-mouth made him a rich man until a Dutch pharmaceutical company discovered the hormone, testosterone, shedding light on Voronoff's rejuvenation claims as a complete fraud.

Voronoff died in obscurity in 1951 but it took 35 more years for the book, *Monkey Gland Affair,* to reveal the seemingly youthful effects of

Voronoff's procedures on thousands of men and women was the one of the biggest placebo effects in history.

The Cult of Celebrity – How Wellness Got Gooped

This brings us to actress and self-proclaimed lifestyle brand goddess, Gwyneth Paltrow, or as *The Guardian* described her "the queen of the vagina-industrial complex." While Gwyneth has her acolytes and her detractors, there is no denying she brought wellness into a new era with Goop, her eponymous $250 million valued start-up venture. However, this may be a case study on how to brilliantly brand your way into wellness without any expertise, education and questionable ethics.

Paltrow has encouraged a cult-like following but her proselytizing has gotten Goop into hot water with the watchdog group, Truth in Advertising. The company has had to pay up to six figures in legal settlements around potentially medically harmful claims. For instance, the infamous vaginal Jade Egg was touted as balancing hormones, regulating menstrual cycles, preventing uterine prolapse, and increasing bladder control with absolutely zero evidence of any of these miracle cures. She was also busted by scientific experts for a special essential oils elixir taken orally or used in the bath to prevent depression.

While her fans ignore all these red flag warnings and continue to pay $75 for an orgasm candle, $956 for toilet paper (but it is virgin fiber-provitamin B5-essential mineral-coated!) and $125,000 for 18-karat gold dumbbells,[8] perhaps they would be wise to read about Dr. Monkey Gland. They may be devoted Goop groupies but what they may not understand is they are not practicing wellness. Far from it. They are demonstrating a need for social affluence

---

[8] I will admit the Goop endorsed $3,750 cedar bathtub is on my fantasy wish list.

by proxy. Wellness is about self-empowerment and developing an authentic identity not a disciple-like fervor that fuels ridiculously expensive retail therapy of sham products. And, as noted, wellness is *personalized*. She may be a wellness agent provocateur, but what works for Gwynnie does not work for all.

This may be one reason Gen Z is moving away from faux celebrity experts and replacing beauty and body perfection with a personalized, science-based wellness plan. They have ditched the booze and bars loved by boomers and replaced the crystals and cleanses advocated by Millennials to practice wellness that especially addresses mental health.

Meanwhile, Millennials and Gen X cannot get enough wellness marketing and the more eco-friendly the better. They embrace the consumerism driven by the beauty and fashion industry: take this supplement, do this cleanse, meditate and wear these $118 yoga pants.

Boomers are the original "Question Authority" generation who have also created the $120 billion anti-aging industry that is fueling ageism – probably the only "ism" left unchallenged today. Ageism is a term coined in 1969 by the late gerontologist, Robert Butler. But it is only in the last few years it has found mostly fearless females putting a spotlight on this denigration of becoming older including: author Ashton Applewhite, singer Mary Chapin Carpenter and fellow gerontologist Becca Levy of Yale School of Public Health. If you really ponder what anti-aging means, it means death. What happened to just aging gracefully?

The other area for scrutiny is in the language used for caregiving. Marketing messages tend to focus on caregiving as a problem to be solved. Since wellness is about positivity not problems, a *Harvard Business Review* article found the way for marketers to reach family caregivers is to acknowledge their efforts. The contradiction in marketing to caregivers is if a product or service is positioned as making a caregiver's life easier or able to spend less time caregiving, there was guilt associated with the potential purchase. However, if marketers messaged the product or service as underscoring the care and love caregivers dedicate to their loved ones, the purchase intent increased significantly.

The purpose of looking at the woeful side of wellness is to help you tune out all the noise pollution about wellness trends. I will take you back to the beginning of wellness: simple, cost-free, nature-infused, easy to do in a few minutes that will make you feel seven times better than Dr. Monkey Gland or Goop could have ever imagined.

When you replace "I" with "We"
Illness becomes Wellness.

chapter 4

The Alchemy of Wellness: The BioPsychoSocial Model

"If you believe yourself worthy of the thing you fought so hard to get, then you help the soul of the world . . . and you understand why you are here."

— Paulo Coelho - *The Alchemist*

Alchemy is defined as the process of taking something ordinary and turning it into something extraordinary, sometimes in a way that cannot be explained. Often associated with medieval times, alchemists were thought to be magical practitioners who could transform base metals into gold. In a spiritual sense, alchemy is a transformative process to find awareness, harmony and contentment and provide a universal elixir for a longer life.

For many family caregivers, health and happiness are often sacrificed or ignored while caring for others. Finding rest stops along the caregiving journey boosts your health and wellness that may even result in a longer lifespan. The GPS for finding balance and wellness in life: Me Time Monday.

> Wellness is not about fixing problems, it is a prescription for maximizing your personal strengths.

Every idea or story has to start somewhere. The origin story of Me Time Monday was a concept I created in 2011 with a mission to help family caregivers find the balance between caring for loved ones and caring for themselves using three steps:

1. Define your Me Time and make a plan on how to achieve it every week (7 days, 7 ways);

2. Track your progress using Mondays as a weekly check-in with yourself but more importantly, reward yourself or reset yourself for success in the coming week;

3. Commit to yourself by making it fun and easy.

What you will learn in this section is what it means to create a balanced life; why neuroscience, nature and sensemaking are essential to understanding wellness and how stress challenges your well-being. The Me Time Monday program is broken down into why seven elements of wellness help you achieve balance in life; why colors spark joy and make a difference in the emotional side of wellness; how to define and create Me Time (finding value) and how to use Monday science for behavioral change. Mostly, Me Time Monday is also a plan based on ephemeral activities – small, short routines to easily fit into a busy life.

Even though much of my research, writing and online education programs have focused on caregiver wellness, it was not until I was in graduate school for gerontology that I realized there is a scientific formula for living longer and better: the BioPsychoSocial (BPS) framework. I found the BPS framework to be the alchemy caregivers need for happier, healthier, longer lives.

Gerontology is a critical expertise, not only to the practice of health care and wellness, but actually in multidisciplinary fields including: financial gerontology, corporate gerontology, social gerontology, urban gerontology, environmental gerontology, gerontechnology and other aspects of professional and social life. Therefore, it helps to understand the evolution of how gerontology and wellness were founded.

Most people confuse gerontologists with geriatricians who are medical doctors who treat older people with health issues associated with aging. However, gerontologists are not medical doctors, we are experts at holistic health using the BPS framework to uncover the secrets for longevity. As a gerontologist we consider both genetics and lifestyle choices along with life course examination from fetal development through end of life – from the womb to the tomb – to uncover why some people live longer, healthier and happier.

We think of gerontology as being a 20th century development but the practice of holistic health with the intersection of biology, psychology and sociology had been in existence for thousands of years. Today, we are refocused on practicing health on an individualized basis not the one-size-fits-all approach that has defined modern medicine.

BIOLOGY: The Greek word *diaita*, from which we have the modern word *diet*, means the starting point of the healing arts involving an entire lifestyle and not just a food diet and nutrition. A friend of mine said, "Just call the book the *Me Time Monday Diet* and it will be a huge hit." In many ways this program is a diet but a diet as defined by Hippocrates of holistic health and well-being not our modern definition of what we eat.

It is not just about the body, it is about how you feel, about the relationships and environments in which you live as well as the belief in a higher power – all of these are the weapons you have to fight disease and disability.

When you look at wellness and the BPS model of balanced health, it is a diagram of all three circles or *spheres* of life equal in size and at their intersection is where you find optimal wellness. It is how plants, animals, humans and other organisms survive by achieving stable and harmonious equilibrium.

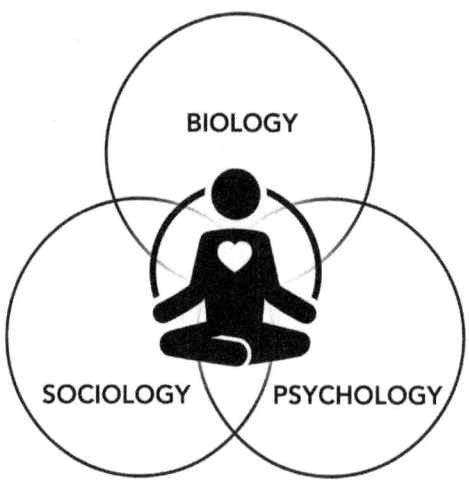

Figure 5: BPS balance for optimal wellness.

Our U.S. health care and long-term care systems have focused mostly on medical care that only looks at biology. It is a sick care system of disease, disability, decay and decline. Most modern medicine still focuses on problem-solving through prescription drugs that only mask the problems. The future will be about functional medicine: patient-centered, personalized and holistic.

In gerontology, and especially in wellness, the focus is not on solving problems, it is about maximizing the positive strengths in your health and life. The focus is on lifestyle practices for your lifespan, not quick fixes. For some the lack of instant gratification, such as taking a pill to cure your ills, is exasperating. But if you experience stress, anxiety, depression and other health issues, the Me Time Monday wellness program will patiently lead you to a happier, healthier, longer life.

PSYCHOLOGY: Another area of science taking center stage in health and wellness over the last few decades is neuroscience. In the 1960s, Joseph Altman made a transformational discovery that broadened the work of those in health care and gerontology. His research identified adult human neurogenesis, known as *brain plasticity*. This revolutionized previous scientific study that held neuronal cells in the brain were fixed from birth and could not be regenerated. Altman proved otherwise. This has led to a huge body of research providing insights into mental health and neurodegenerative diseases such as Alzheimer's and related dementia, Parkinson's disease, epilepsy and traumatic brain injury (TBI).

The continuous discoveries in neuroscience, help fuel the focus on brain health as well as mental health and your psyche. Psychology is a science that had received little attention since Aristotle up until 150 years ago. In the mid-1800s and early 1900s transformative research and theories by Herman Ebbinghaus on memory; Ivan Pavlov on classical conditioning (his dogs and the Pavlovian reaction) and perhaps most well-known, Sigmund Freud on psychoanalysis, dream analysis, sexuality and transference have given us a newfound appreciation for psychology. We know anxiety, depression and other mental and emotional health states can prohibit us from practicing good physical health and vice versa. You will also discover how a lack of movement and good microbiome nutrition affects psychological health.

SOCIOLOGY: And then there is social health. Within the last few years, sociology has taken on significant meaning as it relates to biological and psychological health. As you will read in the Social Wellness section, Harvard University's Adult Development Study is research that has been ongoing since 1938. It sheds light on how your social relationships may be the most important factor in living longer and healthier. In 2023, the U.S. Surgeon General Vivek H. Murthy published the report, "Our Epidemic of Loneliness and Isolation," that found 1 in 2 adults in America reported being lonely. His introduction stated, "Given the profound consequences of loneliness and isolation, we have an opportunity, and an obligation, to make the same investments in addressing social connection that we have made in addressing tobacco use, obesity, and the addiction crisis."

Rather than looking at each of these three areas of life in siloes, it is the intersection and balance of biology, psychology and sociology that leads you to optimal wellness. When you think of the BPS model, you can think of the solar system and the relationship between the Sun, the Earth and the Moon known as spheres. Each sphere has a unique function that interacts with the other sphere. To lose one sphere means life does not exist.

With no Sun, there is no light nor heat and thus no energy for the Earth. With no Moon, there is no nightlight nor stability as the Moon helps Earth remain steady on its axis and provides lunar pull to control our natural circadian rhythms relating to light and dark, wake and sleep cycles. With no Earth, there is no solid foundation on which life can flourish. Its distance from the Sun is in the middle of the solar system not too close where it will burn up and not too far where it will freeze. Earth owes its lifeforce to this equilibrium – balanced in the middle of the solar system line-up.

The attention you now give to balance and equilibrium in your health and wellness pursuits is found everywhere. Consider these words you probably use or hear frequently: balanced diet, checks and balances, work-life balance, balance of power, and the one I use to describe family caregiving: balancing act. Balance has been part of our world since the beginning of time and remains at the core of what wellness is all about.

Neuro-Happiness: Nature and Sensemaking

According to scientific research on the *savanna hypothesis* 2-3 million years ago, the origin of human beings known as *hominins*, lived on the wide-open savannas of the Sub-Saharan African plains. This ecosystem consisted of a mosaic landscape of grasslands dotted with acacia trees where our ancestors were incentivized to walk upright through the grass and found shelter and protection from sun, rain and predators. During this time (and actually for millions of years before) we operated with what neuroscientists call the "old brain" (also called the ancient brain or reptilian brain). Throughout the book I reference certain areas of the brain relating to well-being including:

o   Amygdala – regulates emotions, processes fear and threatening stimuli, encodes memories
o   Hippocampus - embedded deep in the temporal lobe, its major role is in learning and memory consolidation

The old brain is part of the autonomic nervous system that includes both the sympathetic nervous system (responsible for the stress response for survival) and parasympathetic nervous system (returns the body to balance after stress response). The old brain harbors primal motivations such as food, sex, relationship seeking and status.

Today, we have two brains acting together – the ancient brain but also what we call the *new brain*. It works closely with the parasympathetic nervous system and is tied to imagination and creativity, analysis prior to decision-making, self-reflection and language. It is known to create a *top-down* theory of responses where sensory input receives more decision-making analysis before taking action whereas the ancient brain is a *bottom-up* process of instant response. It is the new brain that provides the rest and digest needed after stress to achieve homeostasis (balance).

The old brain houses emotions such as anger, anxiety, sadness. The old brain is reactionary while the new brain is more analytical and proactive. Also, the old brain *sees* first and *thinks* second. This means the old brain will process visual stimuli before it interprets words or numbers because it relies on *sensemaking* which is the use of the five senses – sight, sound, smell, taste and touch. It is actually these sensory data points that help you make good or bad decisions. While sight is the most dominant of your senses, new studies on the power of multisensory activity are driving most wellness practices today.

When we encounter a crisis event, the old brain kicks into gear. The brain engages the sympathetic nervous system to signal to the muscles to react just like stepping on the gas pedal in a car. The senses are heightened and energy is focused on surviving the threat. Breathing accelerates, the heart beats faster, you become highly sensitive to sights and sounds and smells. Energy is diverted from non-essential bodily functions such as

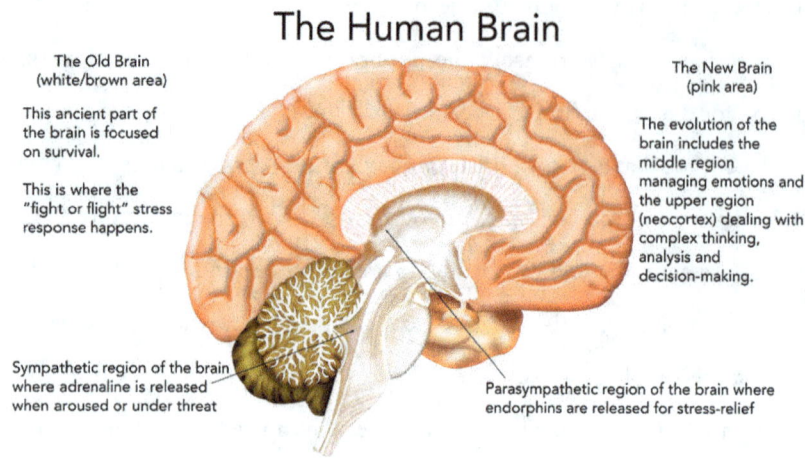

Figure 7: The "Old" Brain and "New" Brain

reproduction, immunity and cellular repair. You are at full throttle and all the energy in the body is vigilant and poised for the attack and ready to respond for survival. Typically, threats are resolved quickly and the parasympathetic nervous system kicks in and acts like a brake to calm the body back into homeostasis. Thus, *fight or flight* is followed by *rest and digest*, also known as *defend and mend* that ultimately is connected to your longevity.

However, in some crisis situations, the threat remains or you encounter constant anticipatory stress (this is commonly seen in those who have post-traumatic stress disorder or PTSD). This constant vigilance does not allow the body to resume to a peaceful, restful state meaning anticipatory stress can ultimately take years off your life.

Our ancient natural environment involved all five senses that are all powered by the brain: views of grasslands and trees and other flora and fauna signaled food sources (sight), sounds of the outside world such as birds chirping, leaves rustling in the wind, ripples on a river but also predators approaching provided safety (sound); soothing scents of fragrant flowers or fruits or the warning crisp air of coming rainfall helped survival (smell); the feel of wood reminds us of protective trees and shelter (touch); and the ability to distinguish between sweet, salty, savory foods helps survival instincts as to what is healthful or deadly to eat (taste) – all of this combines to tell the modern brain we are home and we are safe. These fleeting sensory moments of happiness are what Aristotle called *hedonia,* we call them moods. You will read why these ties to nature are critical for wellness practices.

However, thinking of our five senses in siloes is yesteryear. Today, it is about the blending of all five senses to achieve optimal wellness known as *immersive experiences.* As you will learn in the Spiritual Wellness section from experts such as Charles Spence's work at the University of Oxford, it is the integration of multiple senses that bring about the most happiness and ultimately healthfulness in your life.

Gerontologists understand the aging process begins before birth (in the womb) and your sensemaking ability also begins in utero. At eight weeks, fetuses in the womb start to respond to senses and by 25 weeks all five senses – sight, sound, smell, taste, touch – are present and functioning. One study found babies in the womb at 36 weeks responded with differing facial expressions after their mothers had eaten either carrots or kale. Carrots received what researchers called "laughter-face" while the kale had responses deemed "cry-face" (I can relate).

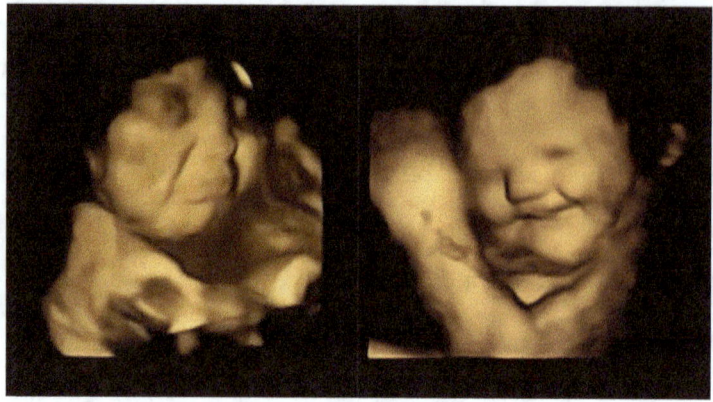

Figure 6: "Crying" kale baby face vs. "Laughing" carrot baby face. (Durham University)

After birth, we engage with external stimuli and the brain breaks down this data into bytes. Some estimate the human brain can store between one terabyte (10,000,000,000,000) to 2.3 petabytes (1 petabyte is 1,000 terabytes). To give these vast numbers context, one petabyte is the equivalent of 500 billion pages of standard printed text making the brain the largest filing cabinet ever created.

Your adult brain is a high-functioning machine that continuously improves performance and ramps up capability. Just a few decades ago, the brain could consume 28,000 words per day. Today, it has more than tripled to 100,000 words, which is like reading a 325-page book *every day*. While we talk about normal cognitive aging and slower recollection speeds as we age, think about how much more your brain is doing. Even though there may be some decline in later life, it still puts us ahead of where we were at our peak in the 1950s.

According to a 2006 article in *Science*, even though one terabyte of stimuli hits the retina every second, the brain computes all this data into manageable portions – only 6,000,000 bytes of data go from the retina to the optical nerve and 10,000 from there to the visual cortex of the brain.

From there about 100 of the 10,000 bits of data are actually what we see. The brain, an awe-inspiring machine, analyzes and acts on this data in just milliseconds for survival.

All of this activity is driven by the brain's sensemaking ability. While some sectors, including academia, business and the military, define sensemaking as a unique problem-solving and decision-making tool, sensemaking in its most basic form is what you were doing as you made your transition from your mother's womb into the real world.

Sensemaking is your brain's response to unexpected stimuli. You encounter these new stimuli through your five senses – you see it, you smell it, you hear it, you taste it or you touch it. From there you perform a swift assessment on whether it is positive or negative and you react. After this initial encounter, you build up intelligence so you know how to react similar to the babies in the womb who liked carrots but not kale. This continual assessment of external stimuli encountered by your five senses is analyzed against existing intelligence. The brain then recognizes the stimuli or recalibrates the brain to understand a new stimulus that in many ways mirrors what we currently see in technology with machine learning and artificial intelligence (AI). The brain keeps building upon stimuli and responses to start to predict patterns.

Most brain development occurs before age five and according to neuroscientists 85% of brain development occurs the first three years of life completing its formation in the early 20s. Through neurogenesis you can repair or grow new brain cells continuously throughout life making the mind-body connection the foundation of wellness.

As referenced, sensemaking is tied to your environmental surroundings and especially nature scenes since our earliest beginnings as humans 100,000 generations ago. The old brain desires these nature environments in our modern lives. According to Ari Peralta, who writes about multisensory integration in the Global Wellness Institute Trends Report 2023, "We subconsciously associate many wellness activities with one sense or another… spa is touch, wellness music is sound, chromotherapy is color, healthy food is taste and thermal is temperature."

chapter 6

Wellness Begins In the Womb

You may believe the stressors of today are the challengers to your wellness. But what you may not know is stress can begin even before you are born and have lingering effects throughout your life. This is epigenetic effect and throughout your younger life, your DNA can be negatively impacted through things such as adverse childhood experiences, smoking, pollution, depression and even what is happening when you are in the womb that can all lead to health issues in later life.

Perhaps the best example of stress and fetal epigenetic effect was a study conducted on the children of mothers who were pregnant during World War II in Holland and experienced the "Hongerwinter," a six-month period during 1944-1945 where Nazi occupying forces restricted food delivery to Holland. Some of these pregnant mothers were trying to sustain themselves on only 400 calories a day as 20,000 Dutch people died from starvation and malnutrition. The late actress Audrey Hepburn was a young Dutch child during this time and remembered eating tulip bulbs to survive. Her childhood malnutrition led to anemia, respiratory illnesses and other health issues for the remainder of her life despite her accessibility to a nutritious diet throughout her teens and adulthood.

Sixty years after the end of the war, researchers studied the effects on these now older adults whose mothers were starving while they were in the womb. What made this cohort of Dutch children scientifically unique is prior to the Hongerwinter period and immediately after the Allied liberation of The Netherlands, the Dutch people had sound nutrition. Thus, the Hongerwinter children experienced the same deprivation at the same time and were not influenced by previous generations of malnutrition nor improved nutrition after the war ended.

Despite these babies achieving mostly normal birth weights, the results of the study in later life were distressing. These Dutch hunger babies, who were studied in their 60s, had higher rates of obesity and twice the risk of cardiovascular disease. They also had higher prevalence for Type 2 diabetes, showed higher rates of depression, schizophrenia and accelerated aging of the brain seen more commonly in adults who were in their 80s and 90s.

The researchers hypothesized these adults had an epigenetic effect of decreased glucose tolerance where they metabolized food differently holding on to calories instead of using them for energy. Their older bodies and brains remembered the starvation period they experienced in the womb that was still affecting their health many decades later. This demonstrates how stress to fetuses in the womb may not reveal its deleterious effects for years.

Before you panic and call your mom about how she was feeling, what she ate and what she was doing while pregnant with you, remember the magic of epigenetics is it does not change DNA, it only means you read the "on" and "off" switches differently based on external influences. Think of it like dyslexia where letters and numbers are transposed, words are harder to pronounce and spelling is difficult, yet with the right tools and training dyslexics can learn to read.

You have the power to change your health even later in life no matter your genetic lottery ticket. By adopting healthier behaviors and other psychosocial tools to help you overcome health risks faced from your earlier life, you can change your wellness outlook for the future.

The Stress Effect on Caregiver Wellness

Not since 1918 had an entire global population lay awake at night stressed about dying of a virus (except maybe those who saw the 2011 movie, "Contagion"). Despite conquering cholera, influenza, pneumonia, typhus, tuberculosis and even death from childbirth that plagued our ancestors 100 years ago, COVID-19 became our black swan event[9] -- events that are unpredictable, have widespread impact and are random or unexplainable.

The conundrum of the recent pandemic is it increased stress about the virus that lowered immunity thus putting us more at risk for contracting the virus – a vicious circle that would make Dorothy Parker and the Algonquin crowd proud. This resulting unpredictability, lack of control, devastating impact and indiscernible completion to chaos is what creates chronic stress. Traditional stressors were amplified during the pandemic because we added social isolation from our comfort sources (family and friends), disruption to our routines (school, work, church), continuous threats to health and life not to mention conflicting and confusing information about vaccines,

---

[9] "Black swan event" was first coined by Wall Street financier, Nassim Nicholas Taleb.

therapeutics and the efficacy of mask-wearing as well as financial concerns, bereavement grief over lost loved ones and general fatigue.

While the COVID-19 virus was scientifically and biologically threatening, the psychological impact and devastation to our sociological needs may have an even more deleterious effect and last longer than the two worst years of the pandemic.

Many young children were removed from school and friends, afraid to venture outside into the fresh air and nature that would help heal their psyches. Some of these children watched their role models – mom and dad – become anxious and fearful. This fear coupled with the lack of peer socialization may be more damaging to these children than the virus. Studies are showing babies in the womb during COVID-19, who are currently toddlers, are developmentally delayed. They are behind their age group norms for walking, talking and social interaction and have more emotional outbursts, separation anxiety and physical aggression.

But it is not just the youngest generations who are suffering. Surveys and studies conducted during and as the pandemic was waning show tremendous negative health effects for caregivers. One study, the Carer Well-Being Index, indicated 72% of family caregivers felt more burnout than ever before with 8 in 10 of the younger age caregivers –Millennial and Gen Z (ages 18-38) – stating the same. Research by Archangels found 52% of Sandwich Generation caregivers (caring for children and older parents simultaneously) reported suicidal ideation.

Even before the pandemic, family caregivers were at risk for chronic stress-related health problems. While not all caregivers feel stress, most research ties the burden and intensity levels of the caregiving experience to increased levels of stress. A study found Alzheimer's caregivers have 24%

more stress hormones, 15% less antibodies for immunity and 2-3 times depression compared to other caregivers.

Since caregiving is a marathon, not a sprint, with the average time spent caring for older loved ones such as parents or grandparents 4-5 years (and for dementia caregivers the average duration is double that figure at nine years), the need to decompress and find periods of rest and digest become lifesaving.

Elizabeth Blackburn's decades of research into telomeres showed one year of chronic stress equated to *six years less of life*. Blackburn compared this phenomenon to fraying shoelaces where your chromosomes – the long chain of DNA that contains all your genetic make-up and helps build and maintain your human structure – have protective end caps called telomeres and with chronic stress telomeres begin to shorten. As stress starts to decrease the length of these protective caps, the DNA strand starts to unravel leading to disease and illness that can take years off of your lifespan.

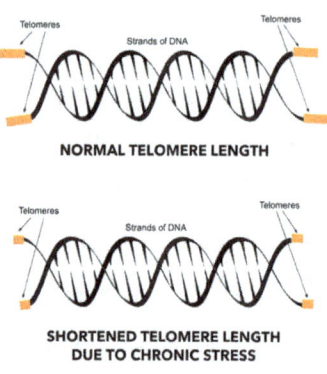

Figure 8: Difference between intact and shortening telomeres of DNA caused by stress.

Robert Sapolsky, the Stanford University neuroendocrinologist who is a global expert on stress research, advises humans "marinate in stress" and as opposed to other animals, we worry and stress more about future events instead of only stressing about imminent threats. This anticipatory stress throws our equilibrium off creating allostatic overload and negative health effects. *Homeostasis* is balance the body figures out on its own; *allostasis* is where the brain engages and thinks through the problem and tells the body how to solve it including possible behavior change. Allostasis is about adapting to achieve balance in life.

I illustrate how invisible stress can be in the Me Time Monday wellness workshops through an interactive test with participants. First, I ask participants to see if they feel their tongue pressed up against the roof of their mouth without trying. If the tongue had been pressed against the roof of the mouth, it may have been minutes or even hours before I asked the question. This is a sign of chronic stress.

The second test is about anxiety. If you thought your phone just rang, chimed or vibrated and you check your pocket or where it is sitting near you and there is no notification nor message, this is called *phantom phone syndrome* which is anxiety based on anticipatory stress.

When the body has a physical problem you can see a wound, a rash or other visual representation. When you break a leg, you immediately get a cast put on the limb. This allows the leg to heal properly and reminds you not to use the limb as you did before the break.

But with stress you keep it hidden inside. It may result in more gray hairs[10], headaches, irritability or insomnia – but you do not realize the mind-body connection as you would with a physical problem. With stress you compound the problem by not relieving or managing the sources of stress *because it appears invisible*. Part of the problem is the ancient brain interprets and discovers problems by *seeing* it first. But this invisibility

---

[10] Just look at photos of U.S. Presidents when they enter office and when they leave – the gray hair is the parting gift to being the leader of the free world.

affects brain health: One study found higher levels of the stress hormone, cortisol, was associated with lower brain volumes and impaired memory in otherwise healthy younger to middle-aged adults, especially women.

The good news is by managing stress through wellness, the body creates an enzyme called telomerase that can help repair the damage to the protective telomeres of the DNA strand and begin to deposit back into your longevity bank account for a healthier, longer life.

However, the solution to stress is not universal. Not everyone experiences or responds to stress or threats in the same way. In the last two decades a new theory on stress response from UCLA psychologist Shelley Taylor is called *tend and befriend* and defines social support during stressful events.

In situations of stress, instead of fight or flight, researchers found females would respond by protecting their young and seeking the connection and comfort of friends. Through social interventions, stress was reduced and homeostasis returned. The researchers found this was partly due to females secreting the hormone oxytocin (the bonding hormone) during stress that was enhanced by estrogen prompting more social contact.[11] While tend and befriend appears to be a more comforting and transactional approach to stress, fight or flight can sometimes be a better mechanism for survival. If you have an abusive relationship or lack strong social support, tend and befriend may not work.

This is an important teachable point about stress. It is not the stress that is killing us, it is the stress response. And that stress response can damage the cells or prohibit cellular renewal and immunity-fighting warriors to combat disease. This is why balance – through homeostasis or allostasis – is essential for wellness.

---

[11] In males there is also a release of oxytocin, just in smaller amounts, and it is inhibited by the dominant male hormone of testosterone.

PART TWO

ME TIME MONDAY

Me Time Monday

F. Scott Fitzgerald ended his brilliant 1925 novel, *The Great Gatsby*, with the line, "So we beat on, boats against the current, borne back ceaselessly into the past." A century ago, the world was emerging from a global pandemic, a devastating world war and economic instability. Then came the Roaring '20s ushering in celebrations, libations, economic prosperity and great social and cultural change. Technology was taking hold with TVs, radio, automobiles, airplanes, telephones and electric appliances changing how we communicate and connect. The era became known as the Jazz Age based on youth culture, dancing, music but mostly it was about finding joy again (even if a little hedonistic).

Today, the world is experiencing the Roaring '20s 2.0. Emerging from another global pandemic as well as great social and cultural changes, life as you know it is changing rapidly and it is all you can do to keep up. And while some of the changes you face are positive, others are paralyzing. For instance: We are living longer making more of us caregivers. We have more choices in everything we do, wear, and eat but choice overload is becoming overwhelming. We are tethered to digital tools but what we really crave is getting outdoors into nature and away from our wireless lifestyles. We want color and fun and we want to connect – or as the Global Wellness Institute says, "not URL but IRL" (in real life). As we emerge from the *cave syndrome* of social distancing, we want to celebrate. And our happiness goals are changing: we value relationships not things, we want meaningful not meaningless lives.

This is what Me Time Monday is all about - a new wellness era I call the Journey of Joy. It is not about the wellness consumerism of the past, it is about returning to the foundation of wellness – holistic and balanced. This book will help you Marie Kondo your life and create a wellness self-care plan that not only sparks joy but helps you create a continuously joyful life. The theme of Fitzgerald's great novel was that despite accumulating all that money can buy, it does not buy happiness. Wellness Past is about consumerism. Wellness Future is based on a happiness economy. Welcome to the new Joyconomy.

chapter 8

7 Days & 7 Ways to Find Balance and Joy for a Busy Life

So far, you have read that achieving balance in life means focusing on a BPS model. You have also learned how neuroscience and nature play a role in your well-being and that stress can begin before you were born but you can control your stress response to improve physical and mental health throughout life.

The remainder of this section will provide you the context behind the Me Time Monday program: Why is the number seven critical? How do colors affect your wellness? What is Me Time? And why is Monday important to making a wellness plan successful?

In my workshops and webinars, participants ask me if they have to perform their Me Time on Mondays. The answer is both "yes" and "no." Yes, you have to pause on Mondays and either have a Me Time moment (you will soon learn I call these microflows) or at least plan for a time during the week when you can accomplish your Me Time. You may have Me Time on Monday as well as Friday. While I want you to take it slow – because part of this program is slowing life down to actually enjoy yourself – eventually you may build up to Me Time every day. You are the architect of your Me Time Monday plan.

Nature, Neuroscience and a New Wellness Era: The Joyconomy

Throughout this book, two concepts are intrinsically entwined in most of my research and recommendations: nature and neuroscience. Much of your life is connected to your senses as evidenced by these idioms:: "a feast for the eyes," "turned a blind eye," "play it by ear," "touched by an angel," "smelled fresh as a daisy," "left a bad taste in your mouth."

The wellness challenges you face in modern society with technology gives you too many choices, too little time spent in nature and too-few in-person interactions that are a barrier to well-being. Technology as a *supplement* to your wellness diet is needed but technology as a *substitute* for what has worked for thousands and even millions of years is perilous. To ignore history and abandon tools and techniques simply because there is a new trend or some celebrity is peddling a new method is to cheat yourself of the vast knowledge and wellness wisdom handed down from the ages.

Our modern wellness era began in the 1950s with Dr. Halbert L. Dunn who explained health is defined by the medical community whereas wellness is defined by each unique individual. It is this powerful theory that paved the way for Dr. John Travis to open the first U.S. Wellness Center in Mill Valley, California in 1975. His mission was to provide individuals with biofeedback on their stress to help people discover and understand why they are sick and devise holistic helpful solutions on how to change things to achieve a better quality of life. In a 1979, Dr. Travis was interviewed on "60 Minutes" with the opening statement, "Wellness. There's a word you don't hear every day." But that was all about to change.

According to the Global Wellness Institute (GWI) 2022 report, wellness is a $4.5 trillion global economy. However, as discussed, healthspan is not matching lifespan. Our 20-30 bonus years may not all be lived in good health. With so much focus on physical health over the last 50 years, today's mission is to also address mental health and social health – two vulnerable areas given the high rates of mental and emotional distress, burnout and loneliness.

In gerontology we look at the *longevity economy* ($8.3 trillion driven by people over age 50) and the *care economy* (identified by the World Economic Forum as the fastest growing economy over the next few years). But now we are ushering in a new era: the Joyconomy. People are ready for surprises, celebrations, loving embraces, smiles, soulfulness and laughter. Too much of life is spent worrying about your career, your weight, your caregiving performance, your parenting, climate change, criminal activity in the streets, corruption in government, financial implosions and FOMO (fear of missing out). You need to step away from the constant digital static that invades your Joy space. You need to be aware of what is going on in the world but you also have to be humble in how much control you have over everything. You control very little of these external factors, but you can control how much joy you have. And, as opposed to most economies that are driven by consumer spending and business investment, the Joyconomy is driven by consumer adoption of wellness practices and both personal and business investment in a balanced life where physical, psychological and social health support each other. The index for measuring the Joyconomy will be societal happiness and well-being.

As you just read, much of this neuro-happiness is based on how your brain is comforted and calmed by nature. The great American writer, philosopher and teacher Ralph Waldo Emerson, led the transcendentalist movement in the mid-19th century and was most famously known for his essay, *Nature*.

He believed each person's soul was linked to nature. Emerson also believed in individualism, championed freedom and was a well-known critic of the pressures of society. A quote from Emerson, captures the Me Time Monday concept beautifully: "It is not for the teacher to choose what the pupil will know and do, but for the pupil to discover his or her own secret."

Me Time Monday and the Power of 7

My research for Me Time Monday showed throughout many millennia, seven has been associated with divine power and a sense of contemplation and completeness. In Christianity, the world was created in six days with the seventh day being spent in rest and reflection. In Judaism as in the Quran, there is reference to the seven heavens. Muslim pilgrims walk around the Kaaba in Mecca, considered Islam's most sacred site, seven times. In the Hindu religion there are seven higher worlds and seven underworlds, and in Buddhism the newborn Buddha stands up and takes seven steps. Thus, every seventh day should be a prompt for every caregiver to get respite breaks every week.

However, the number is not just seen in theology but also in science, literature, astronomy, geography and more. Our planet has seven continents and seven main oceans along with seven wonders of the ancient world. There are seven main constellations in our Northern skies. The Pleiades, known as the Seven Sisters in Greek mythology are called *subaru* which in the Japanese culture means "coming together" or "uniting." To avoid social isolation by maintaining valuable relationships and finding support and resources on the caregiving journey, you have only to look up at the seven stars cluster as a reminder you are not alone.

There are also seven colors in a rainbow (live colorfully!) and seven notes in a musical scale (enjoy music therapy!). In gaming, seven is the most common role of the dice with each of the sides of the die adding up to seven, thus the term "lucky seven" (caregivers can embrace the power of 7 as your lucky number!).

In pop culture, samurai and gunslingers are "The Magnificent Seven," Britain's famous playwright, Shakespeare, wrote of the seven ages of man and the U.K.'s most famous spy was 007. Another famous Englishman, David Beckham, wore the number 7 on his soccer jersey for most of his career (or football in Brit-speak). Even Snow White had seven older, height-challenged men protecting her and keeping her company.

While I focus on five senses in this book, some scientists believe we have seven senses: sight, sound, smell, taste, touch plus mental perception and spiritual understanding. When it comes to the days of the week, seven will become your magic number for wellness you will practice, the numbers of days you have for Me Time and the number of minutes a day (7 minutes) which is all it takes to increase your well-being.

Me Time Monday is for Self-Care Resolutionaries

A lot of people limit the scope of wellness to exercise or nutrition or meditation but those are only the tip of the iceberg when it comes to holistic wellness practices because wellness is multi-dimensional. While studying the BPS framework, I dissected the three areas of biology, psychology and sociology into seven domains of life that I believe help achieve optimal wellness: Physical, Emotional, Social, Intellectual, Financial, Environmental and Spiritual. Me Time Monday uses the power of seven elements for both balance and variety giving you options and flexibility in your wellness plan to avoid the complacency or boredom that can derail your self-care practices. When you focus on just one area of life, such as the physical or social aspects, this does not bring balance to your life. Think of your wellness journey like cross-training in a typical exercise program. You do not want to only work one muscle group or only do cardio or only do stretching. You need all of these to achieve maximum health results. As you will see, you do not have to do all seven elements each week, you just have to mix it up for fun and what your needs are for that week. Think of your Me Time Monday like a mixtape – the old-fashioned way to compile your favorite songs.

I think of those who practice the Me Time Monday program as *resolutionaries* because as opposed to a New Year's resolution, Me Time Monday is a life plan that means experimenting and stretching yourself to do little things in all seven elements of life's wellness needs. Me Time Monday is not a goal it is a lifestyle. How things fit together, how you organize and optimize and personalize these seven aspects of life is what Me Time Monday is all about.

As you analyze your seven elements of wellness, the visual imagery evoking balance is critical, which is why I chose a wheel to instill the idea of forward motion and action because it represents propulsion and movement. This makes Me Time Monday about rolling forward fueled by the seven spokes or elements in the wheel.

Your Brain and Me Time Monday Colors

For Me Time Monday, I use color psychology for my version of the seven colors of the rainbow to represent the seven elements of your wellness plan. Life's stressful events, such as a challenging caregiving situation, can sometimes suck the color out of life and turn it into emotional shades of gray. Rainbows are signs of new beginnings, a symbol of hope, growth and opportunity.

Most neuroscientists agree you do not really see colors, they are a reflection or absorption of wavelengths of light interpreted as electrical impulses – alpha brainwaves - by your brain. All human eyes use cones, a type of photoreceptor that interprets red, green and blue in your retina to detect 100 shades in each cone giving your eyes the ability to "see" more than 1 million color combinations for a full Technicolor life. Along with the cones, your other photoreceptor is rods to detect low light and take control at night. Rods do not see color, only grayscale, but there are 100 million rods in your retina to create the most detailed imagery possible. Experts agree personalized experiences and preferences are key to interpreting color.

For instance, in 2015, "the dress" fueled a global social media debate: was the dress black/blue or white/gold? Scientists believed the dress looked different colors depending on whether you viewed it indoors or outdoors in daylight. Research showed night owls and more men saw black/blue whereas early risers and more women saw white/gold.[12]

Figure 9: 2015 dress that started a global debate on what colors we see

---

[12] As a woman and night owl, I saw the dress as white/gold. It was actually black/blue.

Me Time Monday 3-Step Program

Step 1: Me = Ikigai

Me Time Monday is based on *ikigai* (pronounced ee-key-guy), a Japanese word that means "a reason for being" (*iki* means life and *gai* means effect, result, worth or value). The Me Time part of the program is a concept about finding your ikigai - what brings you joy, a smile to your face, a happy heart. Many define ikigai as having three main areas: what you love (your passion), what the world needs (your mission), what you are good at (your special skills). In the animal kingdom, humans are unique because we can create value and meaning.

No one can dictate your Me Time, both wellness and Me Time are completely personal. As you explore your ikigai, another important principle of Me Time Monday is it is not based on what you *should* do, it is based on what you *want* to do. This is a critical distinction. Most of us have a tendency to feel like we *should* get to gym, we *should* eat more nutritiously, we *should* meditate. But if you are feeling stressed about Me Time, it is not Me Time. Me Time is based on letting go of all the *shoulds* in life and just feeling and doing what you want at a given time. It is about being kind to yourself. It is giving yourself permission to do what you want. Instead of *I should do this* it becomes more about *I get to do this*.

Part of the value proposition of Me Time Monday is the value you place on self-care. While self-care is a positive activity, it has been getting a bit of a beating these days. Similar to wellness, the term has been taken hostage by those who feel it is a selfish, "me before everyone else" pursuit. These self-care haters get it all wrong. I look at Me Time as both a solitary *and* a social activity. It is a way to rediscover yourself. Me Time in the Me Time Monday program is not about indulgence it is about enlightenment and the ability to be self-reflective and self-aware. You may lack empathy or kindness and do not realize these deficits defeat your wellness goals. It is crucial for caregivers to practice Me Time Monday because a life out of balance will eventually make you ill and unhappy.

Me Time can include pampering yourself such as getting a massage or pedicure but it is also about inner exploration and finding inner peace. One way to think about Me Time Monday is to think about what you loved to do as a child. Remember those carefree days when running, laughing and having fun were all that mattered? You need this exuberance and joie de vivre in life to make it all worthwhile and to find strength to keep going. And while Me Time, by the very word *Me* is about solo pursuits, many also define it as involving friends and family.

However, when Me Time becomes an excuse to avoid responsibility and keeps you from helping others, you have taken a detour. When Me Time becomes a virtual moat around your life that no one else can penetrate or you make others conform to your schedule and your barriers, then it is not Me Time. Me Time does not give you permission to be selfish, rude or mean. Me Time is not an entitlement concept, it is a balancing act philosophy. If Me Time is practiced correctly, it underscores a wonderful quote from Maya Angelou,

> I learned a long time ago the wisest thing I can do is be on my own side, be an advocate for myself and others like me, if I do that well enough, then I'll be able to look after someone else -- the children or the husband or the elderly. But I have to look after myself first. I know that some people think that's being selfish, I think that's being *self-full*.

This quote is the essence of the Me Time Monday program – it is about creating a self-full and **ME**aningful life. It is about agency and what fuels your motivation to continue on the path of wellness. What science has shown us is humans are not motivated by charts, data or logic, but with aspirational messages and images that appeal to your emotional state and help you accomplish tasks meaning you have earned it. The emotional first aid of self-care is not just about affirmations but action.

The Me Time Monday program for family caregivers should be seen as a way to maintain physical stamina and energy, strong mental and emotional health to allow you, the caregiver, to stay in your valued role without taking a tremendous toll on yourself. Wellness becomes a gift you give to yourself and your loved ones.

For many who have taken a psychology or business management course, you know of Maslow's hierarchy of needs. Developed by Abraham Maslow in 1943, it is an ascent through adult life that resembles a pyramid with the peak of the pyramid achieving happiness and self-fulfillment. The foundation of the pyramid is the basic function of life, essentially *physiological and survival needs* including food, water, shelter, sleep and sex. The next level is *safety and security* focused on health, employment, property, social stability. The third level is *love and belonging* relating to the quality of relationships including friendships, family, intimacy, sense of connection and support.

> Self-care is first aid for wellness that includes affirmations *but also* actions.

Once you move past these basic foundational levels, Maslow starts to move you in a more self-focused pursuit with the fourth level of *self-esteem* that encompasses achievement, confidence, respect of others and a sense of your individualism. The fifth level is *self-actualization* where you find morality, creativity, spontaneity, acceptance, purpose, meaning and fulfilling your inner-potential. What is interesting is most people only learned these five levels.

However, shortly before his death in 1970, Maslow added a sixth and lesser-known top of the pyramid called *self-transcendence*. This pinnacle is focused on intrinsic values to show self-actualization is not the final goal. This sixth level is about the continued motivation to achieve greater good and the need to understand, to embrace spirituality, to seek truth, to admire aesthetics including beauty and harmony. Part of this is what Maslow called *peak experiences* in his sixth level of self-transcendence, also known as *metaneeds* and *metamotivation* two decades before Neal Stephenson's 1992 novel, *Snow Crash*, and 50 years before Mark Zuckerberg declared dominance over the metaverse. According to Maslow, it is metamotivation that drives individuals to pursue meaningful lives.

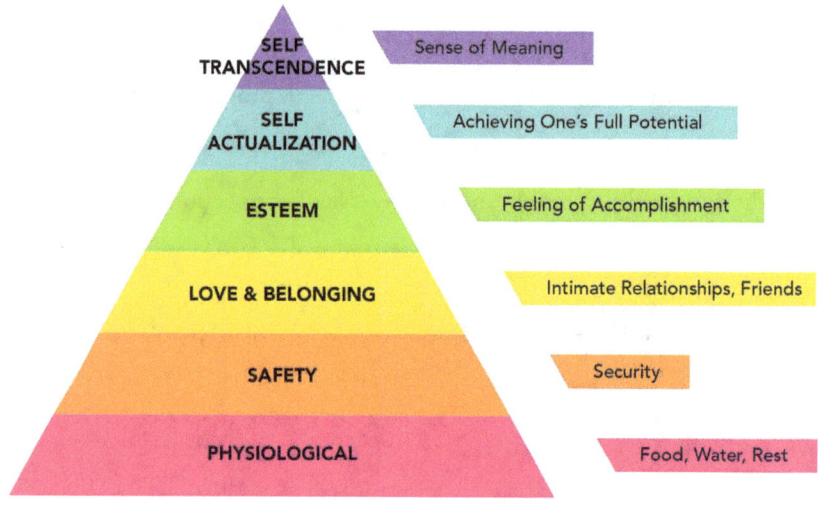

Figure 9: Abraham Maslow's 6-level pyramid of motivation

Maslow's pyramid offers the building blocks of making you a better caregiver. The crucial message is you cannot be a good caregiver if you have abandoned your lower level of needs. As Socrates said, "The secret of change is to focus all your energy not on fighting the old but on building the new." Let Me Time Monday be your *new* road to wellness and a healthier, happier life.

Step 2: Time = Microflows (Baby Steps)

The biggest question I get in my workshops with family caregivers is how do I do Me Time Monday when I do not even have time to take a shower or cook dinner? The dilemma is with all the digital dominance of your free time – where every second there can be a chime, tweet or call – you are suffering from time poverty. Me Time Monday will help you overcome this deficit by building your time affluence. You do this through baby steps or what I call microflows.[13]

The average infant requires 12 months to learn how to walk. At first it may be a few wobbly steps before you land on your nicely cushioned bum (baby fat exists because it is our miniature sumo wrestler protection gear) or into a loving parent's arms. Most children have a fierce determination to move faster and explore as they observe older children and adults doing. You do not want to be left behind.

However, learning to walk does not mean you have learned how to run. Or dance. Or to clear high hurdles or charge down a basketball court. All of that will come but it starts with those first tiny steps. In your wellness journey, you may encounter minor setbacks along the way, but baby steps help you avoid feeling defeated. If babies gave up trying to walk after the first wobbly falls, human beings would cease to exist. Do not feel defeated in your efforts, stay committed and hopeful.

This is the visual I want you to have when you begin your Me Time Monday plan: baby steps or what I call microflows. In the context of a lifetime of wellness, you cannot rush the process or simply take a pill and

---

[13] You will learn about Flow Theory in the Emotional Wellness chapter. Microflows are based on tiny wellness minutes or moments that are part of your flow state.

find instant well-being. If you master things too fast, it takes away the satisfaction of accomplishment, the reward of feeling more in control, the joy of wellness. Earning your accomplishments is what brings joy. *Easy, small* efforts are part of the microflow formula.

> Me Time Monday helps you go from
> time *poverty* to time *affluence.*

One woman from my workshops illustrates how microflow can work. Angela was a 47-year-old woman who was juggling a lot of balls in life. She was caring for her two teenage children as well as her 78-year-old mother who had recently undergone heart surgery and also suffered from foot and leg neuropathy due to diabetes. Angela also had a senior-level job as a vice president for her company and she had a 55-year-old husband who recently had spinal surgery to relieve pain from his college football days. You may wonder where in this woman's overpacked schedule is she going to find Me Time Monday?

Angela said she tried to do a few minutes of meditation but there was nowhere in her house (this was during the pandemic when everyone was home) that was quiet. Ever. She was also trying to schedule a walk with a friend but various crises forced her to constantly cancel plans. In addition, she also was continuing to put herself last on the list of needs because of the priorities of all those around her.

First, I applauded her accomplishment of attending my workshop – that was the first baby step and it was a big one given Angela's time poverty with all her caregiving and life responsibilities. Next, we discovered she was trying to do too much and thinking of Me Time like an exercise program or something she had to create instead of just enjoying life for a few minutes. She was trying to: meditate (Spiritual Wellness) but felt she had no quiet place to do this (lack of Environmental Wellness). And taking walks (Physical Wellness) with a friend (Social Wellness) kept getting cancelled. You can see where this was a recipe for feeling deflated not elated. She was trying to shove four wellness elements into her schedule instead of focusing on just one step.

This is where the neuroscience of microflow kicks in. Your brain is hardwired to take the path of least resistance. You default to doing the same things (or nothing) because it frees up your brain from choice overload to focus on the more critical decisions you need to make.

The world today is overloaded with choices. Here is my personal example. I was recently at the grocery store and needed to buy more laundry detergent. As I looked for the same detergent I have bought for years and realized they were out of stock, I found myself scanning the shelf for an alternative and I realized how many options there were for something as simple as laundry detergent. There were more than 12 options with several fragrances in addition to fragrance free. Some had fabric softener included, others were specifically for white, light or dark colors. One was just for delicate fabrics. All of a sudden, something as simple as automatically grabbing my detergent became something I had to think about. I could feel the stress of the choices caving in on me.[14]

And it is not just detergent choices cluttering our brains. Think about our world today. We have more than 1,700 TV and cable channels plus streaming options (when I was a kid we had six TV channels). More than 122 million viewers consume more than 1 billion hours of video watching on YouTube *daily*. The average adult receives 50-75 texts per day; reads more than 100 emails per

---

[14] I am a stress eater so this situation made me give in to external local of control and go to the in-store Starbucks after 10 minutes of debating which detergent to pick.

day and spends 2-3 hours on social media. Teenagers are spending on average seven hours per day on a mobile device – not including homework time.

No wonder Angela was overwhelmed and could not get to her Me Time Monday plan. All her energy was used in just making numerous choices every day rather than simplifying her routines and schedule to allow for even a few minutes of self-care that could become more automated. I recommended she begin her Me Time Monday plan with choosing one element a week, not one element a day or several elements in one week. She chose spirituality since she felt that would help all other areas of her life. Next, I asked her to focus on her one line of gratitude a day – that was it – nothing else for one week. A simple 15-seconds to say to herself what she was grateful for today.

To make it even easier, Angela, who said she liked routine and was someone who liked schedules, realized she is a morning person so I told her to try to start each day with one line of gratitude. I told her to open her eyes but not get up yet. Stay calm and relaxed in her bed (a place of sanctuary and warmth) and think of what makes her grateful while breathing deeply and slowly. I also asked her to close her eyes while she said her gratitude line and picture the scene. Was it a warm fire and cozy home? Her husband wrapping his arms around her? Her children's laughter? Her mom's smile when she visited? I wanted her to see the images and imprint them in her brain for the rest of the day.

Angela also told me she loved music and loved to dance but could not remember the last time she had really enjoyed either. After a couple of weeks of daily gratitude practice, I told Angela to alert the household that mornings would become Me Time Monday - Mom Time Music. While getting ready for the day and while grabbing breakfast, she would be playing her favorite tunes. She chose Motown and soon the kitchen became like the scene in the movie, "The Big Chill" with classics "Ain't Too Proud to Beg" and "Heard It Through Grapevine" filling the house. Her teens initially rolled their eyes at their mom and dad doing the bump but soon joined in. It started everyone's day with more happiness and energy.[15]

What I also loved about Angela's plan was the Me Time Monday Mom's Music Plan also involved sensemaking: sight (activity in the kitchen), sound (music), touch (dancing) and it was during breakfast (taste and smell). This application of neuroscience into a Me Time Monday plan helps not only with brain health but with awakening your feel-good hormones to go to work as well.

While the above example of Angela may work for you, remember Me Time Monday is a personalized program. I probed Angela on what brought her joy (music, dancing, quality family time) and what gave her a sense of control (routines) along with her current habits (being more of a morning person).

When you feel stuck and unable to embrace your own wellness needs, you need to remember smaller is better. One line of gratitude a day is better than 20 minutes of meditation only once a month. One walk with the dog to the mailbox every day is better than trying to schedule a 30-minute walk with a friend. You have to move past the boundaries that keep you from your wellness needs and enjoy the small victories. Eventually your strength in achieving these small steps will help you add a bit more during certain days or weeks or after a period of time. Like Angela, you will become focused on what you have accomplished rather than feeling you are failing.

The other roadblock to finding Me Time goes back to ikigai and value. By placing value on *things* you will not be as motivated to pursue your wellness goal. You have to start by placing value on *yourself*. Your time, your needs, your wellness requirement for balance means you have to be at the center of the plan. This is how we made it work for Angela.

---

[15] You will learn more about musical menus in Spiritual Wellness.

Wellness – and especially Me Time – is very personalized. I cannot answer the questions for you because it is about your value system. But I can help guide you by asking the questions to start to create a roadmap for where you will go with your Me Time Monday wellness plan.[16] Ultimately, this wellness road trip will lead to a happier life that is not just about how to survive but how to thrive.

Shifting Gears: Routines & Habit-Stacking

"People of the future may turn out to be victims of overchoice."
-- Alvin Toffler, *Future Shock* (1970)

Fifty years ago, futurist Alvin Toffler predicted our societal choice overload epidemic. He cautioned overchoice can actually paralyze you into no action at all. One of the ways to overcome choice overload is to shift the gears in your brain and use microflows (baby steps) to find time to practice Me Time Monday. To make a new behavior or activity easy, it has to be small (microflow), easy and able to be added it to an existing activity.

This is called *habit-stacking* and it has become popular through advocates and authors such as S.J. Scott, James Clear and B.J. Fogg. Habit-stacking taps into Pavlovian triggers for better health and wellness practices by using a prompt or trigger for the new behavior. The way it works is to take an activity you already perform as part of your regular daily routine and stack the new behavior on top of the existing habit.

---

[16] The final chapter in the book is the beginning survey for you to create your Me Time Monday plan.

This also relates to taming and trimming the choice overload you feel in life. Too many choices create complexity in your life that can lead to stress or stagnation. And ultimately, all these choices or non-choices make you unhappy.

Limiting the number of decisions needed throughout the day is an important part of creating established routines and habit-stacking. Think of it this way: If you have a choice to brush your teeth every morning so every day begins with a decision on whether to brush or not, your brain is already being taxed and you just got up! Now, if brushing your teeth is automatic, then the decision is eliminated, you perform the task without thinking and still feel refreshed for what lies ahead in your day. And, the message to the brain is you accomplished something without too much effort or thought and this adds mastery over your life.

Here is how I began to use habit-stacking. Prior to the pandemic, my gym had been located a mere 7-minute car ride from my home. Getting to the gym had a low threshold of time and traffic pain so I was pretty successful at maintaining a class workout schedule. Right before the pandemic, my gym closed and the nearest fitness center was a 25-minute car ride *each way*. Needless to say, adding 50 minutes of transportation onto a 1-hour workout became a big barrier and I stopped going to the gym. I felt physically and emotionally awful.

This is when I embraced habit-stacking. I missed the stretching I would do in my gym classes but I just could not find 20 minutes a day or even during the week to do a good stretch (or so I told myself). I felt my flexibility waning and stiffness invading my body. My solution was to take my daily morning routine of brushing my teeth and habit-stack my stretching on top of it. I throw one leg up on the counter (which is waist high) and during the electronic toothbrush cycles I stretch, changing legs when a new cycle begins.

It is not 20 minutes, more like 2-3 minutes, but the idea is I get in 14-21 minutes of leg stretching a week. It felt so good, I added stretching my back, shoulder and arms to my hair brushing routine. I brush my hair then I do my 3-minute "IYt" stretches inside the doorframe (I hold my hands on the top of the doorframe in an "I" position and push against the doorframe for 1 minute, then move to a "Y" position for another minute and a small "t" position with elbows bended in at my sides for the last minute). This stretch has been found to help decrease risk of osteoporosis and the dreaded "dowager's hump" for women in addition to releasing feel-good endorphins. At the end of the week I have done 35-42 minutes of stretching – about the same amount I did in my exercise classes a week prior to the pandemic. But more importantly I am consistently releasing endorphins that give me a boost of "feel-good" on a daily basis.

My example above shows how obstacles to your Me Time will always be present. The obstacles may be environmental (having to get to a fitness class), or it may seem it will take too much time (thinking of a 20-minute stretching session versus 2-7 minutes a day), and becomes overwhelming to your cognitive load of choices on what to do. Habit-stacking overcomes this choice overload because you do not even think about the behavior, you just do it automatically.

My toothbrushing/stretching habit-stacking example actually has a basis in neuroscience. It is important to note habit-stacking is not multitasking which is powering two activities at once putting your brain into overload. Because the routine activity is a habit, there is no choice involved so adding to it is a "no brainer."

Neuroscientists at the Massachusetts Institute of Technology found daily routines, such as brushing one's teeth, activate the basal ganglia – part of the "ancient brain" that evolved with our nervous system – when you start the routine. The basal ganglia refer to a group of subcortical nuclei responsible primarily for motor control such as eye movement, talking, listening as well as other roles such as motor learning, habit learning, executive functions as part of cognition, and emotions. During the habit activity the basal ganglia go into rest mode but fire up again once the habit is completed.

Neurobiologists, cognitive psychologists and other scientific experts estimate 50% of what we do every day is out of habit. This leaves energy in our brains for other choices – often challenging and taxing – we need to make during the day. While not all of your Me Time Monday efforts can become habits and will need to be mindful and maybe even planned, some others, such as my toothbrushing/stretching routine, may be accomplished through habit-stacking.

The Power of Fun and Play

*"We don't stop playing because we grow old;
we grow old because we stop playing."*
– George Bernard Shaw

Most people experience childhood as a carefree, curiosity-driven time of life. We explored and immersed ourselves in play. Yet playtime is not something many adults practice. With overwhelming responsibilities and so much technology to eat into your free time, you may have abandoned your need to play. Childhood development depends on play and fun but throughout the life course these elements are important to adult development as well. Play and fun release endorphins, dopamine and with the social connectivity that comes with playing with others or with your pets, you also receive a boost of oxytocin and serotonin.[17]

The trick is learning how to make time for fun and play in the day. For children, it is easy. As a student, there are recess breaks between classes often declared by a loud bell – Pavlovian permission to go play. Once you begin working, even if you are a stay-at-home parent, how do you find your recess breaks?

The benefits of play are abundant. Besides the social connectivity you also build your social skills such as showing compassion, even in competitive activities, and you increase your social capital. Through the bonding of play you find intimacy and learn to trust. You learn about body language, teamwork, cooperation, rewards and resiliency. Researchers believe our ancient ape ancestors discovered play 16 million years ago as a bonding exercise through oxytocin release.

In the Me Time Monday program, the colorful wheel reminds you to be a seeker always pursuing new ideas or ways to find wellness in these seven areas of life while also seeking play. And like all good exercise plans, Me Time Monday helps you cross-train your wellness needs. If you are strong in one or two areas, then this helps you also find strength in other wellness areas by inserting fun or "gamification" into your efforts so it becomes more like a game rather than a program.

A wellness plan is not about perfection but progress.

---

[17] You will learn all about what I call "The Four Hormones Against the Apocalypse" in Emotional Wellness.

It is also important to note your wellness needs and desires change with age. What made you happy in your 20s and 30s will probably change in your 60s and 70s.

There is a psychological condition that typically occurs after a stressful or depressing event where the person feels they are no longer able to control their environment so they give up trying. It is called *learned helplessness* and can often affect older adults. Because they have given control to external factors rather than building resilience, they despair and no longer even try to change their situation even if they are physically capable of doing so.

Forty years ago, Harvard social psychologist, Ellen Langer, conducted a research study that demonstrated what she called "psychology of possibility." She had men in their 70s and 80s live in a home-type environment that mirrored 1959 when these men would have been in their 50s and 60s. Most of the men were declining in health and had abandoned many of the social and physical activities they once loved. Langer immersed them in a 1950s world with books, TV news and sports, board games and household appliances of that era removing anything that existed in the modern world.

Amazingly these men began to wash their dishes, make their beds, climb the stairs to their rooms and even get into an energetic debate over a 1959 football game. By time traveling, Langer showed how these men shed the despair and despondency of the health limitations they perceived with getting older. In health data taken after the experiment, these men had improved memory, hearing, grip strength, gait and posture. They also had increased flexibility and reduced arthritis pain, had gained on average three pounds and 64% scored higher on intellectual tests.

This is a powerful example of how mind-body connection can urge your body to behave as you did in younger years to overcome or reduce physical limitations. It also reinforces how your environment can influence your internal locus of control. For family caregivers, it is important to not play into learned helplessness of older loved ones. You may want to be empathetic but you also have to be encouraging. Aging does not mean decline is imminent and by thoughtful engagement and conversations you can help improve your loved one's health status. This same theory of learned helplessness can also be applied to your wellness efforts. While wear and tear on the body can make it more challenging, your brain has amazing resiliency to help the body push past some of these physical limitations.

A lot of behavioral science is focused on correcting bad habits or unhealthy activity. However, wellness is not about fixing things. When we focus on positive areas of our lives, we can achieve what was otherwise thought to be impossible. Wellness is about how we gain strength in certain areas of life. The nuance is when you are fixing a problem you are focused on a weakness. This contradicts positivity psychology. Instead, I want to help you focus on how to build your strengths. There are two reasons people are motivated to change: to avoid pain (fear) or to gain pleasure (something with positive value). Most experts agree gaining something positive is a greater motivator than avoiding something negative. Me Time Monday will help you avoid learned helplessness and gain learned happiness.

Step 3: Monday = Science of Sustainable Wellness

Many people associate Mondays with the blues and despondency or resistance to starting another busy week. We are reluctant to give up the relaxation and restoration unfettered weekends provide therefore Monday becomes a dreaded day that starts invading our mental health on Sunday evenings. The term "Sunday scaries" captures this feeling of reluctance about the impending Monday which in gerontology we call *anticipatory anxiety*. You may have experienced the restlessness or irritability common of this syndrome while others report more serious stress-related health issues such as gastrointestinal upset, headaches and overall malaise. A 2018 LinkedIn survey of 1,000 adults showed on average 80% of Americans have the Sunday scaries: younger generations experiencing more of this anticipatory anxiety (Gen Z = 94%, Millennials = 91%) than older adults (Gen X = 72%, Boomers = 69%).

However, scientific studies have found there is a connection between Mondays and *healthier* behaviors. Gallup found while many people talk about the "Monday Blues" in actuality Monday was just as happy as Tuesday, Wednesday or Thursday for most people.[18] Gallup also found consistently over the last decade, people who love their jobs do not hate Mondays.

Part of the theory of why Mondays are beneficial is for the same reason so many are unenthusiastic about this day. Mondays are part of our cultural DNA of fresh starts: start of the work week, start of the school week, the day to dive back into a busy life with refueled energy after a restful weekend.

---

[18] Not surprisingly there was an uptick in happiness on Fridays that extended through the weekend.

A study conducted during the pandemic by the Monday Campaigns and Researchgate found many Americans were abandoning healthy routines due to work from home and what became known as "blursdays." This national never-ending Groundhog Day experience was based around the disruption of normal routines where work knew no beginning or end, routines and calendars became upended and we became unfocused. We seemed to do the same things every day in a way the days became less and less distinct. In the survey, almost 4 in 10 reported a lack of structure made achieving health goals harder, most people missed a weekly routine and they lost track of time during the week.

When your environment and routines dramatically change, good or bad habits are formed. In fact, environmental cues are essential in habit formation. Were you one who during the pandemic created the surge in Peloton bike sales and online fitness classes? Or were you in the camp that languished and chilled out with Cheetos, chocolate mocha chip ice cream washed down with bottles of rosé wine while binge-watching your favorite TV shows? Did you find athleisurewear preferable to tighter pants and jackets, a new-found freedom from office attire?

You may not have realized the anxiety and fears of the pandemic were actually triggering your stress response and the creation of new habits. This indulgence in obsessive workouts or conversely seeking comfort in food and loose clothing that forgave the extra pounds, was not dissimilar to what the leisure class experienced in the 1800s that led them to fat farms and wacky wellness solutions for their malaise.

The USC Center for the Digital Future conducted a survey on pandemic trends and found 41% were eating more, 33% were drinking more, 32% were exercising less and 38% were dulling their confinement at home via CBD oils and even more powerful medicinal marijuana. For women, the negative impact of the pandemic was the new role and added responsibilities of becoming immediate homeschool teachers, caregivers to older loved ones, along with abandoning any privacy at home as everyone jockeyed for kitchen table or living room space to create virtual classroom and office set-ups. A 2019-2020 study found 41% of women increased their drinking to four or more drinks in one day. The big concern is even moderate drinking (considered 1-2 drinks not four or more) can accelerate aging. Other studies have shown six months of daily alcohol consumption reduces brain volume by 30%. While you may have been alleviating stress, you were also assaulting your brain and increasing your risk for Alzheimer's.

How do Mondays help when faced with anticipatory stress? When the Monday Campaigns public health initiative was founded, its intention was to change behaviors for the better using Monday as a day dedicated to improving health and wellness. The initiative was associated with Johns Hopkins, Columbia and Syracuse universities based on research showing Mondays showed more promise than other days of the week for healthy behavior change. Other research showed using a weekly rhythm for healthy behavior awareness and practice was more beneficial than annual (New Year's resolutions) or seasonal (slimming down for bikini weather) or special occasion (weddings, reunions) efforts because it kept health front and center of life's daily and weekly activity all year. Numerous studies have shown how the annual reset game just does not work. University of Scranton psychology professor, John Norcross, found less than 10% of New Year's resolutions are actually achieved. One 2020 poll found 8 in 10 abandon their grand resolution plans by February. Me Time Monday will make you a resolutionary overcoming annual goals with weekly microflows.

Me Time Monday makes you a wellness resolutionary.

More recent research found people were most likely to start exercise routines, eat healthier and schedule doctor's appointments on Mondays, more than any other day of the week. Sixty-four percent said if they start with a positive frame of mind on Monday, they are more likely to stay positive for the rest of the week.

By using the Me Time Monday program, you instead become a resolutionary whether you start in January or May or September. Monday becomes part of your resiliency tool kit – the day to reflect, reward and reset a wellness plan depending on how the previous week played out.

One tip from my Me Time Monday workshop is to write down all the things you feel you have to jump on for Monday morning or for the next week. By writing it down on Sunday night or at the end of the day on Friday, you release the anxiety onto the paper and can return to enjoying the remainder of your weekend knowing it will be there to address on Monday. This literal "letting go" is a powerful exercise used in stress-related situations and is akin to meditation where you free the mind of the concerns and return to balance to conquer the Sunday scaries.

You can flip the script on Mondays making it more of a TGIM (Thank God It's Monday) day of the week. By becoming a Me Time Monday resolutionary, you learn to master the wellness journey by achieving microflows one week at a time. And Monday becomes your take charge day in planning a wellness week ahead. You can actually look forward to Monday as *your* day.

Refueling Wellness With Rewards

Psychologists and gerontologists know the success of Skinner's pigeons and Pavlov's dogs experiments was to change behavior that relied on reward. For Skinner, the actors are who create the reward through a learned behavior of the birds tapping a button with their beaks which then releases a food pellet. This is an example of operant conditioning where encouraging or discouraging a behavior is learned through positive reinforcement similar to how I taught my dog to sit by giving her a treat. It is a voluntary behavior change.

On the flip side we have Ivan Pavlov whose experiments with dogs and a metronome focused on the dog's behavior becoming conditioned. We call this classical conditioning that after hearing a bell (a neutral trigger), the dogs begin to salivate involuntarily in anticipation of the treat. These reward systems are powerful because it actually is not about the reward itself, but the anticipation of a reward that greatly influences your emotions and creates lasting memories. When you experience a reward, you want to repeat it and this reinforces routines. Refueling your brain's reward system helps your dedication to wellness.

In the Me Time Monday program, there are two key reward triggers: 1) The dopamine release when a pleasurable action occurs; and 2) The anticipatory dopamine trigger when Monday rolls around and we know this is our reward and reset day (or celebrate and continue day) for another week. The Me Time Monday program offers the best of both worlds when it comes to rewards. The instant gratification we get from performing a new wellness habit, such as my daily stretching routine, is supplemented by my weekly Monday reward – which I call the Monday celebration – for achieving the new routine. Arthur Brooks, a Harvard researcher on happiness says your reward should be satisfaction in achieving your weekly goal rather than a treat or gift for yourself. Once you make the reward transactional, he says you fail to feel the self-satisfaction and only focus on the reward (I say it is OK to choose a celebratory reward if that makes you feel good).

This instant and latent gratification plays into both the ancient and modern brain. When the brain's reward system elicits a dopamine release it travels along a neuronal highway called the ventral tegmental area (VTA) located within the midbrain area of the limbic system where we also find the hippocampus (memory, learning, mental maps) and amygdala (emotion center). Scientists believe dopamine is tied to our ancient brains as we evolved more 4 million years ago when your ancient brain became conditioned to immediate rewards while surviving on the savanna. Finding food or warmth brought about an instant dopamine release in the brain. As well, the modern brain analyzes and uses executive functioning to think through challenges and finds its reward in the anticipatory Monday conclusion to a week's worth of wellness practices. These become embedded in your brain like maps.

What Me Time Monday teaches you to do is revert back to your existing cognitive map. In the Me Time Monday program, you recognize the environmental cues (a sunny day means I can take a quick walk outside) and routine prompts (I am habit-stacking my toothbrushing with stretching) that help guide you to another Monday. You get instant gratification (habit-stacking) plus weekly rewards on Mondays for both instant and anticipatory dopamine release.

But what if you have a bad week? This is why habit-stacking on top of more thoughtful wellness practices helps keep you going. The automated habit-stacking activities give you small victories even if the more planned wellness practices (taking a walk, soaking in a bath, seeing a friend) do not happen. You avoid derailment with small achievements.

We often abandon new health behaviors because of the obstacles (not enough time, chaotic schedule, too tired, not seeing immediate results so discouragement sets in). Me Time Monday teaches you resiliency. We all have bad weeks. We all have times when we want to curl up in a ball or stay face-down on the mat and not get up. But knowing Monday awaits and Monday is kind and forgiving and gives you another chance makes you hopeful and optimistic and overcomes any self-defeating tendencies you may have. And Monday becomes the day to celebrate you so you begin to develop a love for Mondays and look forward to that feeling of "I earned this." The key is building in your *rewards* (celebration) and recognizing you may have to *reset* (course correct and carry on).

One of my workshop participants, Joe, has a great story about rewards. His wife was always complaining that Joe would never get to the small things he said he would fix in their home. His wife also hated his beloved country music. Before the pandemic, Joe got his country music fix during his commute to work. But when work from home became the norm for more than a year, he lost touch with Travis Tritt, Toby Keith and other country crooners in deference to his wife.

While outwardly he did not blame his wife for his having to abandon his country singers, internally he was upset by what he saw as a compromise and this subconsciously led him to resent wanting to do the handyman honey-do list and never finding time for it. What we explored is how he could achieve helping his wife (a motivator) with something that gave him a Me Time Monday pick-up (playing country music). Joe decided his garage would become his workshop and virtual Grand Ole Opry. He plastered posters of his favorite stars on the walls for visual encouragement, blasted his country tunes, had a pair of cowboy boots next to his workbench that made him feel empowered (similar to Batman's utility belt) and went to work fixing things on Mondays. For fix-it items that could not be done in the Grand Ole Opry garage, he invested in headphones so he heard Tritt while his wife heard silence.

This sensemaking environment (sound, sight) instantly boosted Joe's dopamine release on hearing his music and gave him an oxytocin release when his thankful wife hugged him in appreciation (touch). He also got a serotonin infusion of happiness upon accomplishing his tasks. Whereas he had felt put upon by his wife and punished for his musical tastes now became fun while fixing things and the hugs and kisses from his wife became all the reward he needed. Joe found he looked forward to Mondays that became his favorite day of the week.

Neuroscientist John Gabrielle, a professor at MIT's Integrated Learning Initiative, presented at one of my online graduate courses on how we learn. He reinforced that assigning value to what you learn is key because it engages the amygdala that drives emotional learning. He also believes in reward systems and engaging the five senses to create the neuronal scaffolding you need to maintain a wellness plan.

Trouble With the Curve

When you embrace a wellness lifestyle plan, the challenge becomes how to make behavior changes last. Wearable biometric sensor companies, such as FitBit, have learned there is a drop-off to positive behavior despite receiving daily digital data feedback, similar to how we abandon New Year's resolutions. A few years ago I attended the Consumer Electronics Show in

Las Vegas. During a panel discussion it was reported 42% of fitness tracker owners abandoned usage within the first six months, a statistic that mirrors fitness center dropout rates. Despite technology's assistance to track your progress, you need more to motivate you into sustainable good behaviors.

This is where the assignment of value (ikigai or Me Time) and rewarding yourself when you have achieved a milestone or microflow (celebrate yourself on Mondays and reset for the next week) will help you maintain the momentum toward ever greater wellness. Research has found it is routines not repetition that build new behaviors. Even if you study or practice doing drills over and over – the behavior is only sustainable through routines. While you now know Monday gives you a weekly reset and reward cadence, you also have to ensure you do not fall prey to the Ebbinghaus curve.

Have you ever read a few pages in a book or watched a webinar or sat in a meeting and the next day you cannot remember what you learned? This was the pioneering research by Hermann Ebbinghaus in the 1880s that became known as the Ebbinghaus Forgetting Curve. His learning theory illustrates that knowledge transfer from oral or written information to being imprinted on your brain can fade over time with the sharpest loss after one hour (56%), after one day (66%) and loss of new learning after six days (75%). Yet, memory and knowledge retention are keys to survival so what makes you remember things?

Ebbinghaus felt the only way to overcome this loss is to assign value to what you want to achieve (Me Time), ensure there is variety in the experiences to make them each memorable (7 Wellness Elements) and to connect something new to something already learned (habit-stacking). He also believed your biological and psychological states affect learning. If you feel stressed or you do not get enough sleep, you will find it harder to retain new learned information.

The Me Time Monday approach is to layer your learnings over time:

- You blend and cross-train your wellness behaviors in seven different elements that have personal meaning (Me)
- You engage multisensory inputs (all fives senses) through habit-stacking and small microflows to consistently imprint the memories in the brain (Time)
- You reinforce your efforts with rewards and reminders every seven days to overcome the forgetting curve (Mondays)

One of the questions I get asked a lot in the workshops and webinars I do for Me Time Monday is how long does it take to form a new habit or behavior? The scientific answer is an average of 66 consistent days but the realistic answer is "forever." Do not become discouraged because your ancient brain is wired for instant gratification. Your wellness efforts are not like taking a pill to be magically and instantly transformed! Remember toddlers take 12 months to learn to walk. Patience is key for Me Time Monday. Learn to *slow down* your life. Trying to walk too fast means more falls. Again, this is not a road race, this is an enJOYable road trip.

In the next few chapters I will take you through the 7 Elements of Wellness to spark ideas you can use for Me Time Monday.

PART THREE

7 ELEMENTS OF WELLNESS

Physical Wellness

17th century Martha Stewart: Hannah Woolley (1668)

The wellness innovations of the ancient Chinese, Indians and Romans somehow got lost until the 1600s when we see the first written appearance of the word *wellness* in the Oxford English Dictionary. During this period we meet the predecessor to Martha Stewart: lifestyle guru Hannah Woolley. In 1668, she published her compilation of cooking recipes along with medicinal balms and elixirs to cure rickets, dropsy, "trapped wind," headaches and childbirth pain, *A Guide to Ladies, Gentlewomen, and Maids*.

Since women at this time were not allowed to attend university to become physicians, they instead became trusted healers within their households and their communities. Many healers and individual housewives kept their notes to pass down to younger generations on treating sore throats with violet-based syrup, using ginger root for nausea and valerian root for insomnia or reducing smallpox scars with a tincture of lemon juice and sea salt.[19]

Upon her husband's death, the widow Woolley became famous as the most well-known healer of her era because she took the initiative to publish her compiled recipes for the broader public. In fact, she is known as one of three women who were the first published female authors making a living from their writing including almanac author Sarah Jinner and Lady Jang Gye-hyang who wrote the first Korean cookbook in 1670.

Beyond her healing advice, Wooley also dispensed how-to guidance: how to run a tidy and efficient household, how to create your own perfume, how to engage in the proper etiquette for dining and more. She used her published works to gain greater awareness for her services at a time when books were still a novelty since literacy rates were at 30% for men and half that for women. But word of mouth grew and just like the Instagram stars of today, Woolley became a celebrity for women seeking domestic goddess advice along with better health and wellness for their family. Wooley is also a symbol for the role women play today: chief medical officers of their families.

---

[19] My maternal grandmother's sore throat concoction was whiskey, honey and rock candy made of pure sugar. A couple of sips and you never even knew you had a sore throat.

chapter 9

Night Shift:
Body Goes to Sleep, Brain Goes to Work

As you start this journey through the seven wellness elements, let us begin with the vehicle you are using which is your physical body and how your body operates which is biology. Over the course of a lifespan, the average American will own eight or more cars. Every few years, we swap out the old model with one that has upgraded bells and whistles. Yet, in your lifespan when it comes to your body, you only get one car — the body and brain you are born with stays with you.

In cellular beings, such as humans, the cumulative wear and tear of every year of life creates DNA damage, an aging process called *senescence*, that results in increased disease and disability risk. For instance, spending time in the hot sun without sunscreen or other protections for most white western European-descended people can create freckles as early as ages 2-3, but also often leads to age spots that arrive after age 50 for many racial groups. For some it can also manifest as skin cancer decades later. Other signs of senescence include wrinkles, graying hair, hearing loss, vision changes, joint pain, loss of collagen and slower metabolisms.

According to the National Human Genome Research Institute, all humans are 99.9% genetically identical, despite a wide variety of racial backgrounds. The remaining 0.1% of a person's genetic makeup is what makes each of us unique. And, certainly lifestyle choices determine your health outcomes as much as your genome.

Many wellness programs begin with diet and exercise while others focus on sleep and meditation. For Physical Wellness, I am focusing on four critical areas that also impact brain health: sleep (letting the body/brain recharge), diet and nutrition (fueling the body/brain), hydration (ensuring the body/brain have enough lubrication) and operating for optimal performance (how to move it or lose it and practice brain balance).

We start with sleep. You have heard it many times: you need 7-8 hours of restorative sleep for good health. For family caregivers burning the midnight oil often juggling one (or two) full-time jobs, means sleep quality may be affected. With all the books and articles on sleep health and sleep science, why are we still sleep deprived? I answer this question in my workshops and webinars by showing *why* restorative sleep is so important to wellness.

I often refer to your body during sleep like charging your smartphone. If you miss a charge, the phone's battery will be low or dead. Most people cannot imagine life without their phone. Now think of your body performing day after day without enough battery life because it is not getting charged every night. Typical comments such as, "You snooze, you lose" or "I'll sleep when I'm dead" underscore society's value for those who can achieve peak performance on a paltry 4-5 hours of sleep. But, if you apply the same dedication of recharging your phone to recharging your body through sleep, you will optimize your body and brain performance.

The CDC reports only 31.6% of Americans get enough sleep and fewer get *restorative sleep*. In addition, other studies show up to 50% of people over age 65 have *sleep debt* to a point it has a negative effect on overall physical and mental health. For family caregivers, another survey showed 62% were not getting needed sleep during the pandemic adopting a "later to bed, later to wake" pattern and one-third encountered chronic sleep disturbances brought on by anxiety about COVID-19.

This growing body of research on lack of sleep and mental health suggests one may cause the other. A meta-analysis of 170,000 people showed insomnia at the beginning of a study period indicated a more than the two-times increased risk for major depressive disorder. And health issues such as sleep apnea have been shown to increase Alzheimer's risk by as much as 30% if unaddressed.

> Your body is like your smartphone,
> it needs recharging every night to work the next day.

Even before the pandemic, technology – including everything from electric lights and streaming services to scrolling social media before bed – has reduced your average sleep time by two hours from what your body was able to get 100 years ago.

The reason why certain hours of sleep – typically 7-8 hours for adults, 9-12 hours for younger children and 8-10 hours for teenagers – are needed is because when the body goes to sleep, the brain goes to work. While your body does a lot of the work during daytime, the night shift is when the brain takes over as the janitorial service to clear out the toxins and debris from the day. It literally does a deep cleanse on your emotions modulating intense feelings or experiences from wake times and tempers them at night so you wake with a more balanced outlook on your anger, desires, frustrations and pleasures the next day. Maybe this is why our mothers told us, "Just sleep on it, it will work itself out by the morning." Who knew moms were neuroscientists in disguise?

Sleep is also when long-term memories imprint themselves on the brain. During sleep hours, our short-term memories are transferred from the hippocampus to the neocortex as the archival repository of these memories. This transforms the short-term memory into a long-term memory.

Many people believe they are OK with less than seven hours of sleep per night. I have people come up to me after a speaking engagement or workshop and tell me they have been getting by on 4-6 hours of sleep a night and do just fine. And this may be true because each of us are physiologically unique. But for most of us, you have to look past the present into the future. I touched upon how your actions today could have disastrous effects later in life. Bad habits such as overeating, over-indulging in alcohol and smoking may not have immediate effects but later in life will take years off your life. Sleep is the same proposition.

While 4-6 hours a night does not seem to hurt you now, studies have shown you are less alert and focused. Those getting less than 5.5 hours of nightly sleep have the equivalent of a .05 blood alcohol level the next morning. Other studies have shown healthy adults who only sleep 5.5 hours a day quickly developed abnormal insulin levels and slowed metabolism. The researchers estimated the metabolic changes could translate into 12 extra pounds a year.

During sleep the brain is also helping other organs repair damage. For instance, during sleep is when your pancreas breaks down sugar allowing a protein to suppress insulin release. If you have poor sleep habits or do not get enough sleep, your blood sugar levels spike and this leads to Type 2 diabetes risk. Even one night of partial or inadequate sleep can increase insulin resistance which is a precursor to diabetes and Alzheimer's. While only anecdotal, both President Ronald Reagan and Prime Minister Margaret Thatcher only slept 4-5 hours a night, yet in their later years both were diagnosed with Alzheimer's.

If you think of your body as a vehicle, the mechanic (aka the brain) is working on the wear and tear on the car from the day's ride. When you sleep your breathing and heart rate slows, your body temperature lowers and your muscles go into temporary paralysis because they are not being asked to make you walk, climb, hold things or run as you do during the day. Sleep is when muscle repair occurs and if you do not give the mechanic enough time to get the repair job done, when you drive the car out the next morning the tires may still be deflated or the engine not running as it should.

During sleep we have two stages: REM (rapid eye movement) and NREM (non-rapid eye movement) that require multiple cycles for your brain to clean and repair the day's wear and tear. REM is when your eyes dart around quickly under your closed eyelids in a range of directions, but do not send any visual information to your brain. The visual cortex area of your brain is awake, your heart rate speeds up, and your breathing becomes irregular. In contrast to other stages of sleep, when your brain waves slow down, your brain is highly active during REM sleep, and your brain waves become more variable. Some scientists believe this is when the brain is performing its memory processing. The REM cycles happen every 90 minutes with optimal sleep requiring four REM cycles per night.

While your brain operates as a mechanic on wear and tear damage to other organs for cellular repair, like any good union worker, the brain also needs standard break times known as NREM that happen in four cycles (N1, N2, N3, N4) making your brain similar to a car wash. NREM sleep makes up about 80% of total time spent in sleep, and REM sleep constitutes the remaining 20%. N1 lasts 1-7 minutes as you lay down and your body prepares for sleep. During this stage you can be easily disturbed by noises or awakened (think of the slow drive through the sudsy car wash flaps) where the body is not completely relaxed yet and may still twitch or have small movements such as turning to your side but heart rate and eye movement start to slow. This is followed by N2, typically lasting 10-25 minutes. During N2 sleep is when everything really slows down: heart rate, breathing, muscle relaxation and a drop in body temperature and eye movement completely stops.

Finally, we have N3-N4 (also known as slow wave sleep), the last deep cleaning cycles with N3 only a few minutes and N4 lasting about 40 minutes (this is when the car wash workers take time really wiping down the car and making sure all the suds, water and dirt are gone). This is the deep sleep, also known as delta sleep, when slow-brainwave sleep happens and it becomes hard to awaken you in this stage. And this is probably the most critical stage of sleep when the real toxins and emotions are getting washed from the day's cumulative stress and your body is put into repair and healing mode.

I call this the brain's night shift and it is full-time work of 7-8 hours not part-time work of 4-5 hours. If you add up all these repair and wash cycles you get 415-480 minutes which is 7-8 hours. If the car wash only lasts 240-360 minutes a night (which is the 4-6 hours of sleep some say they feel is right for them) you can see how you reduce needed cellular repair time, avoid memory imprinting and disrupt the key cleansing time needed for the mind and body to function optimally. This is why people who get less than 7-8 hours feel groggy, irritable and still fatigued the next morning. Many adults spend years getting less sleep not letting the brain's wash cycles be completed.

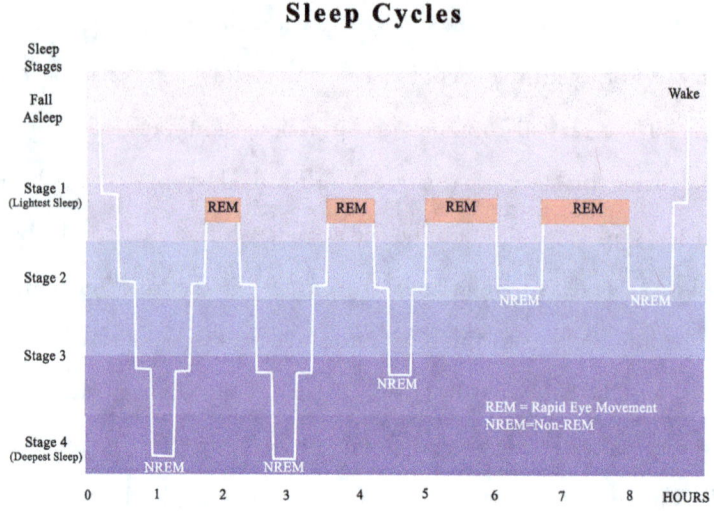

Figure 11: Sleep cycles showing 7-8 hours of REM/NREM phases

One sleep myth is older people need less sleep as they age. Actually, it is the opposite. They need more sleep but this is often challenging because older people have less melatonin, the hormone that tells the brain it is time to sleep. Other studies have shown greater sensitivity to blue light emissions, missed or changing meal times and less activity during the day all contribute to less sleep quality and duration as we age. One solution to add melatonin into your sleep routine is to eat kiwi, cherries or have milk for dinner – all of which release melatonin helping put the body and brain into rest mode.

When it comes to naptime, several studies show the benefit of a quick 20-minute afternoon siesta for younger and older generations can be beneficial to de-stress from built-up pressures of the day. However, a 2022 study showed older adults cannot compensate disrupted nighttime sleep by taking daytime naps. Researchers tracked study participants for 14 years through their early 80s and found sleeping more than one hour every day during daytime increased risk for Alzheimer's by 40%. Sometimes you nap not because you are tired but because you have to decompress. Instead of taking a nap, consider taking a leisurely walk, reading a chapter in a book or chatting on the phone with a friend. All of these activities will alleviate your stress without risking your brain health.

Another area of sleep science is dreams. During REM when we enter dream state is when you have a loss of muscle tone and reflexes (such as punching, kicking, walking, running or yelling) that protect you by preventing you from acting out your dreams or nightmares while sleeping. People with sleep apnea or breathing problems at night also often have nightmares. It is your body's defense system to awaken itself to avoid suffocating. Seven in 10 veterans with post-traumatic stress disorder (PTSD) have sleep deprivation and do not get enough REM sleep, often experiencing fearful nightmares. People with pre-Parkinsonian symptoms develop REM sleep behavior disorder actually acting out nightmares in their sleep. This often happens decades before the signs of Parkinson's, such as tremors, are observed and diagnosed. Improved sleep may reduce risk for this neurodegenerative disease.

Banish the Blue Light

I have mentioned the bad influence social media has had on our lives and while you may feel enlightened or entertained by what you read, it is the artificial light and negative messaging that are disrupting your sleep. While the science is still out on whether blue light emission damages the retina, when it comes to sleep, experts agree the scrolling before bedtime routine has changed sleep hygiene habits in negative ways. A few years ago, researchers in the U.K. reported only 5% of adults were using social media. By 2020 social media addiction had shot up to 70% with younger teens and people in their early 20s on their digital machines 90% of their waking hours. In another study, 90% of Americans were found to use some type of electronic device at least one hour before bedtime several nights a week. With just one minute more of average daily screen time, you get 1 hour less of sleep.

The first problem with scrolling through emails, texts or social media feeds as you lay in bed is the blue light emission from your smartphone is interrupting your circadian rhythm which is your light-dark and sleep-wake 24-hour clock based on our earlier existence on the African savanna. While the light you are seeing appears as white or light yellow, the retina's cone photoreceptors interpret the light as the same blue light as the sun. Yes, the brain actually sees bright sunlight as blue harkening back to our ancient brains when bright sunlight meant harmful UV rays and prompted us to not spend too much time without shade and to not look up directly into the light. When the orangey dusk colors appear, your brain tells your body it is OK to use the last hours of sunlight to safely be in sunlight before getting restful sleep.

More than 140 years ago Thomas Edison flicked a switch in lower Manhattan and changed our lives forever lighting up the night sky with his incandescent bulbs. Today, incandescent and fluorescent lightbulbs mimic the sun's blue light in our brains. When we add all the technology in our modern lives since then – artificial lights, TV sets, computers, smartphones, tablets that use light-emitting diode (LED) – our brains are signaling a retreat from all this light. Light is good but too much light (as everything else in life) is not good. Instead of the brain releasing melatonin, which tells the body to relax and prepare for the REM and NREM cleaning and repair cycles, the blue light confuses the brain into thinking it is still daylight so it suppresses the melatonin release and the body remains awake and alert. Studies show using artificial lights two hours before bedtime decreases melatonin by 23-50% and can delay your body getting to sleep for 2-3 hours. This is known as *cognitive arousal*.

Even getting up in the middle of the night to use the toilet can disrupt your circadian rhythm if you turn on a light or use a nightlight with a blue light emission. Instead, most sleep experts advise using a warm nightlight hue such as soft red, orange or amber that simulates dusk. Amber-orange-red hues resemble the fire light humans used for hundreds of thousands of years at night so our bodies and brains are attuned to not awakening from what is translated by the brain as a nightly heat source. Another tip for getting a good night's sleep is to spend more time during daylight hours outside taking in natural sunshine, according to one study.

This blue light "stay awake" signal is not the only thing going on in the brain. The second problem with the digital messages or content you are viewing is your emotions come into play, especially the mood regulating hormone serotonin. For instance, a late-night email from your boss may make you anxious and worried about responding right away; or you may become upset about a social post or annoyed by a text. This can lead to ruminating for minutes or even hours not allowing your brain to refocus on its cleaning cycles because it is still working out the high intensity emotions you just encountered via technology.

To combat this, the emotional fallout of a text or social media post needs to be replaced with something scientists call *savoring*. Just like it sounds, you need to focus on a visual that brings you pleasure and satisfaction in the same way you enjoy the savoriness of a good meal (thank you umami) by associating taste and smell with positive emotions. These pleasurable scenes in your mind increase the parasympathetic nervous system's return to equilibrium and calm by boosting your serotonin feel good mood hormone. Whether it is an internal movie in your brain of you playing with your dog, going to your favorite vacation spot, remembering your wedding or holding a grandchild – whatever are your "happy" thoughts deserve the last few minutes of your brain time before falling into good sleep.

For family caregivers who are concerned about loved ones and feel the need to have the smartphone nearby in case of emergencies, ensure you set the phone to a night-shift function that changes light quality from blue to amber.

Besides lack of good sleep, family caregivers also can be dealing with situational depression. While many caregivers express sadness and despair over a loved one's health condition or their passing, depression can also be linked to your sleep health. Your cortisol awakening response (CAR) is regulated by circadian rhythms. Your cortisol levels are higher in mornings as you are awakening and decline throughout the day until midnight when it increases again. There is an unregulated release of cortisol during the body's stress response which in turn increases inflammation in the body leading to both short-term and long-term health issues. If you suffer from depression, you have lower cortisol levels in the morning which make you feel sluggish and uninterested in getting out of bed. On the opposite end of your sleep/wake cycle, depression will cause you to have too much cortisol at night which makes you adopt night owl behavior.

It is important to power down from all electronic devices before bed also known as a *cyber curfew* which experts advise is three hours prior to wanting to fall asleep. This is because the blue light stimulation has a latency period that is longer than we may realize for our brains to begin the melatonin release. At dusk, the brain sees orange and reds signaling the end of the day and starts to ease into night hours. About three hours later it begins the process of helping the body to get to sleep.

This power-down is part of what is known as good sleep hygiene: no reading in bed with artificial lights, no watching TV or working on a computer in bed, keep the room temperature cool around 64-68 degrees Fahrenheit,[20] and do not drink or eat at least 2-4 hours before bedtime. Some other helpful sleep hygiene tips include: use sleep masks to keep out light and ear plugs for noise (particularly if you have a snoring partner), try a weighted blanket (the pressure calms the autonomic nervous system and reduces symptoms of anxiety, such as a quickened heart rate or breathing just ensure you get one less than 10% of your body weight) or spritz lavender spray on pillows, a sleep aid originally used by Egyptians thousands of years ago.

For those struggling to get a good night's sleep, taking a warm bath or shower 1-2 hours before bedtime can help because it focuses circulation on hands and feet that drop core body temperature putting you into pre-sleep mode. It is also a meditative exercise where you "wash" the problems and struggles of the day off in the same way your brain regulates toxic emotions during sleep. The warming effect of a bath is also crucial to maintain throughout the night. While you want the ambient room temperature cooler, you want your feet to be warm. Soft socks regulate body temperature and maintain a semi-hibernation state that promotes good sleep without increasing room temperature.

Sound also plays a key role in your optimal sleep hygiene routine. According to the Cleveland Clinic, 70 million American adults struggle with sleep disorders including insomnia. One prescription has been to use

---

[20] This nighttime temperature and the optimal daytime temperature most maintain at home (63-73°F/ 17-23°C) mimic the temperatures of the African savanna our ancient brains find most comforting and comfortable.

white noise found on apps or via sleep machines. But experts agree *pink noise* is actually the best type of sound for restful sleep whether you are a 50-year-old woman going through menopause or a newborn needing restful sleep to build immunity and gain weight for healthful growth. A study found steady pink noise reduces brain waves and increases stable sleep, especially for sensitive sleepers and those who may have tinnitus. It can also increase memory by aiding deep sleep cycles and showed improved memory in those with early-stage dementia. In one study participants remembered almost twice as many word pairs shown to them as the previous night.

Pink noise is of one of several sonic hues, the others being white, brown (also known as red), green, blue, violet and gray noise. While both green and pink noise simulate the ambience of nature with higher and lower frequency levels to help you get to sleep, pink noise is best for staying in restful sleep mode. Think of soft ripples in a stream, gentle waves upon a sandy beach, tiny raindrops falling among a tree's branches or quiet rustling leaves. These pink noise sounds tap into your ancient brain to bring a sense of comfort and soothing found in nature.

Say "No" to blue lights and "Yes" to pink noise.

White noise has been the default for years, providing a consistent hum with the same frequency such as a whirring fan,[21] a hairdryer or TV static. For some the consistent hum is similar to hypnosis and can reduce startling noises such as a door slamming or a humming motorcycle. The

---

[21] Some people use their ceiling fans in the bedroom for sleep noise while also staying cool.

most anxiety-inducing and least sleep-friendly sound is brown noise where deep tones simulate alarming thunder or roaring waterfalls, however brown noise is helpful for those with tinnitus and ADHD.

Innovative companies are looking to capture a portion of the $74 billion sleep science market. 8Sleep uses sensors in its mattresses to regulate body temperature and provide biometric feedback and Dreampad uses a patented technology integrated into the pillow with subtle vibrational frequencies (bone conduction technology) with sounds and music to trigger the brain into sleep mode in a natural way.

chapter 10

Dietary Diversity: Rainbow + Sunshine Diet

Many of the trendy diets that come along are often based on nutrition fiction. Unless you are a registered dietician it is hard to know which new rituals or foods are really helping and most of the time these diets became a recipe for disaster. Yet we still chase the latest fad diet trends: keto, gluten-free, vegan, Flexitarian, DASH, Paleo or the Dukan diet popularized by Britain's Princess of Wales (aka Kate Middleton). We are also being told there are ways to stave off Alzheimer's such as intermittent fasting and adopting the MIND or Mediterranean Diet plan (more on this below).

Somehow, we have this need to think our nutritional habits are innovative breakthroughs. However, many fad diets simply reinvent themselves through the years and complicate what is the simple yet smart science right before your very eyes. To illustrate this, following are the diet crazes over the last 100 years.

At the turn of the century, Horace Fletcher (not a doctor, scientist or nutritionist but an industrialist), created the Mastication Diet. This called for chewing your food until it was liquified in your mouth, a precursor to today's more appetizing blended food movement. I think people lost weight simply by the time it took to chew the food not because this was a remarkable breakthrough in how to eat. A cult of celebrity was attached to "Fletcherism" with Thomas Edison, Henry James, John D. Rockefeller, J.C. Penney and Franz Kafka all adopting his eating plan. And it has not gone away, especially for top executives. In 2013, I interviewed the CEO of Dole Foods, David Murdock, about his proclamation he would live to age 125. He was 90-years-old at the time of our interview. Murdock shared part of his longevity secret is he eats 30 servings of fruits and vegetables daily by blending them – banana and orange peels included – into numerous liquified meals. As he joins the centenarian club in 2023, the billionaire is still on track to meet his age 125 goal.

In the 1920s it was the Cigarette Diet that promised to make those extra pounds go up in smoke. This was before the '60s when nicotine was linked to increased cancer risk. In fact, Lucky Strike, showcased in the hit TV series, "Mad Men," used an advertising slogan in the '20s, "Reach for a Lucky instead of a sweet." Of course, 100 years later we know both nicotine and sugar are killers. In the '30s it was the Grapefruit Diet, also known as the Hollywood Diet, promising to burn fat enzymes. This theory of eating a grapefruit before every meal was rekindled in the '70s as the Mayo Clinic Diet.

It was during the 1940s concerns over pesticides, arsenic-laced herbicides, antibiotics and synthetic hormones ushered in the era of organic foods, also known as natural foods. The movement was kickstarted by Walter James, a British peer also known as Lord Northbourne, whose book, *Look to the Land*, was one of the first to use the term organic farming versus chemical farming. This was followed in 1962 with Rachel Carson's seminal book, *Silent Spring*, that uncovered the effects of the insecticide, DDT, and led to it being banned by the U.S. government 10 years later.[22]

---

[22] Carson was an early activist in the environmental movement that many feel her writing launched.

In the Fifties, desperate housewives turned to the Cabbage Soup diet which mostly flushed water through your digestive system. However, the lack of calories had women fainting, as well as showing deficiencies in essential nutrients and minerals to make the body operate properly. The '60s and '70s ushered in the era of pill popping with the ingestion of diet pills mostly consisting of amphetamines, laxatives, diuretics and thyroid hormones. This continues today with the 2023 fad among tech titans, celebrities and Tik Tokers who are using a diabetes drug, Ozempic, for the off-label use to trigger quick yet possibly harmful weight loss.

While the pills did more damage than good, a positive 1960s movement was the creation of Weight Watchers based on a social support system for losing weight. This weight management philosophy continues to this day championed by the nation's best girlfriend, Oprah Winfrey, who owns a stake in the company she also promotes.[23]

Long before Oprah, the 1970s ushered in the celebrity diets such as the Scarborough Diet (no carbs, no snacks) and the Atkins Diet (high protein, low carb, low fat). Of course, not all celebrity diets go well as Scarsdale Diet creator and cardiologist, Herman Tarnower, learned when his spurned lover, Jean Harris, shot him to death (she seemed to be starving for his attention or maybe she just needed a carb-loaded snack). And both diets are shown to be shorter term solutions as long-term followers suffered reduced kidney function and increased risk for osteoporosis and colon cancer.

Since the 1980s when SlimFast diet shakes became the rage, cleanses and pressed juices remain the latest diet fads. The parade of "master cleanses" are championed mostly by celebrities and while they promise to eliminate the pounds, there is not much promise in creating better

---

[23] Incidentally Weight Watchers jumped on the wellness bandwagon rebranding itself WW International for "wellness that works" in 2018 based on body positivity rhetoric.

health. In fact, the only guarantee in a celebrity-promoted cleanse is it will eliminate dollars from your wallet.

And although it was introduced in the '70s, it wasn't until the start of the new millennium that everyone got excited about an ancient nutrition plan: the Paleo Diet. Based on foods humans might have eaten during the Paleolithic Era of 2.5 million to 10,000 years ago while hunting and gathering, it includes fruits, vegetables, lean meats, fish, eggs, nuts and seeds. Not included are grains, legumes and dairy products – foods that only became more common when small-scale farming began about 10,000 years ago.

What does work? We would all love a pill we can take that would photoshop our bodies in real life and not just for our Instagram feeds. As you have learned from previous chapters, the answers are simple: a balanced diet based on long-term lifestyle choices, not short-term solutions. For some, a vegetarian diet (also followed by vegans who adopt a vegan lifestyle rather than just a diet), which took hold during the '60s counterculture movement includes rejecting mass-produced, commercially packaged foods and meat and has been shown in some studies to aid longevity.

But as you age, decade by decade your nutritional needs change and by your 50s, you need more protein in your diet to counteract the loss of muscle mass and hormonal disruption, such as menopause in women. And while diabesity (obesity+diabetes) is a growing societal concern, you may experience weight loss after your 70s given the decreasing sense of taste and smell that can occur with medications for aging health issues.

We have long known good nutrition is tied to energy, stamina and feeling good. But you often do not think about how food is tied to your mental and emotional health. For some, indulging is part of the reward center of the brain – even the anticipation of a salty or sugary treat triggers your dopamine response. For others (like me) it is part of the body and brain's stress response. You feel pressured or anxious so you soothe your emotions with food known as *emotional eating*. This is why so many diet and nutrition services – from the Diabetes Prevention Program to Noom – use psychological and behavioral science to moderate food intake and teach you how your brain is the key to healthful nutrition. The food choices are in your head not your stomach.

Nutrition is a personalized pursuit but as with all wellness plans, it requires balance to be successful. The takeaway is to forget the fads and focus on filling your body with the right fuel for you. After talking to nutrition experts and evaluating the history of nutrition, Me Time Monday focuses on two diet philosophies that reinforce the principles of the program: colorful, fun, easy and connected to nature. I call them the Rainbow Diet and the Sunshine Diet.

The Rainbow Diet

Eating the rainbow means you are eating more flavonoids which are foods that protect your cells from oxidative damage that can lead to disease. If you "eat the rainbow" every day, you are getting at least seven servings of healthy fruits and vegetables into your diet. Think of it as your nutritional DEI – diversity, equity and inclusion – plan for eating.

It helps to visualize the rainbow as you plan meals or decide what to eat because you do not see browns or beiges that are often the colors of packaged foods such as cookies or potato chips or pasta (whole grains, oats and mushrooms are the exceptions for those brown foods are healthful). Instead, you see apples, tomatoes, oranges, bananas, green bell peppers, grapes, blueberries and eggplant - all healthful and good for various brain and body functions.

Each plant-food contains many phytochemicals, vitamins, minerals and other nutrients that work to improve health. But the key is the *variety* and balancing multiple food colors. Visualizing the rainbow keeps you on track for the choices that make you feel and perform better, and also highlights the color psychology to make things more fun. Studies show stress changes eating habits and appetite in 80% of adults. Counting colorful food rather than points or calories adds fun into stressful days and reminds you of playing a game. Adopting a diet that is fun increases the chance of healthier food choices.

Because of the ancient savanna where our brains were hotwired to seek colorful food, sight sense it also critical. One tip is to have a clear bowl or container of red or green apples, purple grapes, avocados, blueberries or raspberries, carrots or oranges in your kitchen or refrigerator where you cannot help but see the colorful alternative to a brown cookie or tan cracker.

The Rainbow Diet

Red = Lycopene

Red and pink foods, such as tomatoes, watermelon and grapefruit, keep your heart healthy and decrease your risk of stroke. These foods can also prevent and even fight cancer, especially prostate and breast cancer. They are also good for urinary tract health and memory. When free radical levels outnumber antioxidant levels, they can create oxidative stress. This stress is linked to certain chronic diseases, such as cancer, diabetes, heart disease and Alzheimer's. Many red foods lower heart disease risk by 26% and stroke by 31%. One tip from nutritionists: Processed tomatoes contain lycopene that is better absorbed than fresh tomatoes.

Orange and Yellow = Carotenoids

Orange and yellow foods have carotenoids that decrease inflammation in the body and can help prevent cancer because they have high antioxidants. Carotenoids also keep your immune system strong, your skin healthy and are good for vision. A leading cause of vision loss after age 55 is age-related macular degeneration (AMD) and a study found carotenoids reduce AMD by 25%. Carotenoids, which have high levels of Vitamin A, can help alleviate chronic dry eye affecting 4.8 million people over age 50. Foods, such as carrots, cantaloupe, oranges, mandarins, mangoes, papaya, pumpkin and yams, are also good for lowering inflammation. One 7-year study of over 500,000 participants found oranges, papaya and bananas to be protective against Type 2 diabetes.

Green = Lutein

Lutein aids brain health (memory, learning efficiency and verbal fluency) and protects your eyes by preventing cataracts while slowing down AMD. Lutein-rich foods also contain folic acid to prevent neural tube defects in infants and a study showed 7 servings of leafy greens a day may protect against Alzheimer's. Green foods such as kale, spinach, broccoli, parsley, kiwis, green peppers and avocado also strengthen bones, teeth and nails and prevent blood clots. Most adults only get 30% of the recommended daily 6 milligrams of lutein-rich foods.

Fun green food fact: While Bugs Bunny munched on carrots for eye health, maybe he should have snacked on guacamole. Avocados, which are actually berries, are as beneficial for eye health as carrots. They help filter harmful blue light that attacks the healthy cells in your eyes from over-use of digital devices. A single ounce of avocado gives you eight times more lutein than found in a daily multivitamin.

Blue and Purple = Anthocyanins

Blue and purple foods contain anthocyanins that help improve memory and keep skin looking young. Eggplant, purple cabbage, blue cauliflower, figs, grapes, blue and black berries have been shown to reduce blood pressure and lower risk of stroke and heart disease. Anthocyanins also help fight cancers, especially those in the GI tract (mouth, esophagus, colon). They modulate the composition of the gut microbiome and may help prevent and treat cardiovascular disease, cancer, neurodegenerative disorders and age-related bone loss.

The Sunshine Diet

When it comes to good nutrition, eating the rainbow is not my only nature metaphor. A good plan to follow is what I call The Sunshine Diet. It starts with the role of vitamin D, known as the sunshine vitamin, necessary for the absorption of calcium. Vit D plays a key role in maintaining bone strength and helping older adults avoid fractures and osteoporosis. However, up to 40% of Americans are vitamin D deficient.

During the coronavirus pandemic, sales of vitamin D supplements surged as some news reports indicated increased intake of this vitamin may help boost immunity against the COVID-19 virus. While most While scientists are still weighing this hypothesis, most medical experts agree vitamin D is one of the few dietary supplements shown to boost immunity to fight colds and seasonal flu. Eating foods high in vitamin D such as salmon, sardines, tuna, egg yolks, orange juice, oatmeal and milk (or a lactose-free milk if you are intolerant) can help your health with increased immunity and bone density.

Another element of the Sunshine Diet is based on a Mediterranean-style diet. As opposed to trendy fad diets, since the 1950s this method of eating has been identified as one of the scientifically healthiest diets you can adopt. Its roots are based on a lifestyle for many centuries practiced in Italy, Greece, Spain, Croatia and other countries along the Mediterranean Sea. The Blue Zones research found eating foods nurtured in sunshine and eating socially with family and friends are key reasons why some people in Sardinia, Italy have lived to 100 years and beyond. In addition to these food groups, studies have found eating during daylight resembles our ancient beginnings from 2 million years ago up until the era of living on farms in the 1800s. And eating during daylight hours taps into the trend in intermittent fasting to optimize digestion and metabolism.

The Sunshine Diet

1. **Eat foods kissed by the sun.** Fruits, berries, vegetables and nuts contain the powerful vitamin D of sunshine that is locked into these foods grown outside. Also, eat the skin of the fruit or vegetable when you can. Where the sun touches the food is where many nutrients reside.

2. **Eat during sunlight hours.** Sometimes called "farmer's hours" eating only during daylight hours has been shown to be one of the most efficient ways to maintain or lose weight. A study showed metabolism is more efficient during daylight hours since it is tied to your circadian rhythm. Researchers found you metabolize 10% more calories in the late afternoon compared to any other time of day. Eating after dark makes the body think it must stay awake since it takes a few hours to completely digest the food. Also, eating during an 8-10 hour window means less time to consume more calories and is advocated by intermittent fasting experts to possibly prevent Alzheimer's.

3. **Eat a Mediterranean-style diet.** Think sunny Sardinia, Italy for inspiration. This type of diet rich in seafood such as salmon as well as olive oil, nuts, avocado, whole grains, legumes and red wine. It was first popularized by Dan Buettner in his book, *The Blue Zones*. It provided a prescription for living longer and from a nutritional standpoint highlighted the diets of centenarians across the globe, including those in Sardinia. Contrary to many modern diet fads the Mediterranean Diet says it is OK to eat small amounts of poultry and dairy, including eggs. In fact, eggs are making a comeback, polishing their tarnished reputation over the years as leading contributors to cholesterol. Now, nutritionists are pointing to new research that shows eggs are essential to good nutrition offering a little bit of almost every nutrient you need in a daily diet.

An evolution of the Mediterranean Diet is the MIND Diet (Mediterranean-DASH Intervention for Neurodegenerative Delay) specifically designed to improve brain health and possibly prevent dementia. The DASH Diet (Dietary Approaches to Stop Hypertension) targets blood pressure stability where one of the leading causes of dementia is hypertension. By combining the two, the MIND diet plan is perfect for those concerned about brain health but who also want to improve heart health and manage or prevent Type 2 diabetes.

Some of the subtle differences between the original Mediterranean Diet and MIND Diet are: fruit is encouraged but the MIND Diet has an emphasis on berries (raspberries, blue and black berries) as they are shown to be more neuroprotective than other fruits. The other two differences are the MIND diet emphasizes plenty of servings of leafy greens as a main vegetable, while also increasing fish consumption to three times a week, especially fish with omega-3 fatty acids such as salmon, trout, mackerel, tuna and sardines. A 2023 study published in *Neurology* found in post-mortem brain autopsies of the participants who adhered to the MIND diet, their brand scans had average plaque and tangle amounts – the hallmark signs of Alzheimer's – that appeared 12 years younger than those who did not stick to the diet. Even more remarkable, the participants who ate seven or more servings per week of green leafy vegetables, had plaque amounts in their brains corresponding to brains 19 years younger.

And, do not forget to floss your teeth after eating – it reduces bacteria tied to inflammation in the body that leads to chronic diseases such as heart disease and Alzheimer's.

On my podcast I spoke to Dr. Annie Fenn, a physician and culinary expert who runs the Brain Health Kitchen. Dr. Fenn talked about how her culinary classes and her book, *The Brain Health Kitchen Cookbook*, came from caring for a mother with dementia. "Food choices are at the core of the Alzheimer's epidemic, which also makes food at the heart of the solution," advised Dr. Fenn. "Taking steps to protect and improve your brain can start at any age."

Bon Appetit – How to Master Mindful Eating

Beyond rainbows and sunshine there is no one-size-fits-all or miracle diet for any of us. Since age typically ushers in a more sedentary lifestyle and lower metabolism level as well as less muscle and more fat, eating less every decade of life is recommended. A quick calculation is to decrease your calorie intake by 10% every decade after age 20. This means if you consume 2,000 calories at age 30, you want to be eating only 1,450 calories at age 60.

This brings us to the French way of eating. I know you are saying to yourself, what about cheese and cream sauces and chocolate and bread – how can eating like the French be healthy? It is because the French people eat petite (small) portions and practice what is known as *social dining*. And while David Murdock once proclaimed butter to be the equivalent of death, Julia Child, the famous American cookbook author who trained at the famous Parisian Cordon Bleu cooking school to become the "French Chef" on PBS-TV in the '60s, once advised, "With enough butter, anything is good." (And she lived to be 91).

But how does a French diet rich in butter work? In the '80s researchers began studying what is known as the *French Paradox* that showed despite a diet higher in saturated fats – the culprit in LDL "bad" cholesterol – the French people had a *lower risk* of cardiovascular disease. The studies continued 20 years later and found possible links to moderate red wine consumption as a mitigating factor for the higher fat diet. While some experts point to any alcohol intake as detrimental to heart health, both the French Paradox and Mediterranean Diet indicate moderate red wine may actually be good for you.

Another advantage to French cuisine is the way in which the French dine known as *mindful eating*. As outlined by Mireille Guiliano's best-selling book, *French Women Don't Get Fat: The Secret of Eating for Pleasure First*, eating in France is not a frat house sport to see who can shove the most food in their mouths in the least amount of time. Instead, it is a social activity first - the French rarely dine alone.

While the French focus on *mindful* eating, Americans are intent on *mindless* eating. The U.S. is suffering from an obesity crisis because we eat a ton of food – literally. Data from the U.S. Department of Agriculture found in 2011 the average American consumed nearly 1,996 pounds (one ton) of food a year. About 300,000 people die each year from being obese or overweight, second only to smoking. For every pound of food you eat, you need to burn 3,500 calories. Simple food digestion burns 10% of the calories, sleep burns 50 calories an hour (this is why the more sleep, the more calories burned). The rest is your activity level.

The other reason the French beat Americans when it comes to mindful eating is they have perfected fashionable, unplugged dining. French people do not eat in their sweatpants and do not scroll and dine on their smartphones. If you are dressed properly and eat socially you consume food at a slower pace that aids digestion and allows satiation to occur so you eat less. From first hunger pangs to satiation is 20 minutes – our brains need that long to process that we no longer need more food.

As stated earlier, a key rule for French dining is to make it petite and a multisensory experience. Everything from smaller plates to smaller bites are the antithesis of eating in America where "super-size" me has become a way of life. And the French savor their foods because eating uses sensemaking: taste, smell, sight, touch.[24]

French cuisine is known for its quality gastronomics and artful presentation. In America, one in four adults eat fast food regularly and 2 in 10 meals are eaten in the car, what nutritionists call "car cuisine." In 2022, Americans spent more than $110 billion on fast food – more than we spent on movies, books, magazines, videos and recorded music combined. One survey showed the McDonald's golden arches are more widely recognized than the Christian cross.

The Brain-Belly Connection

Scientists are discovering a diet lacking in balanced micronutrients has significant effect on your mental health. The most scientific way to eat better and cleaner for your brain health is outlined in *The Better Brain - Overcome Anxiety, Combat Depression, and Reduce ADHD and Stress with Nutrition*, authored by Bonnie Kaplan, PhD. and Julia Rucklidge, PhD. The biggest lesson from this book is your diet can reduce or replace pharmaceuticals that are so easily prescribed, even at young ages, and can have harmful downstream effect on health. Adopting the right micronutrient plan, may help you be drug-free and mentally heathier.

I interviewed Kaplan for my "Caregiving Club On Air" podcast where we talked about the growing incidence of mental health issues.

"It's very clear that my grandparents who lived through WWI, the Dust Bowl and the Depression, WWII and the Holocaust, and grew up

---

[24] You will learn more about music and multisensory dining in Spiritual Wellness.

through the pandemic of the Spanish flu in 1917-1918, that their life was not easier, my life has been easier. Yet in my lifetime we have seen the prevalence of mental health challenges increase dramatically. Today, 1 in 5 Americans will experience mental illness in a given year. Yet, when I was getting my PhD in the 1960s, it was less than 3%. To go from 3% to 20% in my lifetime – that is really crazy," said Kaplan.

Over the last 10 years there is growing evidence mental health is connected to the microbiome where trillions of microorganisms such as bacteria, funghi, parasites and viruses live within your body mostly housed in your belly area around the small and large intestines known as your "gut." These microorganisms are often called microbiota or microbes and while seen as "bugs" they also have a positive purpose in digestive and mental health.

Your microbiome is unique to you similar to how your DNA is distinctly yours. If you are healthy, microorganisms co-exist without problems and the digestive system is in balance. When this balance is tipped – bad nutrition, infections, over-prescription of antibiotics – the body is susceptible to disease.

Scientists have been exploring the microbiome's role in gastrointestinal disease but also other chronic diseases such as arthritis, cancer, diabesity (obesity and diabetes) and even Alzheimer's. Two recent studies in *Nature Communications*, found a possible causal link to depression, depending on the type of bacteria levels in your body,[25] because 95% of serotonin resides in your gastrointestinal tract not in your brain. Researchers believe these bacteria interact with serotonin levels to regulate mood. These latest findings also showed the connection between bad gut bacteria levels and depression is similar across ethnic groups. Another study led by Keck Medicine of USC

---

[25] Such as higher levels of *Lachnospiraceae* and the genus *Eggerthella* and lower levels of *Ruminococcaceae*.

researchers showed a relationship between inflammatory bowel disease (IBD) and mental health – those with IBD were nine times more likely to also suffer from depression, those with depression were twice as likely to develop IBD.

While some experts feel increased stress is the culprit in the exponential growth of mental health cases, Kaplan disagrees. She believes it has more to do with our lack of resilience due to not getting enough natural vitamins and minerals into our diets. Her research and a review of current diet information shows we get enough *macro*nutrients (fats, proteins, sugars, carbohydrates) into our daily diets, but it is the *micro*nutrients – the natural vitamins and minerals – that we lack. She also advises when it comes to government spending, we can save as much as 90% of health care costs for mental health by adopting sound education and treatments for mental health problems using nutrition.

"During this period where we saw an increase in mental health disorders, we have chosen as a society to cut our nutrient intake in half," explained Kaplan. "The recent National Health and Nutrition Examination Survey showed 57% of the caloric intake consumed by adults and 67% of the caloric intake consumed by children is not real food, it's ultra-processed chemicals. So that is a big change from when I was a child and we ate real food."

Kaplan, along with other nutritional experts such as integrative medicine pioneer, Dr. Andrew Weil, believe nutrition is the foundation of our resilience because we are made up of nutrients. And while medications may help some of those with mental health issues, Kaplan writes they do not restore everyone to normal mental health whereas better nutrition continues to promote healthier brain function. Another concern is many psychiatric medicines approved by the FDA went through only a few weeks of clinical trials yet doctors are prescribing these drugs to patients for most of their adult lives. Kaplan cites a New Zealand government report, "We cannot medicate . . . our way out of the epidemic of mental distress."

In addition to less nutrients in your diet, the indiscriminate use of antibiotics and other over-sanitary measures (antibacterial cleaning agents) has had a deleterious effect on your brain-gut health. By removing bacteria, you may reduce the pathogenic microbes but you also remove the helpful microorganisms that provide protection. A recent journal article found the unintended health effects include higher risk for liver disease, diabetes, asthma and C.diff diarrhea.

Your nutrition, just like your overall wellness plan has to be personalized, including knowledge of family health history. For instance, we were told for decades to avoid egg yolks otherwise we would have an instant heart attack. Experts now agree the entire egg, not just the whites, is mostly beneficial in increasing metabolism, stabilizing blood glucose and insulin response. The zinc in eggs help your immune system, create calcium for bone strength and are packed with protein that you need more of as you age. In 70% of people, eggs do *not* raise cholesterol as previously thought. However, in the remaining 30% of the population, eggs may mildly raise bad LDL cholesterol levels and be harmful to those with a family history of hypercholesterolemia or the 25% of the population who have the APOE-e4 gene, the same gene connected to Alzheimer's risk.

chapter

11

Nature's Cleanse

There is something amazing about water, health and a balanced life. The Earth consists of 70% oceans and our bodies are 70% water – how is that for balance? While you will read about blue wellness and your primitive need to be in and near water in the Environmental Wellness section, in this chapter I am focusing on water as a nutritional tool.

Drinking the proper amount of water is nature's cleanse to help fight inflammation that can cause arthritis, angina, asthma and Alzheimer's. Adequate hydration also helps with headaches, hunger and weight loss because it increases metabolic rates by turning food into energy. It also helps regulate your body temperature and nourish your skin – the largest organ of your body.

A study published in 2023 conducted over a 30-year period and involving more than 11,000 White and Black adults showed proper hydration can slow cellular aging and may help prevent chronic health issues such as heart failure, stroke, diabetes and dementia. Yet, research shows 50% of people worldwide are not getting enough water on a daily basis and are basically dehydrated.

One study found if you are 1% dehydrated, you experience a 5% decline in cognitive function and even have some short-term memory loss. Your brain needs water to perform and if deprived of hydration for long periods of time or over years of not getting enough water, your brain cells start to shrink in size and can lead to severe brain fog, depression, sleep issues and inability to focus.

One of the reasons why older adults get dizzy and may succumb to falls is because they may be dehydrated. While some medications, such as those that treat high blood pressure, may cause water retention (edema), other medications may cause dehydration. It is a best practice to always ask this question of your doctor before taking the prescription so you are aware of the side effects.

And of course, water, not just liquids, is the cure. Some people think they can get around the daily water intake by having tea or sodas or flavored water. None of these options replace your standard water intake needs because their chemical compositions alter the effect of good water hydration. Also, since we are talking about liquids, we know self-medicating with alcohol to alleviate stress may be trendy ("All day rosé" clubs) but alcohol, even light versions, can accelerate aging. Six months of daily alcohol usage reduces brain volume by 30%. And be careful of turning to marijuana as an alternative to alcohol. Marijuana abuse accelerates brain aging by 2.8 years, and this includes both THC (tetrahydrocannabinol) and CBD (cannabidiol). Also, a recent study showed older people and marijuana may not mix well with reports of increased falls, anxiety, confusion and medication interactions.

50% of adults are dehydrated affecting brain function.

When it comes to how much water you need, the old one-size-fits-all formula for water intake per day – 8 glasses of 8 ounces per glass – is out-of-date. Those 64 ounces fall woefully short of the 80 ounces of water we typically lose daily from sweating, breathing and eliminating the body's waste. The latest data from the National Academy of Medicine is for females to drink 91 fluid ounces daily while males should consume 125 ounces daily. However, this prescription still does not adjust for your body type, activity level or age. To personalize your daily water plan and achieve a true nature's cleanse use this formula:

1) Take your body weight in pounds and cut that number in half to identify the ounces of water you should have per day. If you weigh 160 pounds; drink 80 ounces of water daily.

2) When you workout, ensure you drink more water to replenish water loss from sweat (the National Council on Exercise says to drink 16-24 ounces of water for every 1 pound of body weight lost during exercise).

3) If you have edema (swelling of legs, ankles, wrists or fingers) or water retention issues – talk to your doctor first about your daily water intake.

4) Remember - caffeinated sodas, coffee, tea, sports drinks do not count. However, most nutritionists agree carbonated water is as hydrating as regular tap or bottled water.

5) Drink water at room temperature and ditch the ice. Iced water does not allow your digestive system to work at optimum levels.

The Matthew Effect of Health

Matthew 25:29: For unto every one that hath shall be given, and he shall have abundance: but from him that hath not shall be taken away even that which he hath. (KJV)

The Matthew Effect is based on the theory that initial success drives future success – a concept known in gerontology as *cumulative advantage*. Initially presented as a theory on why certain scientific researchers received grants and others did not, the Matthew Effect is also seen in childhood literacy where a child who learns at an early age to love reading and becomes proficient, finds subsequent learning easier and success in life is tied in part to that early education and literacy.

If you apply the Matthew Effect to healthy aging, the theory should be healthful behaviors will cumulate over months and years making you healthier longer to achieve a healthspan equal to your lifespan. While starting healthy habits in childhood is beneficial, it does not mean if you start at age 50 you will not reap the benefits.

In gerontology there is a phrase we use called the "move it or lose it" philosophy. Keeping the body moving improves blood flow to the brain and improves circulation. Think about the day you were born. You moved your arms, kicked your legs, squirmed a bit – this is what we have to keep doing throughout life – we need to keep moving and it only takes a few minutes a day to increase blood flow 15%.

The good news is research supports the Me Time Monday mission in taking microflows (baby steps) and spending 7-15 minutes a day moving to improve well-being. One recent study showed 10 minutes of walking a day is all it takes to boost your metabolism, slim down, lighten your mood and help you live 7% longer than non-walkers. Even performing small amounts of exercise five days a week will improve muscle tone and bone mass more than a single longer weekly exercise session. Remember the Me Time Monday mantra: Smaller is better.

One of the godfathers of easy, simple and short minutes-per-day physical routines was J.P. Müller, author of *My System – 15 Minutes' A Day for Health's Sake*, published in 1904. The system was built around physical exercises such as knee bends, leg swinging, torso twists and touching your toes, as well as wellness practices such as hygienic bathing, rubbing the muscles (massage) and deep breathing. More than 2 million copies of *My System* were sold and translated into 25 languages read by doctors, kings, business titans, fellow athletes and celebrities such as Franz Kafka.

Müller was on to something. First, you have to softly swing or push (like in tai chi) your arms and legs to gain range of motion. Second, you need good posture to support proper breathing, digestive health and balance of your internal organs. Most people spend hours a day sitting which is abnormal based on our evolution. You hunch over and get "tech neck" and all this works against you in maintaining a strong frame to keep your body in balance. Desk exercises are helpful – raise your arms above your head several times, lean right then left all while still sitting or do chair yoga. You should also stand up every 20-30 minutes. Look at a beautiful vista – perhaps a nature scene outside your window. This exercises your eyes from screen fatigue. Then bend over to touch your toes or lift your legs left and right all while breathing with good straight posture.

Müller's approach to wellness is that he felt as a society we were conditioned to think of a doctor first rather than ourselves to address health issues – he wanted to flip that notion. What made Müller a trailblazer is his focus on women, older people and even children. He customized his system for these special populations and even wrote a version called *My Sunbathing and Fresh Air System* that blended biophilia and exercise. Today we call this connection of moving in nature "green exercise" and it is an ageless solution to build both your physical and mental health. A 2023 study in *Nature* found a 15-minute walk outside on a leaf-canopied or tree-lined path rather than inside on a treadmill, improved cognitive test scores and calmed anxious nerves.

The aerobic activity of walking just 5,000 steps a day, improves blood flow and lowers blood pressure to reduce risk of cardiovascular disease and Alzheimer's. And, as mentioned above, walking outside in nature is a double boost – it is your supplement to your regular routine where you get more wellness benefit. One study found taking a walk where you can view trees, beaches or other nature scenes, reduces oxidative stress and can lower Alzheimer's risk in adults over 60. Other researchers found adults in their 60s who exercised outside spent 30 minutes more a week working out than did the indoor gym group.

The speed of your walking may also be a diagnostic indicator for dementia. A recent study of 16,855 older yet fit people in Australia and the U.S., showed having a slower gait as you walk is associated with increased risk of Alzheimer's. This risk was highest in people age 65+ who had both gait and memory decline. But people who walk about 5% slower or more each year while also exhibiting signs of slower mental processing were most likely to develop dementia. In another study of older adults who had mild cognitive impairment (MCI), the participants showed no signs of progression in cognitive decline after 12 months if they either did an aerobic exercise such as walking or swimming, or if they stretched or did yoga. Part of this may be that exercise increases the size of the hippocampus, where you capture memory in the brain and is one of the first areas to atrophy with dementia.

Walking your pet may also reduce risk for dementia for both of you. Studies show dementia affects between 14% to 35% of older dogs and more recently the Dog Aging Project found dementia is more than six times higher in inactive dogs.

While you may think of today's social workout as a Soul Cycle class[26], the precursor of modern fitness and sports clubs was Jack LaLanne who opened his first health club in the 1930s. An evangelist for fitness, weight lifting and nutrition calling it "America's salvation," LaLanne became a household name with his fitness TV show in the '60s and '70s. He is credited with encouraging women to join gyms (including the 200 he operated across the country) and to lift weights. Jane Fonda must have been tuning in. In the 1980s Fonda, the Academy Award-winning actress and political activist, healthified her image by donning leg warmers and kick-starting the aerobics craze with books, studio classes and VHS cassettes (the era before DVDs and streaming) using her catchphrase "feel the

---

[26] In Social Wellness, I cover Soul Cycle founders' latest Peoplehood social fitness trend.

burn."[27] But what LaLanne and Fonda gave us was not just sweat equity in our own wellness, but the focus on flexibility, as well as bone and muscle strength that is critical for any physical health program.

About 45% of people ages 40 to 59 years old are obese. Even being 10 pounds overweight increases the force on your joints and especially your knees by 30 to 40 pounds with every step. This wear and tear on your body leaves you feeling like the Tin Man in "The Wizard of Oz." Using my car analogy, your knees and hips are the shock absorbers for the body. After decades of use, those over age 50 often need hip and knee replacement surgery.

There are also bone density aging health issues, such as arthritis and osteoporosis, affecting more than 32 million adults – men (42%) and women (47%) – after age 50. To address stiff joints the prescription is "motion is lotion." Cartilage is the connective tissue where our bones come together: knees, elbows, shoulders, ankles and along the spine. Repetitive motion keeps blood and nutrients flowing to the tissue. When you are sedentary, you are breaking down cartilage health and putting yourself at risk for other injuries and for stiffness. Cartilage is also 80% water which is why staying hydrated means more lubrication equals less pain. When it comes to "forgiving sports," former tennis enthusiasts who gave up playing due to elbow bursitis, knee aches and stamina issues, have picked up the pickle ball craze with more than 36 million players, many in their 50s to 80s. This trending sport is both joint wellness and social fitness.

Some cross-training hacks for your body and your brain exercises are also essential.[28] For instance: sleeping on the opposite side of the bed

---

[27] An 84-year-old Fonda is continuing to leverage her fitness persona as the brand ambassador for an ageless athleisurewear line called H&M Move. I wrote about brands with younger audiences embracing influencers like Fonda, who could be their grandmothers (and the "coastal grandmother" Tik Tok trend), for PBS Next Avenue.

[28] You will learn more about brain exercises in Intellectual Wellness.

(either every other night or every other week) makes you use muscles on the *other side* of your body to get up. It also jumpstarts your brain because you have to think about how to get up instead of just rolling out of bed as usual. Another hack is switching the shoulder on which you carry a purse, backpack or laptop bag. The wear and tear to just one shoulder over a lifetime will catch up with you in mid-life. Balanced use of muscles is key to overcoming joint pain that can begin in your 40s.

Back to basics workouts, such as Müller's *My System*, dominated 2023 Google and Pinterest searches with terms such as primal movement (140% increase) and mobility stretches (120% increase). Driven mostly by Gen X and Millennials, everything from knee and hip mobility exercises to neck hump stretching to avoid "tech neck" are trending in this era of an endless cycle of work and screen time that keeps your body cramped in one position for hours at a time. If you use the Me Time Monday microflows approach and spend 5-10 minutes a day on fun, easy exercises that increase heart rate or strengthen bones and muscles, in one week you will have performed 35-70 minutes of exercise.

Emotional Wellness

How Sully found his flow in the "Miracle on the Hudson"

The afternoon of January 15, 2009 was a brisk yet beautifully sunny winter day in New York City. As U.S. Airways flight 1549 took off from La Guardia Airport the 150 passengers on board had no idea their pilot would use his flow state of positive psychology to save their lives.

Only two minutes into the flight, the airplane was struck by a flock of geese causing both engines to shut down. Captain Chesley "Sully" Sullenberger had only 208 seconds to make a fateful decision. After consulting his options, Sully felt the only recourse was to hopefully glide the airplane to a safe water landing on the Hudson River, what aviation experts call "ditching" the aircraft. With one minute until the plane made contact with water, he announced to passengers and flight crew, "Brace for impact."

Drawing on his 42-year airline pilot experience, his expert knowledge of aviation safety and his passion as a glider pilot he successfully landed the plane saving all 155 souls on board. He was 57 ½ years old, only 2.5 years away from the mandatory retirement age for pilots at that time (the age limit has been increased and is currently 65).

In a "60 Minutes" TV interview shortly after what has been called "the Miracle on the Hudson," Sullenberger admitted it was "the worst sickening, pit-of-your-stomach, falling-through-the-floor feeling" he had ever experienced. However, he later wrote about that day where he explained he immediately transferred his airline pilot thinking to glider pilot thinking. Sully's flow state from flying gliders created calm and empowerment and gave him the internal locus of control that became the determining factor in saving lives that day.

Glider training teaches pilots to overcome fear of engine failure because there is no engine. These pilots find calm in the silence whereas other traditional airline pilots might panic. Most glider pilots define the serenity of floating on air as spiritual and meditative.

The experience of Flight 1549 was far from serene but what Sully's heroic management of this potentially devastating event shows is finding your flow may just be life-saving.

From FOMO to Flow to JOMO

One of my favorite theories I studied in my graduate gerontology courses was *flow* – the state of consciousness leading to optimal experiences and positivity identified by Mihaly Csikszentmihalyi.[29]

As opposed to what some people believe is flow – the languid, "go with the flow" mantra embraced by most California surf bums and Zen masters – Csikszentmihalyi's flow theory is an extension and evolution of Maslow's peak experiences. It is defined as combining *effort* with *energy* in an *enjoyable* pursuit, where the journey and achievement creates a flow state of mind over body. I call it the E^3 formula for happiness. Many participants in Csikszentmihalyi's decades of research across several countries and cultures, describe their flow state as "floating in happiness."

Csikszentmihalyi found that flow happens during a heightened state of consciousness – a psychic awareness and energy – where the discipline of the mind can overcome the limitations, distractions or stress responses felt physically. Flow provides internal locus of control, where achievement is in the hands of the individual rather than being shaped by outside forces.

---

[29] One of my fun hacks was to train myself how to phonetically pronounce his name – it is ME-high Chick-sent-ME-high.

It is the achievement of control over attention, the ultimate state of what many call "being in the present." But unlike its cousin, meditation, where attention can be distracted and you must bring your mind back to focused breathing, flow state is where the distractions do not exist. In flow, you are so centered on the task at hand that all time, outside stimuli and physiological activity is on pause until the task is completed. It is such a sublime state of happiness that longer-lingering joy courses through your body.

In today's world, we celebrate spontaneity and going with our gut instinct. And while breaking out of confining routines can have its benefits, being governed by instant gratification leads you to be less happy. The pursuit of flow helps you gain mastery over your life based on achieving meaningful personal goals that take time and patience. When the effort is earned, it is not only enjoyable but also joyful.

Part of our wanting instant gratification is the dopamine release in the brain, such as posting on social media. However, social media posts rely on external locus of control – feedback from others with "shares" or "likes" – for fulfillment and happiness. This is the opposite of flow.

When you become an addict under the power of others who dictate your emotions you are doomed to be less healthy and less happy. In fact, "doomscrolling" where people spend endless minutes or hours scrolling through their phones or laptops, is another aspect of this unhealthy behavior. It is why studies show people who spend 2-3 hours per day on social media have higher levels of depression and anxiety. Ironically, there was a great tweet that captured everything you need to know about social media screen time: "Scrolling is the new smoking."

Most obsessed social media addicts are driven by FOMO (fear of missing out) to achieve a sense of relevancy, meaning and inclusion. But

FOMO is based on a nameless, mostly unknown audience. Becoming enslaved to a digital machine is external locus of control not flow. It is this false sense of fame (and perhaps the incentive of Kardashian levels of cash) that ultimately leads social media junkies to higher levels of depression than those who monitor and limit their social screen time. Abandoning FOMO for flow will lead to higher levels of life satisfaction and ultimately a sense of accomplishment better than any social media feedback.

Csikszentmihalyi analyzed how Olympic athletes, grandmaster chess players, prima ballerinas, concert pianists and avid mountain climbers are all experiencing flow in their efforts. But you do not have to be a world-class performer or athlete to find flow. People who enjoy their jobs, thrive in their gardens, learn a new language or how to play a musical instrument, adopt a new hobby or perfect a new recipe can all embrace flow in their life. In Csikszentmihalyi's research, reading was one of most frequently mentioned enjoyable activities that can achieve flow state. The key is to find the balance between a challenging task with the ability and skill needed to complete the task and to find enjoyment during and after the process.

One of my favorite examples of flow is an experience I had watching a special ballet performance. Ever since I was little, my Mom and I have attended the ballet.[30] Every season I would be enthralled watching the exquisite ballerinas and powerful male dancers perform "Giselle," Swan Lake," "The Nutcracker" and more. When I think of flow, I think of a particular performance out of all the ballets we attended. The *prima ballerina assoluta*, Alessandra Ferri, was at the height of her dance mastery in the 1980s. On this night in 1985, she was dancing a role that would become her signature: Juliet of the star-crossed lovers in "Romeo and Juliet."

---

[30] My Mom had been a talented young ballerina while I was more of a Fosse-esque jazzy hip rolls, finger snaps dancer.

While Ferri had danced this role numerous times[31] this night would be magical because I watched her flow state in person. She was formidable yet fluid, precise but pliant, innocently joyful and vibrantly passionate. She was not performing for an audience, she was living and breathing Juliet.

Figure 11: Ballerina Alessandra Ferri finds her flow during "Romeo & Juliet" performance

I was not the only one mesmerized. She received 18 curtain calls and even three decades later, my Mom and I still talk about that special night. When asked by a reporter about her stellar performance, Ferri answered, "I just feel it, Juliet is inside me, I am her when I'm on stage."

One of the difficulties in finding flow is the need to abandon your multitasking life. Being able to juggle numerous attention-seeking activities at once is a badge of honor and is a skill society admires. But multitasking defeats flow state. Scientists have found you can only manage seven

---

[31] 31 years later Ferri would make "Romeo and Juliet" her last performance at age 53 dancing to a sold-out crowd at the Metropolitan Opera House in New York City in 2016 where she received a 20-minute standing ovation.

different stimuli at once: different sounds or visual images, emotions and thought process. When all of your senses are engaged in one activity, you are able to control your consciousness, be focused and present, and successfully accomplish the task or activity. This is why flow is not about productivity, it is about mastery.

The result of flow state is a sense of accomplishment and achievement. It boosts confidence, resiliency and satisfaction. For caregivers, whose multitasking capabilities are on display every day, finding flow becomes essential in helping to tackle other challenges that are less satisfying or enjoyable. It also provides the mental tool caregivers need to focus and eliminate distractions in accomplishing caregiving responsibilities.

Finally, flow allows caregivers to avoid being tied to the judgment of others. The more you practice flow, the more you become trained to achieve self-care. You also accumulate the internal locus of control to not only rely on how you feel, but to appreciate the quality of the caregiving experience. The essence of flow is enjoyment, not necessarily pleasure, which is a more fleeting emotion and temporary state. Flow allows caregivers to enjoy caregiving even if the situation is not a pleasurable one. Flow also allows personal growth, satisfaction and provides the energy and endurance for caregiving. Csikszentmihalyi explains during flow state, "Concern for the self disappears, yet paradoxically the sense of self emerges stronger after the flow experience."

This correlates to many caregiver studies that show despite the challenging, time-consuming and emotionally draining nature of caregiving, these family members report being grateful to be in their role and happy they were able to give back to their loved one. For these caregivers, flow has replaced FOMO with JOMO (Joy of Missing Out).

When Sully transformed a would-be disaster into a case of survival and celebration of life, he was using flow state to make it happen. "The physiological reaction I had was strong and I had to force myself to use my training and force calm on the situation," Sully said during one TV interview. He said it was not hard to do, it just took some concentration. "I was sure I could do it."

Now that is what I call going with the flow.

Happiness is both a Right and a Choice

> We hold these truths to be self-evident, that all men are created equal, that they are endowed by their Creator with certain unalienable Rights, that among these are Life, Liberty and the pursuit of Happiness.
>
> — United States Declaration of Independence
>
> (July 4, 1776)

When Thomas Jefferson drafted the unalienable rights in America's most profound statement about its freedom and liberty, he was borrowing substantially from the Enlightenment philosophies of John Locke. Regarded as the father of classical liberalism, Locke defined the concepts of identity and self. He also believed we are born with our minds as a *tabula rosa* – a blank slate upon which knowledge is gained through life's experiences by way of sense perception, a concept known as empiricism. Empiricists believe we use our five senses to gain experiences and observations that shape our knowledge and determine who we are and how we live our lives.

What is profound about the establishment of happiness as a right is it is seen as equal to life and liberty and firmly establishes the principle of the individual's rights over the rights of the state. This is the essence of wellness: your right to pursue happiness however you define it.

Of course, happiness has been a goal long before Locke and the founding of America. The ancient Greeks had a term, *eudaimonia,* which translates to "good life," "flourishing," and "happiness." Aristotle believed this practice of well-being was tied to nature's fulfillment of realizing one's potential. In our modern world, Martin Seligman in his book, *Flourish,* feels happiness is passé and so overused as to be meaningless. He believes it is flourishing we should be pursuing.

Whether you define this state of life satisfaction and fulfillment as happiness or flourishing, in the world of wellness, happiness is more than a moment or isolated event. It is also entirely personalized to each of us. My happiness goal may not be the same as yours. And this is one of the prescient messages the Founders left in the Declaration of Independence. It was not only a consensual group declaration on freedom but it was also an independent declaration that anyone and everyone has a right to pursue happiness as they define it. Happiness typically means emotional well-being, a pleasurable – and more importantly, meaningful – life that brings satisfaction over the life course instead of just for transitory moments.

The big question is whether happiness is sustainable. Many people define their lives as happy. But that does not mean grief, disappointment, frustrations and pain do not enter the picture. Most psychologists believe learning to cherish happiness and a happy life means having to experience the downsides and bad times as well. The ability to look beyond the negative and find the silver linings or lessons from these difficulties and challenges makes the happier times even sweeter. And science tells us it takes three months for feelings of happiness or unhappiness tied to life events to dissipate where we go back to "normal" or our baseline of everyday life emotions. More life-altering (having a child) or traumatic (losing a child or parent or spouse) events can have longer lasting effect, but most of the research shows the happy times are never as good as you expect and the bad times are not as bad as they initially seem.

This is the balance and equilibrium foundation for both happiness and wellness when caregiving. Harvard physiologist, Walter Bradford Cannon, coined the phrase *homeostasis* in his 1930 book, *The Wisdom of the Body* to define the necessary equilibrium of the body's processes needed for survival. Once again you see through Cannon's research and writings that the body is an amazing engine maintaining steady, balanced levels of vital conditions such as temperature, water, salt, sugar, protein, fat, calcium and oxygen contents of the blood to create the perfect environment for health and the optimal physical and mental performance. And this also brings you back to nature because this equilibrium of the body's processes is mirroring what you see in nature where the Earth dynamically maintains steady-state conditions to allow life to flourish. As individuals we mirror the equilibrium around us.

As you apply homeostasis theory to mental and emotional health, the constant balance of pursuing happiness in a way you can flourish becomes the recipe for better wellness. This is different from seeking things that give you pleasure or transitory moments of elation. When you have a desire for something and that desire is fulfilled, you are instantly gratified but often the gratification dissipates over time, particularly if the object of your desire is of the material world such as a red Ferrari or a Sprinkles cupcake. This is known in gerontology as *hedonic adaptation*. Both of these desires will not replace the value you seek such as quality relationships, a spiritual fulfillment or a life of meaning. These objects will not make you free. In some ways, they enslave you more with expensive car and insurance payments or added pounds and a sugar-high followed by a sugar-crash you will regret. This enslavement reaches only the lower emotional vibrational frequencies you will learn about in this section.

What Locke and Jefferson and many enlightened psychologists like Seligman understand is happiness is a lifelong pursuit for aims that are higher and more meaningful to your soul. Seligman early on in his research identified the three levels of life: *pleasurable* (includes creature comforts and companionship); *engaging* (reveals each individual's unique virtues and strengths and how to put them into action to enhance one's life); and *meaningful* (taps into an individual's unique strengths and virtues for the good of others). When your life has meaning, you have sustained wellness and freedom.

Think of a passion project. Typically, these pursuits are not accomplished in one hour or even one day but your sense of purpose keeps you going. Anything worth pursuing - people and projects – takes time. Pleasure is like winning a raffle or a good hand at poker. But if you pursue purpose, passion and meaning, it is more like a savings account or investing in stocks. The reward is not instantaneous but so worth the wait and keeps building on your happiness returns year over year.

Scientific research over the last 20 years is captivated by how to maintain this state of happiness but like wellness – it is not a trend. Humans will never stop wanting happiness, wellness and joy.

In my Me Time Monday workshop, we go through an exercise called "Refueling Happiness" that you can do on your own. Based on the *affective forecasting* theory[32] from Harvard's Dan Gilbert, a mind-brain behavioral psychologist, and his research collaborator, Timothy Wilson, psychology professor at the University of Virginia, I ask the workshop attendees to look backwards over the last 10 years of life on what made you happy (as well as unhappy)? Did you plan for these happy occasions or did they happen outside of a plan? Now project the next 10 years of happiness as well as unhappy situations to be avoided. Review your future list, how many things are tied to meaning or doing something for others (including caregiving)? This becomes your roadmap for happiness. The lesson is happiness does not just happen, you have the agency to make it a constant in your life but only when you plan a meaningful life.

The U-Curve of Happiness

When most of us look at the life course and aging, we often presume our happiest days were in our youth. They were carefree, mortgage-free, debt-free, job and family life stress-free. Conversely, when people are asked to think about how they feel about growing older, many will moan and lament their lost youth and become almost petrified about what additional years will do to their physical and mental well-being as well as their quality of life (not to mention concern about drooping jowls, crepey necks and bulging middle sections). But the science is showing us the opposite of our fears is true.

In an interview with *The Economist*, Stanford University psychologist, Laura Carstensen, said, "When young people look at older people, they think how terrifying it must be to be nearing the end of your life. But older people know what matters most."

---

[32] You will read more about affective forecasting in Financial Wellness.

One notable 2010 study that got everyone talking showed in our 20s we hit high levels of happiness only to have it decline in our 40s and bottom out in our early 50s. We only to start to rise again with the peak levels of happiness across the entire life course occurring in our 80s. This research by Arthur Stone, a psychology professor now at USC, is called the U-Curve of Happiness also known as the *aging paradox*. In other words, older people are more present-focused and live for what matters now making their futures happier.

Over the last decade, many scientists and researchers have debated the U-curve happiness hypothesis with varying and polarizing results. Researchers struggle with happiness because it is not "quantifiable."

Some of the debate is centered around language and semantics including the terms happiness, subjective well-being (SWB) and hedonic (happiness) versus eudemonic (meaningful) life pursuits that are related but different.

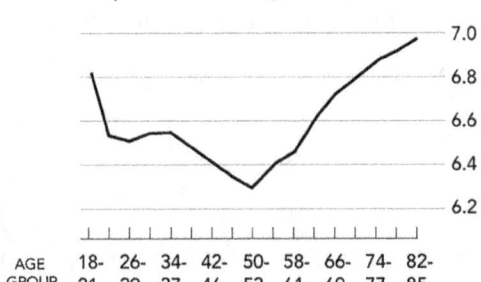

Figure 12: Snapshot of age distribution of psychological well-being in the U.S. (Stone, et.al, 2010)

The question is are people in their 80s expressing more life satisfaction or overall well-being? Does living longer mean you have more to measure in terms of personalized happiness and therefore looking back over life, being older is not so bad? Is it a time of some regained freedom to focus on self? Does it mean you have developed wisdom and patience for things that may have upset you earlier in life? Or is it a time of wanting to leave a legacy rather than stressing over keeping up with the Joneses?[33]

Whatever the motivation, getting older becomes a time of self-reflection and if you believe the science, self-satisfaction. Other studies have also found the U-Curve of Happiness remains stable when applied globally. Researchers expanded this study to more than 145 countries and despite gender, culture, ethnicity or socioeconomic status, the curve remains the same around the globe.

What is concerning is the current state of global emotions as the most recent Gallup survey indicates. For the last decade Gallup has analyzed happiness and life satisfaction across 150 countries worldwide. Despite different age groups and nationalities, feelings of sadness and anxiety are increasing making our world a less happy place.

> The longer we survive and older we get, the happier we become.

In the 2022 report, Gallup found a decline in overall happiness measures and all-time highs for negative responses: four in 10 adults worldwide said they experienced a lot of worry (42%) or stress (41%), and slightly more than three in 10 experienced a lot of physical pain (31%). More than one in four experienced sadness (28%), and slightly fewer experienced anger

---

[33] Interesting fact: the Joneses referenced in this saying were the high society family of Gilded Age writer, Edith Wharton, neé Jones, who famously said about happiness, "If only we'd stop trying to be happy, we could have a pretty good time."

(23%). Although the global coronavirus pandemic influenced the findings, Gallup researchers say happiness globally has been on a decline for the last decade. However, Gallup's methodology states it queried adults over age 15 with no breakdown of respective age groups. It would be interesting to overlay Stone's research of an increase in life satisfaction in older adults from the U-Curve with Gallup's current states of happiness across all ages.

Is Happiness Genetic?

If happiness is the global obsession of science and society, how do we find it? Scandinavian countries such as Finland, Denmark and Iceland always seem to be at the top of the leaderboard in global happiness polls. Besides living near water, what makes these Nordic countries happier than their global neighbors?[34]

The World Happiness Report 2022 found 30-40% of the differences in happiness between people is accounted for by their genetic differences. A new study analyzed why Denmark is always in the Top 3 of countries with high well-being scores.[35] What the researchers found after looking at 131 different countries and various happiness surveys including Gallup's, is the greater a nation's genetic distance from Denmark (in terms of genetic make-up not geographically), the lower the reported well-being of that nation. They also analyzed a mutation of a gene that influences serotonin that affects your moods and mental well-being. The findings show Danes and people from the Netherlands have the variant of the gene that is opposite to scoring lower on life satisfaction surveys.

---

[34] You will learn more about blue wellness and happiness in Environmental Wellness.
[35] Danes are mostly happy people debunking Shakespeare's *Hamlet* that influences our opinions of Danes as being melancholy.

And finally, researchers looked at whether ancestry held true for generations of certain heritages who were born and have lived outside of those countries such as America. What they found is the genetic happiness factor holds true – if you happen to have Danish ancestry,[36] despite being born in America and generations removed from my Danish ancestor, I am genetically predisposed to happiness.

Dr. Andrew Oswald, one of the lead researchers in the study, commented in an article for *PsychCentral* online, "We used data on the reported well-being of Americans and then looked at which part of the world their ancestors had come from. The evidence revealed there is an unexplained positive correlation between the happiness today of some nations and the observed happiness of Americans whose ancestors came from these nations, even after controlling for personal income and religion."

But what is within your control to increase your happiness factor? In an article I wrote for *PBS Next Avenue*, I highlighted how caregivers can find happiness. One resource is through visualization techniques as discovered by Sonja Lyubomirsky, a noted happiness researcher and psychology professor at the University of California at Riverside. She has spent years studying happiness and its health impacts and one of her projects required participants to think about happy events for just eight minutes every day for three simultaneous days. The results showed participants had higher life satisfaction levels for the following four weeks and at higher levels than they felt before they joined the study.

Another idea I use in my Me Time Monday workshop is to have participants do Smile Exercises. For one minute everyone smiles then we track what thoughts came into your mind during that time. Then we do it

---

[36] I can claim 12% of my DNA is Danish.

again, but this time I have participants think of something sad or negative without losing their smile which is very hard to do since studies show smiling boosts your dopamine, endorphins and serotonin levels. I also have the participants use this in their daily lives smiling at least one smile for every waking hour per day – approximately 16 smiles per day. Smiling is also a great facial exercise – each time you smile you are moving 43 muscles in your face giving them a good workout. A Swedish study showed smiling has a "pay it forward" benefit. When you give someone a warm, genuine smile, the involuntary facial feedback triggers in the receiver to return it in kind and pass it on to the next person.

Heaven is the only place where unfiltered, uninterrupted happiness will be found but maybe that is what Jefferson intended when he included the pursuit of happiness in America's DNA. To win a revolution against a formidable enemy, sometimes you need a little divine intervention and hope for a better future.[37]

Arthur Brooks, a Harvard professor focused on happiness science, gave a talk at the Aspen Ideas Festival a few years ago where he shared insights on subjective well-being (SWB) based on a study done with two groups: lottery winners and paraplegics. What researchers wanted to know is what happened to their mindset six months after these life-changing events? Paraplegics returned to almost the same level of happiness they had in the days before their traumatic accidents. However, the lottery winners were found to be less happy because they felt people were abusing their generosity and the grand purchases they had made did not make them any happier than before their change in fortune.

---

[37] Jefferson has been labeled an atheist or agnostic but he is actually a theist believing in a benevolent creator, God, to whom humans owed praise.

Our Founding Fathers realized to be happy you need to be free. Many people think "if only I . . .". (get the promotion, win the lottery, buy the house, have a child) then I will be happy. But happiness does not happen *to you*, happiness is *your lifelong pursuit* just as the Declaration guarantees.

The lesson is you should never stop pursuing happiness despite life's roadblocks such as caregiving. You need to be grateful for the happy moments you have accumulated so far with the promise of more to come. Sustained happiness is not one big thing that makes for a happy life, it is the accumulation of small happy moments that keep you going day to day. Ultimately happiness is about striking balance between the bad days and seeking things and people that bring you the joyful moments in the present.

Good Vibrations:
Emotional & Mental Health Energy

If your body is the vehicle that carries you through life, your mental and emotional wellness is what fuels the journey. For caregivers the emotional part of the journey can be like a roller coaster, with ups and downs, anticipation and fear and everything in between.

Since the body is in constant motion emitting energy 24/7 (even when you are asleep – remember the brain is working), we will explore your emotional vibrations and the energy frequencies associated with emotions that become essential to optimizing your well-being. We start with the difference between mental health and emotional health, terms often used interchangeably. While they are connected to each other they are different.

The National Alliance on Mental Illness (NAMI) reports 1 in 5 Americans are considered to have a mental illness: schizoid spectrum, bipolar disorder, chronic depression, seasonal affective disorder (SAD), postpartum depression, eating disorders such as anorexia, addictions to alcohol, drugs or other unhealthy behaviors such as gambling. In addition, 1 in 5 people have anxiety disorders such as agoraphobia (fear of leaving your home), panic attacks, separation anxiety and other issues that impair daily living and quality of life. Certain mental health issues including bipolar disorder, schizophrenia and depression can be genetic. As well, some scientists believe mental health is tied to nutrition and circadian rhythms.

During the pandemic, rates of depression tripled jumping from 8.5% before the pandemic to a staggering 27.8%. The symptoms of depression can include: unrelenting sadness, despair, fatigue, sleep problems, lack of enthusiasm, complacency and loss of appetite or overeating. It is one of the reasons a divided U.S. Congress came together to pass the national "988" mental health hotline and within the first six months of operation – between July to December, 2022 – it received more than 2 million calls and texts.[38]

One type of depression is dysthymia, a longer-lasting type of low-grade depression typically lasting two years or more. Dysthymia is often associated with other conditions, such as heart disease, cancer, substance abuse and anxiety disorders. Most people do not seek help with dysthymia because the symptoms are not severe as in major depression. But even low-grade depression should be treated to help you avoid longer-term health risks.

Mental health does not have to be life threatening, such as cancer or heart disease, but it can lead to suicidal ideation. Suicide is one of the Top 10 leading causes of death and Kaiser Health News reported a 4% increase in 2021 suicides with teen suicides double that rate at 8%.

While news headlines focus on mental distress of younger generations, 1 in 5 adults over age 55 suffer from mental health issues with men over age of 85 experiencing the highest levels of suicide of any age group. Yet the CDC reports only 40% of assisted living communities offer mental health services. While older men have higher suicide rates than women, it was

---

[38] I take mental illness very seriously. Many of the comments in this chapter are for those who have situational depression not chronic depression or suicidal ideation that needs to be treated by a psychiatrist or psychologist or in emergencies call 988 in the U.S.

female family caregivers who expressed more negative mental health impact from the pandemic (39%) than male family caregivers in a 2022 American Psychological Association survey. And as noted in the Me Time Monday section, 2021 research by Archangels found 52% of Sandwich Generation caregivers (caring for children and older parents simultaneously) reported suicidal ideation and 85% had negative impact to their emotional health.

Mental health is a leading cause of disability and those who suffer from a mental health disorder typically die 32 years earlier with a life expectancy of only age 54 as compared to their mentally healthy counterparts. For instance, chronic depression increases risk for insulin resistance which is why 20% of diabetics have severe depression. One longitudinal study following subjects for nine years found a moderate increase in insulin resistance was linked to an 89% increase in cases of major depressive disorder. In the same study, every 1-inch increase in abdominal fat was related to an 11% higher rate of depression, and increased fasting plasma glucose created a 37% higher rate of depression.

The difference between mental health and emotional health is the latter is how you *react* to information and situations about your mental health. It is how you process information and situations and express emotions and feelings. For instance, how you express your feelings while in the grip of depression – feelings such as "no one loves me" or "no one supports me" or "no one cares about me" – is your emotional health status. It is sometimes difficult to distinguish mental health from emotional health because they are meshed together like twine. When one is out of balance, it affects the other.

We know negative events are part of the human experience, but how you cope and conquer your emotions and allow these events to affect you are crucial to your happiness, health and survival. If your resiliency and strength in addressing emotional health issues seems to be at an all-time low, too often drug therapies are the only solution offered for those with mental health issues.

While feelings are experienced consciously, emotions are displayed either consciously or subconsciously. And even though numerous teletherapy and app-based mental health solutions grew exponentially during the pandemic, data shows usage of these apps is down 30% from 2021-2022.

In the 1970s, psychologist Paul Eckman identified six basic emotions relevant to all human cultures: Happiness, Sadness, Fear, Disgust, Anger, Surprise.

Figure 13: Paul Eckman's research identified six basic human emotions

A few years ago, researchers at UC Berkeley Greater Good Science Center expanded the six basic emotions to 27 different categories. The researchers realized there are subtle gradients in your six basic emotions that more accurately express how you react in various situations. These nuanced emotions include: adoration, anxiety, awe, confusion, relief, satisfaction and joy. Part of this evolution into understanding of emotions is the six primary emotions Eckman identified are triggered by the ancient brain but when interpreted, analyzed and acted upon – those additional gradients classified by the Berkeley researchers – are being modulated from the modern brain.

One of the many silver linings of this pandemic is it made us all *slow down and think about what makes us happy*. In the Me Time Monday workshop, we focus on Eckman's six emotions for an experiment to become more self-aware of your emotions. For two weeks, participants make notes next to the six emotions to evaluate how they are feeling. Are you more happy or sad? Do you have a lot of anger moments or disgust? Were surprises positive or negative?

> You must experience highs and lows to understand the context of happiness.

By evaluating your emotions you can analyze how to create balance between everything you are feeling and experiencing. It is important to experience the spectrum of emotions because balance is what gerontologists know you need for survival. We do not prescribe "good" or "bad" to your emotions. Being able to manage an emotion such as anger, which some may consider negative, is what helps you survive. It is why it is one of the five stages that helps you heal from grief. Anger anchors you back to life and reality and rescues you from denial. And throughout life, you will encounter and should embrace the moments that bring both sun and clouds into your life.

A few years ago, I attended the funeral of a dear college friend. While my heart was heavy over the tragic loss of someone in her early 50s, my friend's memorial celebration of life brought together sorority sisters I had not seen in years. We cried, we laughed, we reminisced and the bitterness and sadness of loss was mixed with the gift of having this friend in our lives. We were also comforted by the sense of belonging and the friendships that were still strong despite the distance of years and time.

Finding Your Vibrational Frequency

Your emotional health is human-powered and energy-based. Have you ever witnessed someone literally lighting up the room when they walk in? Is it their smile, confident posture and gait, engaging eye contact or something else?

One answer may be the study into brain wave patterns and vibrational frequency associated with what are considered "positive" and "negative" energy connected to our emotions. This has led to an emerging health care focus on energy medicine also known as vibrational medicine.

According to Italian researchers, David Muehsam, and Carlo Ventura, "All life exists within a sea of vibration, and rhythm is fundamental to all of life. Diurnal, seasonal, lunar, and solar cycles, and the resonant electromagnetic field (EMF) oscillations of our planet make up the symphony of rhythms in which life on Earth exists."

Everything in the universe is made up of particles: electrons, protons, neutrons, and these particles are what create your emotional vibrancy and vibrational health. In Hinduism and Ayurvedic health practices, these energy fields are called *auras* and in Traditional Chinese Medicine they are known as *chi* (or *qi*). But rather than being dismissed as mystic medicine, emotional frequencies are becoming a growing body of research on resiliency, happiness and emotional health.

Vibrations are often associated with our environmental world – the tidal pull during lunar cycles, seasonal changes in flora and fauna and the electromagnetic energy displayed during a lightning storm. In the 1990s, NASA discovered the "songs of the Earth," an eerie collection of hums and pops where the Sun's vibrational frequency was meeting the Earth's magnetic field. NASA was able to validate each planet in our solar system has a different vibrational frequency or "song." This follows ancient Greek Pythagoras' doctrine of *musica universalis*, where he hypothesized the planets move according to mathematical equations related to musical notes or an inaudible symphony. This doctrine was the foundation for the discovery of the laws of planetary motion.

The same vibrations seen among the planets is true of all living organisms. We each have our unique song that emits energy around us known as sound waves. As humans evolved in our nature environments, our physiological and neurological development integrated with these energy frequencies so the rhythms of breathing, heartbeats and brainwaves have their own energy frequencies.

Here is how it works: humans hear sound via sonic waves that travel through the air to the ear. Bouncing against the walls of the eardrum, a vibration is felt. Those vibrations cause the small hairs – about 10,000 to 15,000 tiny hairs called *cilia* – inside your eardrums to vibrate and act like antennae to turn the vibration into an electrical signal that travels to the brain through the auditory cortex. The brain translates these electrical signals as sounds with different pitch (intonation in a melody) and timbre (vowels and consonants of words and various instruments).

The best illustration of energy frequencies and how we adapted to our environment for survival is found through *entrainment* also known as *beat matching*. Discovered by 17th century Dutch scientist, Christiaan Huygens,[39] the oscillations of two pendulum clocks coincided perfectly due to their

---

[39] Huygens many talents included his invention of the pendulum clock in 1665.

energy fields synchronizing with each other. Entrainment has since been found in various physical and biological systems—from clocks and musical instruments, to cooperative behavior of crickets and fireflies and synchronous firing of neurons. This phenomenon can also be found in greenhouses that use sound wave vibrations to stimulate the growth of cells and nutrients in plants and flowers as well as in sleep science using bone conduction technology to send vibrations to the ear to ease the body into sleep.

When you say you are "in synch" with someone the meaning is literal. Have you been walking with someone where suddenly you are stepping with your right and left legs at the same time? The area you really see entrainment is in circadian rhythms. You are innately programmed to synchronize yourself to these 24/7 cycles. You see this with crossing time zones in long-distance travel. The body takes time to entrain itself with local light/dark cycles which is why you experience jet lag.

Entrainment is what allowed our ancient bodies the ability to adapt to the external changes in our environments of night and day (and to a lesser extent cold and warm temperatures). But it is the social interactions as well as the environmental actions that drive entrainment and influence your health and happiness vibes. One study found entrainment between fetuses and mothers happen inside the womb where researchers were able to observe the synchronization of a mother's heartbeat with that of her unborn child.

GOOD VIBRATIONS: EMOTIONAL & MENTAL HEALTH ENERGY

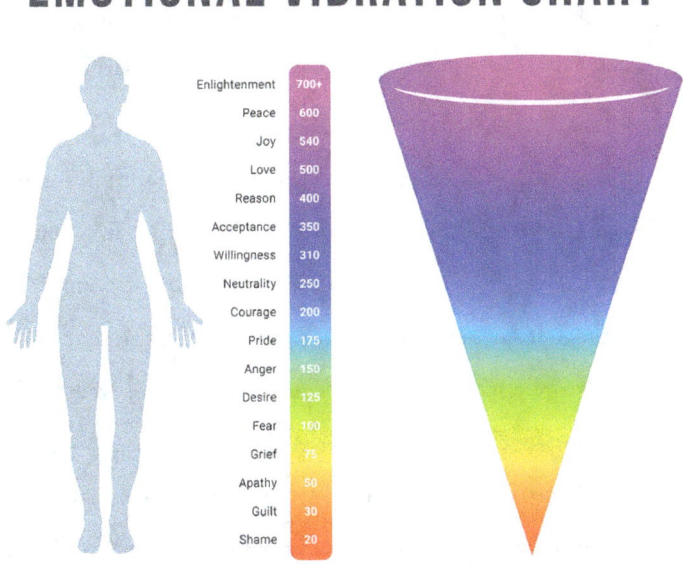

Figure 14: Vibrational Frequency Chart – Energy of Emotions

The graphic shows how some of the top emotions map against the vibrational frequencies they deliver. Your emotional vibrations are tiny molecules made up of water and atoms emitting frequency or hertz levels (Hz). Desire appears lower on the frequency range making it not as "attractive" as Peace or Love. Researchers believe it is because Desire can lead to criminal and transgressive actions (jealous lovers or carjacking someone's Mercedes Benz) and thus, it carries a lower vibrancy. Peace also outranks Love and Courage. Why? Love can be painful and courage can be transitory while Peace is a constant state that stabilizes your energy field and ultimately leads to better health physically and emotionally.

But it is Enlightenment that tops all. Researchers, including Abraham Maslow, believe Enlightenment is about ego-transcendence and once you move beyond yourself your vibrational energy is at its strongest and most stable level. Quantum physics is taking a look at how you can change your vibrational frequencies either by focusing on an emotion higher on the chart when experiencing a lower-level emotion, or by being around others with higher vibrational frequencies where you can synchronize your vibrational energy. Most small children provide strong vibrational levels of happiness and peacefulness and adults tune into this frequency when near them. And spending time in nature will also increase your emotional vibrations because it creates a level of Peace and entrainment with your most ancient, nature environment that calms and soothes the mind.

Emotional frequencies are also associated with empathy. Some people are *emotional sponges* taking on the emotional energy of those around them. You can be a sensitive and perceptive person that offers empathetic support but to take on other's feelings such as pessimism or negativity will lead you to burnout and depression. Compassionate family caregivers can absorb too much emotional energy of others that defeats your wellness needs. This is where Me Time Monday can bring back your empowerment and resilience in a challenging caregiving role and part of that is using four powerful feel-good hormones.

chapter 16

The Four Hormones Against the Apocalypse

Me Time Monday relies on four feel-good hormones. These are oxytocin (love or bonding), serotonin (mood booster), dopamine (reward) and endorphins (pain relief). I call them the Four Hormones Against the Apocalypse as a twist on the four horsemen of the apocalypse in Christian Scriptures who brought death, famine, war and pestilence. When you feel fear, pain, loneliness or stress, these hormones rescue you from your personal apocalypse.

These four hormones are also neurotransmitters, out of the 100 neurotransmitters in our bodies that create the central control for emotional and physical function. Neurotransmitters are chemical messengers that carry messages between nerve cells - think of them as the Fed Ex, email or texting service from your nervous system to other parts of the body. Neurotransmitters also operate like air traffic controllers. They push the messages from cell to cell, block the messages from cells or tweak the message to optimize function.

You can boost these four hormones for wellness. Endorphins, serotonin and oxytocin are released through physical exercise. You boost oxytocin and endorphins by playing music, dancing or singing. You also release endorphins and serotonin through ultra violet light therapy also known as virtual sunshine. Meditation has been linked to dopamine and endorphin release. And laughing and acupuncture also bring pain relief through the transmission of endorphin release.

Throughout the book I refer to how you can harness these four hormones to optimize your wellness efforts.

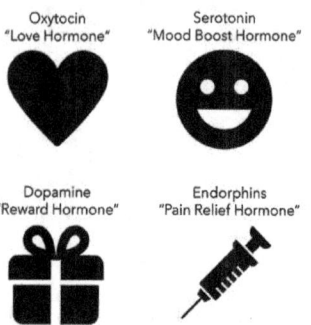

Figure 15: The Four Feel-Good Hormones

OXYTOCIN – It is the hormone associated with love, bonding and physical contact such as hugging. Its main function is to facilitate childbirth. Low levels of oxytocin are linked to postpartum depression.

SEROTONIN – Regulates moods and plays a key role in sleep patterns, anxiety and appetite. Low serotonin levels are linked to depression.

DOPAMINE – Central command for the body's reward center allows for feelings of pleasure and arousal. Dopamine also enables learning by allowing focus and concentration. It also controls motivations.

ENDORPHINS – The body's natural morphine, regulates pain response. Also released when you laugh, fall in love, have sex and eat delicious food. Think of endorphins as euphoria.

chapter 17

Pajama Class Revolt: Positivity and Personality

In 2022, with the passing of Britain's Queen Elizabeth II at age 96, the world mourned a global figure whose dignity, duty and devotion to her country was driven by her positivity and hope. Her outlook on life played a pivotal role in her 70 years as the United Kingdom's longest reigning monarch. From her childhood assaulted by the Nazi Luftwaffe raining bombs down during Britain's Blitz to her "annus horribilis" in 1992 when three of her four children sought divorce[40] and her beloved Windsor Castle was ablaze, Queen Elizabeth's optimism remained even after losing her consort and confidante of 73 years, Prince Philip.

Resiliency and optimism were traits she shared with another great Briton, her first prime minister, Winston Churchill, who lived to age 90. He was a symbol of both remarkable British fortitude coupled with a risk-taking maverick spirit similar to the American revolutionaries, courtesy of his New York-born mother.

Many scientists who study longevity believe and have produced evidenced-based research that positivity and optimism are ingredients to

---

[40] In modern times, divorce may not seem tragic but the Queen was the titular head of the Church of England which is opposed to divorce despite the irony that King Henry VIII created the church so he could divorce Catherine of Aragon and marry Anne Boleyn.

longer, more healthful lives. Does that mean if you do not have an optimistic personality you will not live as long? Not necessarily. Personality traits can organically change with age but one also has the power to change these traits at any age if desired. This topic of personality being fixed or changeable has been debated by psychologists and philosophers throughout history.

Aristotle felt personality could be altered and does change across our life course. However, in the 19th century the father of American psychology, William James[41], believed your personality becomes fixed at about age 30. In *Principles of Psychology*, he wrote, "In most of us, by the age of 30, the character has set like plaster, and will never soften again."

Most psychologists today believe there are no personality *types* but certain personality *traits* can be changed. A majority of the research into personality over the last 20 years has been focused on the Big Five Personality Theory (also called the Five Factor Model). What the researchers, Robert McCrae and Paul Costa, found is personality traits do change over time and are influenced by age and gender. They also found that remarkably these personality traits are consistent across different cultures. In fact, some researchers now believe the universality of the Big Five may point to evolutionary traits from our earliest beginnings as humans. The five factors, are easily remembered with the acronym OCEAN: Openness, Conscientiousness, Extraversion, Agreeableness and Neuroticism.

What various researchers found using the OCEAN theory is throughout most of adulthood – ages 30 to 60 – your Big Five personality traits are fixed, despite difficult or traumatic life events. However, some scientists have observed as people reach their 60s, 70s and 80s, they have a tendency to become less neurotic, but also less extraverted and less open

---

[41] Trivia fact: William James was the brother of famous novelist, Henry James, who wrote poignant portraits of character traits about early 20th Century society.

to new experiences. The experts feel older people compensate with an increase in agreeableness and conscientiousness.

I believe this is typical stereotyping and ageism. Think of the late former president, George H.W. Bush, jumping out of an airplane at age 90 (sounds like extraversion to me) or Anna Wintour, the formidable fashion arbiter and 72-year-old editorial queen of *Vogue* magazine who as of this writing for the last 34 years has dictated fashion trends and anointed successful new designers (sounds like openness). Even Winston Churchill, at age 65, defied these stereotypes during WWII when he showed great openness and less agreeableness executing his Operation Dynamo against advice of other military and political advisors. Churchill ordered the evacuation of more than 338,000 Allied servicemen trapped at Dunkirk using only a flotilla of 800 small boats that most thought was a suicide mission. Not only was it risky but it was also definitely challenging and inventive (and successful). These may be only three examples but we know ageism is rampant even among scientific researchers. If 90 is the new 40,[42] let us hope the scientific community follows what McCrae and Costa believe, "It is the nature of science to be self-correcting."

Martin Seligman, known as the father of modern positive psychology, calls this *learned optimism*. As opposed to what was uncovered in the Me Time Monday section about learned helplessness, you can embrace the opposite called learned optimism. Seligman wrote the epidemic of depression and anxiety in our society will not only put our national security at risk but it also cannot be solved by a dose of Prozac. He felt depression leads to less productivity and worsened health that jeopardizes America's economic and hopeful future and ultimately will hurt our strength as a country.

---

[42] According to Dr. Michael Roizen in his book *The Great Age Reboot*, "90 is the new 40."

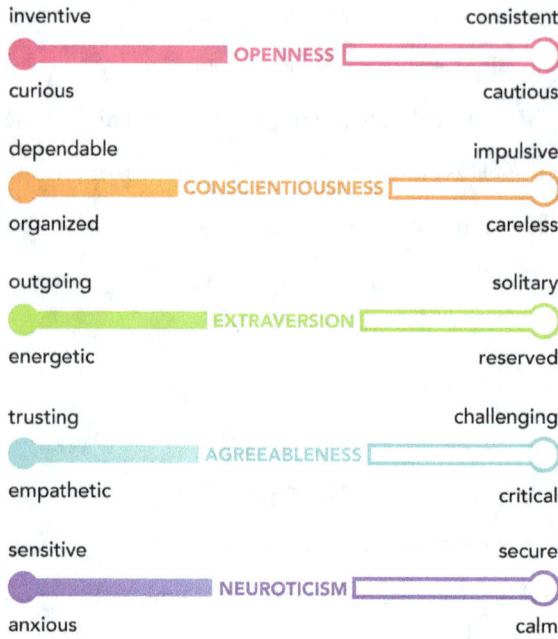

Figure 16: The Big Five Personality Traits "OCEAN." The left side is if you have more of that trait, the right side is if you have less. (McCrae & Costa, 1987)

Studies show people who are optimistic are happier, healthier, live longer, get better jobs or more promotions, have more stable relationships, have healthier children, do better on tests and get elected more frequently. However, just because you may naturally have an optimistic outlook does not mean you are automatically more advantaged than pessimists. You have an increased chance for a happier, healthier, longer life but can Eeyores become Tiggers?

To distinguish between the two groups, optimists are people who do not feel the world is out to get them or that bad events or situations are permanent. They bounce energetically like Tigger from situation to situation. Even when this fun-loving, socially engaging orange tiger creates some chaos or things do not go well, he bounces forward knowing it will be better tomorrow. Optimists do not beat themselves up for problems and if they feel responsible for the problem, they resolve to correct it. They are glass half-full people with more hope and energy.

The Eeyores – pessimists – are glass half-empty people. Eeyore, the famous donkey who wears a gloomy expression and gray coat, believes everything in life is always a problem. Challenges are overwhelming and insurmountable. Pessimists feel a lack of internal locus of control and tend to give up in the face of adversity. They can also engage in the victim blame game: it is always someone else's fault their lives are not going well because personal responsibility is not part of their make-up.

This chronic toxicity flies in the face of wellness. To have little or no hope, to always be in a negative mood, to blame others indiscriminately, to feel a loss of any control and never have any empowerment in the choices to change things leads to stress then inflammation, then chronic health issues resulting in disease and ultimately death. Thankfully the wonderful thing is Eyeores can adopt Tigger traits.

Most people have traits of both optimists and pessimists depending on the situation, although we typically fall into one camp more than the other. If pessimists embrace more positive thinking, research shows you improve your health and wellness. One study conducted among 159,000 women ages 50-79 of different racial and ethnic backgrounds found over a 26-year period, the more optimistic women lived 5% longer and had 10% more likelihood of living past age 90 than their pessimistic counterparts. Psychologists interpreted the findings as both individual optimism but also socializing with other optimistic friend circles as contributors to longevity.

Another eight-year longitudinal study investigating cardiovascular disease risk examined quality of life, chronic disease and ages of death in a sample of 95,000 women. The results found those high on natural optimism were less likely to develop or die from coronary heart disease and had lower mortality overall. And finally, a study conducted among men and women found those with the highest optimism levels increased their lifespans by 11-15% and had a greater chance of reaching age 85 than those who were pessimistic. Further studies suggest optimism may be a protective factor against stroke and improves quality of sleep.

When good things happen, both optimists and pessimists see it as luck or blind fate. But when bad events occur, optimists believe these things are transitory and can be changed or improved while pessimists view these events as catastrophic and self-defeating. In conclusion, pessimists remain down for the count while optimists pick themselves off the mat, bloodied, wounded but determined to keep going. The ability to face adverse circumstances becomes your most powerful tool in pursuing wellness and a longer, healthier life.

Toxic Positivity vs. Victimhood

Recently a new term has made its way into our cultural lexicon: *toxic positivity*. The definition is when someone buries worries, angst, guilt and fears or has someone tell them to "just look on the bright side" or "cheer up things will get better." The proponents of toxic positivity believe it is detrimental to mental health to avoid dealing with emotions, especially when the emotions are negative. On the other hand, it is important to address your sensitivities and achieve a more balanced perspective to escape the victimhood that has become so trendy.

Toxic positivity is a classic clash of pessimists and optimists. It is a balancing act between empathy and hope. If you just lost a loved one or a coveted job, you do not want a friend who immediately says, "It will get better" or "Suck it up, buttercup – that's life." A good friend will be supportive rather than prescriptive. On the other hand, some pessimists wallow in toxic feelings and go tone deaf when anyone tries to help them.

Often how you perceive other's intentions is more about how you feel about yourself. Are you marinating in the hot tub of toxic emotions? Take the opportunity to listen to the person who is promoting self-resiliency and educate them on why this situation is hard for you. Explain your feelings and maybe even ask for help.

Toxic positivity simply labels optimists as toxic offenders. One thing damaging our society is we are engulfed in too much narcissism about how we are hurt, injured or in fear. When you see yourself as a victim, you have no power nor control. You cannot be empowered and strong if you are in victim mode feeling offense even at benign or positive comments. You cannot have it both ways – you either have an internal locus of control that empowers you to neutralize remarks or you are controlled by external factors and have no power. Your choice.

Unfortunately, many women have embraced the victimhood mindset. I witnessed a young woman being told by a young man her eyes were beautiful. Instead of being grateful and accepting the compliment so it could boost her mood for the day, she lashed out at the young man for "objectifying" her. If someone tells you that you have something special, do not turn it into a negative and chastise that person. Again, pause for positivity and let it fill you with strength. Compliments are not micro-aggressions they are social connectors. Everyone encounters comments or problems, the difference is how you react to these situations. Think of victims such as those from 9/11 or the Holocaust. Everyone decides how they will react to evil, horror and adversity with either a hopeful or hopeless future forecast.

Stanford University researcher, Laura Carstensen, showed as your time horizon shrinks, you prune your relationships to focus on more quality than quantity but you also accept or filter positive versus negative messaging as you age. If someone in your life is truly toxic, it might be time to prune that frenemy. On the other hand, avoiding or dismissing negative messaging can have important health consequences.

In many ways, this avoidance of pessimistic messaging may hurt us more than we know. Similar to stress, which is a mechanism for survival, some negativity and pessimism can also improve your survivability. When you are concerned or alarmed, you have heightened awareness that triggers the sympathetic nervous system into action. But chronic pessimism leads to physical health issues, taxes your mental health, bedevils your social health and bars you from spiritual health.

Sometimes even optimists can lose their positive mindset and pursue daily life on auto pilot. But then you misplace your motivation and misdirect your energy. This robotic existence creates complacency and even depression. It is how marriages falter or you become apathetic about a job. You become stuck in melancholic restlessness. Instead of flourishing, you are *languishing*.

This malaise is what so many felt while we escaped into our caves – known as our homes – during the coronavirus pandemic. At first it was safe and comfortable embracing Zoom meetings in our pajamas and avoiding shaving and showering. However, endless months of languishing and avoiding positive daily routines sent us into a slow emotional decline (not to mention hygiene concerns). Anyone who is clinging to or slowly emerging from cave syndrome complex, join the Pajama Class revolt and regain mastery and control over your life.

When you revolt against the Pajama Class, you go from languishing to flourishing.

Taking back control and predictability makes you less distressed. Routines require attention, discipline and deadlines. You have a purpose and you achieve mini milestones that build your confidence. You can also reframe the narrative from languishing to flourishing using linguistic distancing. Psychologists recommend addressing yourself in the third person to create distance. ("Sherri, you are going through a hard time, but you are going to get through this, girl.") This lets you give yourself the advice you would give a friend.

How to Crack the Anxiety Code

In the film, "The Imitation Game," Alan Turing (played by actor Benedict Cumberbatch) and his fellow mathematician code crackers at Bletchley Park in 1940s London were in a desperate race to unravel and decrypt the Nazi cypher called "Enigma." With bombs destroying much of England and German invaders closing in around them, the British scientists were feeling the anxiety of a nation that was on the brink of losing their freedom and way of life. Breaking the enemy code may be their only hope for survival. Good films, such as "The Imitation Game," make you feel the tension and drama of impending disaster or danger.

However, what makes great movies does not make for great quality of life as high anxiety is something you try to avoid. While most people experience anxiety in certain situations, chronic and persistent anxiety that overwhelms daily quality of life requires therapeutic intervention.

Enter the woman who cracked the anxiety code and democratized mental health therapeutic protocols for hundreds of millions of people who suffer from anxiety disorders: Australian psychiatrist, Claire Weekes. Today, there is broad acceptance to understanding the mind-body connection to alleviate and treat stress, depression, anxiety and other mental health disorders. But 60 years ago, this rocked the medical establishment when Weekes published *Self Help for Your Nerves* (1962) that continues to be a top-selling book. Weekes, who called her books "transfusions of hope," came to this breakthrough only after being misdiagnosed. After the loss of her academic mentor to a stroke, she was originally told she had tuberculosis and was sent to a sanitorium suffering chronic heart palpitations. Her six-month institutionalization brought on severe anxiety.

After her release she was talking to a friend, who was a WWI veteran, about her continued heart issues. He told her it was nerves reacting to her fear. If she could conquer the fear, the nerves would calm and the palpitations would cease. She overcame her problem with her self-prescribed therapeutic protocol: *face* the fear, *accept* the symptoms of the fear (heart palpitations, sweaty palms, etc.), *float past* the fear (just like a leaf floating downstream in a lake or river – do not analyze the fear, let it float away), *let time pass* (allowing fear to not panic you means it will disappear more quickly). Most people who suffer from anxiety try to deny it or fight it rather than accept it and this was the breakthrough Weekes provided. I love the *floating* phase, which Weekes called "masterly inactivity."[43]

Clinically, anxiety is a reaction to actual but also perceived stressful situations, also known as *anticipatory stress*. When your sympathetic nervous system is in a constant state of increased anticipatory stress response, the results are feelings of fatigue, frustration, irritability, depression and burnout. The diagnostics manual for mental disorders (DSM-5) criteria for having chronic anxiety is uncontrollable worry and at least three negative physical symptoms persisting from the anxiety for at least six months.

---

[43] You will read more about this as well as digital detoxing and *niksen* in Environmental Wellness.

In 2020, the National Center for Health Statistics reported 8.1% of adults aged 18 and over had symptoms of anxiety disorder, 6.5% had symptoms of depressive disorder, and 10.8% had symptoms of anxiety disorder or depressive disorder. The following year, a 2021 annual survey showed 47% of Americans felt anxiety, especially over their uncertainties of the pandemic. Anxiety topped the list of mental and emotional health issues followed by sadness (44%) and anger (39%). The statistics also show more women than men tend to suffer from generalized anxiety disorder (GAD) and they ruminate more based on chronic anticipatory stress[44]. Some studies point to this difference in brain chemistry between men and women including hormonal fluctuations for women often based on health stages such as puberty and menopause. These brain differences as they relate to anxiety can be observed in children as young as nine years old. With brain plasticity, we imprint emotional responses in the brain if we consistently think of negative or positive stimuli and thoughts. You can train your brain to become more resilient and less anxious if you practice positive exercises, such as Weekes' solution, consistently.

In the Me Time Monday program, we look at anxiety as transactional in order to regain control over your stress response. When you experience anxiety, it is easy to think in terms of external locus of control or things you cannot change. You need to remind yourself that you also have internal locus of control, an ability to control your response to the stress you are experiencing. This is what Weekes' formula is all about – taking back control over the stages of anxiety to return to equilibrium.

---

[44] When it comes to sex differences in neurohealth, males suffer more from neurodevelopmental issues such as autism and ADHD, while women have more anxiety and Alzheimer's.

You can also tackle your response in two ways: 1) Problem-Focused Coping activities such as going on a daily walk, becoming more organized, creating a to-do plan and asserting your needs; and 2) Emotion-Focused Coping such as meditation, mindfulness, seeking emotional social support by talking through a problem with an empathetic friend or therapist.

One of the best ways to address anxiety according to numerous studies is to embrace your curiosity and interest in learning new things. Anxiety is based on fear but curiosity enables a sense of wonder and awe.

How to Predict Your Mental Health Forecast

This section on Emotional Wellness helps you see not everyone can be happy every moment of every day. Just like the weather, you need the rain to appreciate the rainbow. Allowing yourself the grace to have bad episodes is OK as long as you do not hold onto that emotion so it impedes your ongoing quest for happiness. Eckman's original concept of six basic human emotions only had two that were positivity-driven: happiness and surprise (and some see surprise as negative). This is a signal that it takes an effort not to let the other emotions – sadness, anger, fear and disgust – overwhelm you. But it also is a reminder that you need the bad days to appreciate how good the good days make you feel. This is the balance needed in life just like the planet needs sunny day and rainy days to thrive.

You are the weather forecaster of your life. You dictate if it will be cloudy or sunny each day. Some days the forecast may be about survival, other days it may be about revival. Finding this balance in your mental health weather forecast makes for a joyful life.

Social Wellness

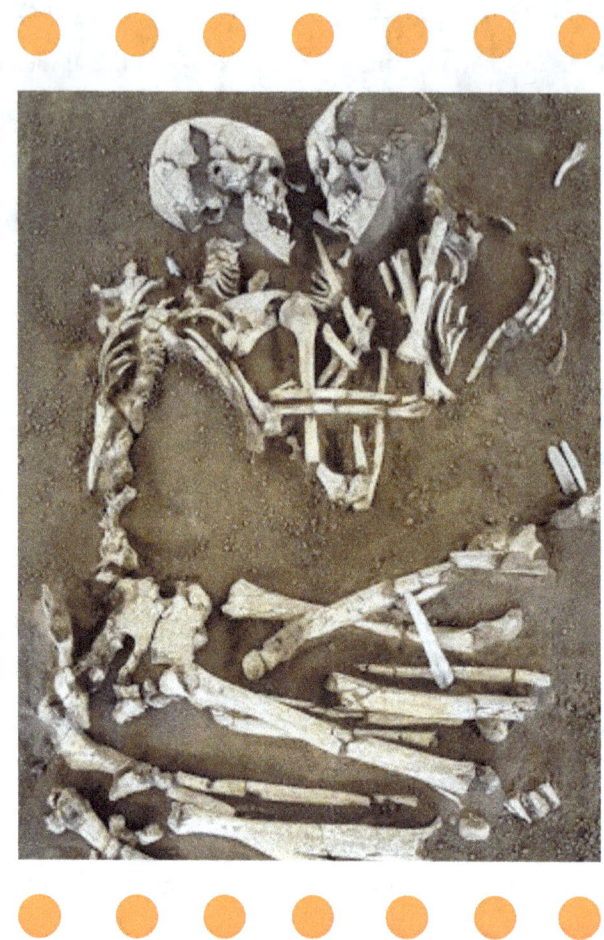

The Lovers of Valdaro "Romeo and Juliet" (4000 BC)

On Valentine's Day 2007, archeologists on a dig in the village of Valdaro in Northern Italy made an historic find. Two skeletons – one male and the other female – were posed in a loving embrace, arms and legs intertwined, facing each other with foreheads touching, a uniquely human emotional expression that typically signifies love and intimacy. Researchers confirmed the skeletons with carbon dating 5,000 to 6,000 years ago during the Neolithic Age, both about 20 years of age but not genetically connected (e.g., not mother/son, brother/sister or father/daughter). It appeared these ancient lovers found comfort in each other during their last moments of life.

What amazed the archeologists and historians is most burial sites and remains found for this ancient period do not consist of more than one person. The male skeleton had an arrow in his spinal column while the woman had an arrowhead in her side. It is unclear if they were both mortally wounded by a predator or if the woman sacrificed herself to join her lover in the afterlife. Archeologists named the couple Romeo and Juliet not just for their youth and romantic death poses but also since the burial site was found near Verona, the city where Shakespeare famously set the story of his star-crossed lovers.

Since ancient times, love, intimacy and bonding with others have been a part of the human experience. As a social species, humans survive and thrive through the cooperation and love of other humans. When we share the risk of threats to our mortality, we gain trust with those individuals. This bond of trust is the most significant influence on both health and happiness. It also allows groups to become stronger whether it is the military where soldiers trust their fellow warfighters to "have their six" or in companies and countries where employees and citizens become loyal and dedicated when the social contract is formed through the trust of each other. Happiness is not found in things, it is found in people and your relationships and without them you will perish. This social bonding is your eternal strength. Shakespeare's "Romeo and Juliet," captured it best, "Thus, with a kiss I die."

Social Convoys: Secret Sauce for Longevity

Dr. Jack Travis, founder of the modern wellness movement and the first dedicated wellness center in the U.S. said, "Connection is the currency of wellness." It is why the Social Wellness aspect of the 7 Elements of Wellness is a critical component of the Me Time Monday program.

It sounds almost contradictory that a program focused on "Me" the individual would require social interactions in order to create a fully balanced life of well-being. Yet, without the Social Wellness element, Physical and Emotional Wellness cannot be optimized; Intellectual, Financial and Environmental Wellness are compromised and Spiritual Wellness is harder to achieve. And as I covered in early chapters, Me Time Monday is both a solo and social pursuit of wellness. It is why the ancient practitioners of wellness understood sociology is as important as biology and psychology to life balance that makes up our BPS framework.

As mentioned earlier, one of the longest longitudinal studies ever conducted[45] is the Harvard Study of Adult Development. It began in 1938 in Boston with a group of Harvard University sophomores - all young men

---

[45] Longitudinal studies are where the same cohort is followed over a length of time.

including some well-known names such as John F. Kennedy and Ben Bradlee. In addition, a group of teenage boys in Boston's inner city – many living in tenements often without running water and who came from immigrant families – were also added to the study. And over the years, the wives and children of these groups have been studied as well. The mission was to follow these individuals for their entire lives, checking in every few years with surveys and interviews to determine how the choices these participants made throughout life dictated their level of happiness and health. What the researchers found was unexpected. Rather than controlling blood pressure or stopping smoking or making a lot of money, the one constant in the men who lived the longest, healthiest and happiest was the quality relationships they had with immediate family and close friends.

"What made this study unique at the time is it did not focus on pathology or psychological issues of the participants, but rather what choices in life lead to human thriving," said Professor Marc Schulz, co-author of *The Good Life – Lessons From the World's Longest Scientific Study of Happiness* and co-director of the current Harvard Adult Development Study when I spoke to him prior to the publication of his book. He explained during our conversation that even after 85 years the study of this group continues despite many of the original men having passed away. In the book, Schulz says he and his co-author, Robert Waldinger, director of the Harvard Study, looked not just at their own research but also the full breadth of scientific literature on happiness and health.

"When we looked across gender, across ethnicity, across ancestry and background, and even across countries worldwide, essentially it is quality relationships that keep us healthier and happier through the lifespan," added Schulz.

And while tech lovers argue the Internet of Things (IoT) has connected us, in many ways it has also isolated us. Many of our activities today are done solo with no physical interaction. No talking to a friend and looking into their eyes, no saying "thank you" or asking advice of an in-store sales person. Gary Turk, a British spoken word artist has a YouTube video called "Look Up" with more than 600 million views and one of the best illustrations of how social media and technology may ruin your life. My favorite line from this poignant commentary illustrates our digital enslavement, "We are a world of smartphones and dumb people." We are talking *at* people not *with* people.

However, Schulz cautions new technologies are not the problem. "There were new technologies for our original young men who were born in 1910-1920s – phones and television – that changed the connections they may have had. In fact, TV was prophesied to be a big disruptor and intruder on family life," added Schulz. "What we do see is young people today are dependent on phones for their real-time relationship interactions yet emojis that replace actual faces and texts that may not be immediately responded to make it harder to socialize and connect."

What is missed in digital-only encounters is the oxytocin release of human closeness and touch that is a key part of the theory of *linked lives* identified by Glen Elder, a sociology professor at the University of North Carolina at Chapel Hill. Elder states your well-being and development is interdependent on the social relationships you gather throughout life. For instance, in the context of caregiving, a loved one's diagnosis does not just impact that person but their family caregiver who may be a spouse or partner, child, parent, sibling or friend. While the impact is felt most acutely by those closest to you, there is a ripple effect felt by many of the associations and relationships in your life.

One way to visualize this interconnectedness is through a *social convoy* model created in 1980 and led by researcher, Toni Antonucci at the University of Michigan. The social convoy model helps explain the protective factor to health and emotional well-being for those with strong social relationships throughout the life course. While relationships can change over time, there are some that stay with us – traveling together in a similar fashion as long-haul truckers or naval ships in a convoy. Think of this graph as your "travel buddies" list on your caregiving journey that is instrumental in helping to define and develop your close-knit tribe. Antonucci acknowledges family dynamics have changed significantly since the original model was created 40 years ago. We have blended families through divorce, widowhood and remarriage; loved ones living longer and our definition of family can include blood kin but also families of choice.

It is important to note this model is fluid and should be reviewed after any life-altering event such as getting married, having children, caregiving for older loved ones or facing grave illness or diagnosis. By updating your social convoy model you can focus on those relationships that give you the most protection, the most support and the most joy at that specific age and stage of your life.

One thing you may notice about your social convoy model from years past to present is certain relationships may not have stayed with your convoy. As noted earlier, Stanford University researcher, Laura Carstensen, has published numerous studies about this life transition called socioemotional selectivity theory (SST). Her research showed as people's time horizons shortened – either because of older age or because of a terminal illness – they automatically pruned their relationships cutting out the more superficial or even toxic relationships you can develop in life and focusing on quality instead of quantity. Emotional sustenance became a primary driver in the social goals of those who felt there was less time to waste on meaningless instead of meaningful relationships.

Using Antonucci's Social Convoy Model below, you can develop your personal social convoy graph. It reinforces for you whom you can count on and the one person you can text or call at 3 a.m. who will be there to help you. It also identifies who you want to spend your limited time with given all your caregiving responsibilities. And it releases tension from having unrealistic expectations of people you should not rely on for support. This graph is important for your Me Time Monday program to ensure you are focusing on the people who count in your life and how to maintain these valuable social interactions in your busy schedule.

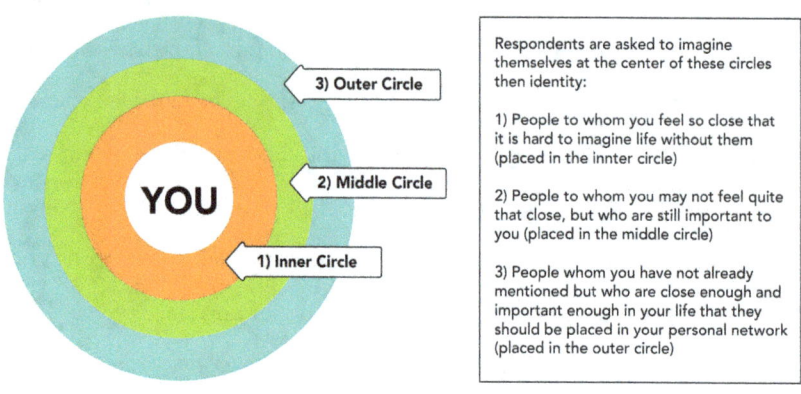

Figure 18: *Convoy Model and Aging Families* Figure 2. The Hierarchical Mapping Technique (Adapted From Antonucci, 1986).

Most importantly, this graph reinforces "You" at the center. It is a reminder that your needs come first and then securing the social support you need to balance self-care while caregiving becomes an easier lift. The graph also helps to identify how many of your relationships are personal and in-person rather than the legion of followers you may have on Instagram. Researchers have identified that more people are reducing their inner circle of this graph and finding only friendships and support through social media or online. Instead of friendships or relationships, I call these "iShips" because you cannot fully bond with someone you only know in the digital world. You are communicating but not truly connecting, like ships passing in the night.

This tool can also be a great conversation starter with an older loved one to find out how they feel about their relationships. A new tool now being used in gerontological research is the Social Frailty Index. Rather than only looking at age and medical condition as predictors of mortality, researchers at Massachusetts General Hospital and University of California at San Francisco revealed eight predictors of death within four years: poor neighborhood cleanliness, lack of control over finances, only seeing children annually or less frequency, not working for pay, not active with children, not volunteering, feeling isolated, and being treated with less courtesy or respect.

Healing Power of Hugs

A few years ago, I was invited to be the keynote speaker at the National Caregiver Expo held in Jacksonville, Florida. One of the topics I talked about was the social connections we need as family caregivers. I told the story of a friend whose husband was going through painful chemotherapy and had many hours and days of constant nausea and weakness. When I visited her during this period, my first question was, "How are you doing?" My friend burst into tears saying no one ever asked about her, they always asked about her husband and while she understood this, she felt invisible and alone. I hugged her to give her comfort which only let loose more tears as she croaked, "Thank you – Jack is unable to hug me because he is so weak and I have been missing those bear hugs."

I was a little emotional as I told the story but I reminded the audience sometimes we all need human connection so if you know a caregiver, give them a hug. Spontaneously the hundreds of people in the audience turned to the person seated next to them and enjoyed a quick embrace. This story demonstrates how much we are craving human physical touch and yes, hugs.

Yet, I am baffled by how criminalized hugs have become. During the pandemic we were warned to not touch each other even for the comfort of a warm embrace we so desperately needed in a time of anxiety and concern. Over the years, I have worked with many human resource professionals and when I prepared my employee educational webinars and workshops and came to the part about the healthful aspect of hugs, they always winced and asked if I could remove the reference or make sure I also talked about personal space and requesting permission to hug. I admit there are times when hugs are a health risk (cancer patients going through chemo, the pandemic) and there are many bad huggers out there and some people are too quick to give a hug or may even seem a bit lecherous. So yes, some people need a hugs training camp and a decent dose of respect for others, as we are not all fans of hugs. However, for you non-huggers you may want to carefully read the next paragraphs so you understand the well-being side of hugging you may be missing.

Science shows hugging has health benefits – physical, emotional and social. One 1950s research study led by University of Wisconsin psychologist, Harry F. Harlow, illustrates the benefits of hugs in the "wire monkey momma" study. Researchers analyzed maternal-child attachments and whether this was based on the mother as a food source or as a comfort, nurturing source. The researchers took one group of infant monkeys and placed them with a wire frame surrogate of their mother with an expressionless block head. The wire surrogate was warmed with radiant heat. The other mother surrogate was a block of wood with soft foam cloth wrapped around it and a more expressive face, warmed by an internal light bulb.

Although both groups of baby monkeys received food, they only stayed with the wire mother long enough to feed whereas the group with the softer, warmer, more expressive mother clung to the wooden surrogate hugging it for hours.

Similar studies were conducted among human infants in a neonatal hospital where one group of babies were held and rocked by the nurses, while the other group were fed and cleaned but not held or nurtured. The second group who were mostly devoid of human contact, cried for longer periods, had less restful sleep patterns, higher levels of anxiety and agitation and ultimately showed lower weight gain as well as less regulated heart beats after the experiment. In one of these studies, the skin-to-skin contact (known as "kangaroo care") of nurses and parents in the earliest infant stages, had beneficial physical and psychological health outcomes even 10 years later for the children who received the physical contact of their caregivers.

And, finally, physical contact and hugs are beneficial for older adults as well. One 2022 study conducted at a nursing home in New York assessed the health benefits, life satisfaction and subjective well-being of residents in a program called "Embraceable You." The premise was to have intergenerational hugging between staff, family and residents. Trained "hug ambassadors" were brought in to administer appropriate types of touch, while residents were given buttons to wear if they were interested in taking part in the hug experiment. The residents were given a token for every hug they received resulting in nearly 1,400 hugs in the first week. The results speak for themselves as the researchers found the residents who received three or more hugs per day were less hopeless or depressed (97%), more interested in social activities (88%), slept better (71%) and felt more energetic (66%).

And yet, the pandemic erased all this validated physical and mental health benefit of hugs in assisted living and nursing homes with no-visitation, no-touch rules. Many desperate families overcame this forced physical separation and contact loss through "hugging booths" that allowed loved ones to hug through makeshift, protective barriers similar to a NICU baby incubator. There was also more attention given to haptic "hugging vests" using tactile technology to simulate human hugs. In Japan, there was an emergence of "cuddling cafes" developed for lonely office workers to receive warm embraces or even be swaddled like newborns for comfort. All of these spontaneous solutions to social isolation shows how strong our biopsychosocial need is for physical contact.

As we attempt to unravel the negative effects from the lack of physical contact during the pandemic, Paul Zak, a neuroeconomist advises in his TED Talk oxytocin gained from hugs is not just our bonding hormone but our "morale molecule" responsible for trust, empathy and other feelings that help build a stable society. He advised you need on average eight hugs per day to actually have the oxytocin, endorphin and serotonin release that result in neuroprotection and boosts your brain health. Author Susan Pinker has called hugs a vaccine not just for loneliness but as "a biological force field between disease and decline." Scientists say 20 seconds is the length of hug needed for maximum oxytocin release to bond two people through embrace. By going "heart to heart" with the hug so your left chest connects with the other person's left chest, this creates the beat-matching emotional vibrations to benefit both parties.

I cannot write about the healing power of hugs without also writing about the healing power of pets. For any pet owner, you know your beloved dog, cat, rabbit, horse or other creature is part of your family. Numerous research studies show our furry companions help with lowering blood pressure, reducing stress, boosting immunity and oxytocin levels. It is probably why more than ½ of Americans ages 50-80 own a pet and 10% became a new pet owner during the pandemic.

Our first animal companions were dogs, actually domesticated wolves, who sought human closeness for mutual survival 33,000 years ago. Scientists believe it was during this time dogs developed what we call today "puppy dog eyes." Researchers from the U.S. and United Kingdom published a peer-reviewed study observing dogs were able to morph their facial tendons to literally create "puppy dog eyes" – bigger, sadder, younger, cuter faces to literally manipulate their human loved ones into a treat, a hug or a walk. This is just one demonstration of why dogs are called "man's best friend." We also know dogs in particular have sensitivity to smells with the ability to smell things 10,000 to 100,000 times more acutely than humans. Scientists and animal trainers can actually teach dogs to sniff out cancer tumors or detect an upcoming seizure in someone with epilepsy that can save lives. Research also shows the emotional vibrations you receive from a pet can boost your physical and emotional health.

The non-judgmental nature of animals is what makes them perfect for numerous therapeutic programs. The ancient Greeks were the first to use animals in therapy by using horses to lift the spirits of the seriously ill. Today, people with Parkinson's, multiple sclerosis and children with autism, cerebral palsy, ADHD or anyone with mental health issues find the horse has the same motion as someone walking and this motion passively exercises muscles and builds core strength as well as calm. In the 1800s Florence Nightingale used small pets to comfort and soothe her psychiatric patients. And the American Red Cross used farm animals in the 1940s to help WWII veterans suffering from shell shock – what we know today as PTSD (post-traumatic stress disorder).

While our pets give us emotional health benefits, we cannot overlook the physical health benefits. How many of us would take ourselves out for a walk three times a day or do beneficial stretching in the morning after watching our dog or cat do a little pet yoga stretch reminding us we should do the same?

The takeaway from this focus on hugs is our physical, psychological and social health needs are the same in our infancy as in our older years. As the Lovers of Valdaro skeletons demonstrated, bonding with others and physical contact is instrumental in our social wellness and supports human thriving from our first breaths to our last.

Laughter Can Treat Loneliness

As you have read, humans are social animals. We thrive on interactions and survive only because we are not alone. Yet a National Academies 2020 report showed more than one-third of adults over age 45 are lonely. The impact of loneliness can be deadly and costly. In a 2017 AARP study, the cost to Medicare of social isolation and loneliness for people over age 50 was estimated at $6.7 billion annually. Other recent studies have found loneliness is tied to an increased risk for Type 2 diabetes, a 13-27% increased heart disease risk for women and a 40% increased risk for Alzheimer's. One often recited statistic is from the seminal research done by Julianne Holt-Lunstad at Brigham Young University showing chronic loneliness has the same negative impact on health as smoking 15 cigarettes a day.

There is a growing global health issue of *friendship deserts*. In 2018, after a British National Health Service (NHS) study identified 9 million Brits (about 14% of the population) were chronically lonely and 1 million older Britons go more than 30 days without talking to a family member, friend or neighbor, the U.K. became the first country to appoint a Minister of Loneliness followed by Japan in 2021. In the U.K. the National Health

Service (NHS) set up "talking benches" and "talking café" tables with signs that if you do not mind people sitting down to chat with you, sit here to encourage more spontaneous interactions.

In the U.S. things are not much better. In 2023, the U.S. Surgeon General Vivek H. Murthy published "Our Epidemic of Loneliness and Isolation" report showing 1 in 2 American adults are lonely. And according to the May 2021 American Perspectives Survey nearly half of all Americans (49%) reported having fewer than three close friends. This is double the number who were surveyed 30 years ago when less than one-third (27%) of Americans had three or fewer close friends. Even more troubling, the study also indicated 12% of those surveyed have zero friends today, four times the number of people who claimed the same 30 years ago. This study shows people are talking less and relying less on important relationships which spells more depression and less happiness for our society. A Gallup poll found 330 million people globally go as long as two weeks without talking to any friends or family members. Loneliness is one of the biggest reasons people report being unhappy.

Many use the terms "social isolation" and "loneliness" interchangeably and while they are connected, they are also very different. When someone is socially isolated – a concern many have for older loved ones who live alone, known as *solo agers* – they may be physically disconnected from social interaction. It may be the person no longer drives or has mobility issues needing help with a wheelchair and thus opts out of social activities they may otherwise have joined.

On the other hand, loneliness is your emotional state of how you feel about the quality of your relationships. You can be married, at work, at a party in a crowded room and still feel lonely. Depression in later years is linked to loneliness causing people to reject social engagements. And while trendspotters report friendship apps are replacing dating apps, technology may help make a connection but it will not solve the lack of in-person human connectedness needed.

What is alarming about loneliness is it can change your brain health. A recent study in *Neurology* among 500,000 adults age 57 and older showed social isolation and loneliness actually changes brain structure showing poorer cognition, memory and less gray matter – all potential precursors to Alzheimer's. Some researchers believe it is because the brain is devoid of dopamine from reward responses while other scientists have discovered those with mild cognitive impairment (MCI) can increase risk of developing dementia or Alzheimer's due to chronic loneliness.

When I have given speeches around the country or led the Me Time Monday workshop, one comment I often get from family caregivers is they feel "all alone." Some studies show family caregivers adopt the loneliness their older loved one feels, almost like catching a cold from someone. Another explanation could be the focus on their loved one's care reduces the time to care for themselves. Thus, these caregivers need and want the attention from their other relationships but do not feel they are having their needs satisfied.

One trend addressing the loneliness epidemic is the social prescription of laughter. There is an ever-growing list of organizations and programs you can join online or in-person with sessions such as laughter yoga – for seniors, cancer patients, special needs children and those with depression – that is practiced in 110 countries. This laughter to address loneliness is in alignment with the wellness trend of social self-care. Social wellness clubs are trending helping us go from solo to social activities.

Laughter is most powerful when experienced in person with someone else. Have you ever found yourself in a giggle-fest with a friend where it becomes less about what made you laugh originally and more about sharing a moment of silliness? I overuse my crying laughter emoji in my texts, but nothing beats a good in-person laugh session with a confidante. You are 30 times more likely to laugh in group social situations than just by yourself.

Scientists have looked at the evolutionary aspects of laughter which has its origins 10 to 16 million years ago when the human brain grew in volume and adapted its increased vocal control that became an essential key to language. Laughter may have started as labored breathing while playing creating noises that increased oxytocin and created trust. A recent study analyzed spontaneous laughter, which tends to be at a higher pitch than forced or fake laughter. Country singer, Reba McIntyre, who is known for her sunny disposition, reflected the need for authentic laughter in our lives: "To succeed in life, you need three things: a wishbone, a backbone and a funny bone."

Behavioral psychologist, Albert Mehrabian, researched communication and the conveyance of feelings and attitudes in the '60s. He identified the 7-38-55 Rule that says 93% of communication is through body language in terms of how we interpret emotions and feelings. Most of the emotional messaging is through facial expressions (55%), then through tone of voice by recognizing emphasis on certain words (38%) and very little by words only (7%). When you rely solely on digital tools or social media you eliminate these emotional cues and your ability to get the in-person physical-based oxytocin levels you need to calm your anxieties, boost your mood and help you thrive.

As one of the key drivers of positivity and communication, it is difficult to laugh when you are angry or in pain because laughter releases endorphins that allow you to manage or get beyond pain. Children start laughing and smiling between ages two to four months although some say they have seen a smile or smirk the day their child was born.[46]

---

[46] Similar to the laughing face in utero image in the Me Time Monday section.

One laughter as medicine solution is called Laughter On Call. I wrote a *Thrive Global* article about the program after I met the founder, Dani Klein Modisett, when we were both featured Alzheimer's experts on "The Doctors" TV show. Klein Modisett designed Laughter on Call after her mother, who had Alzheimer's, moved to a memory care community. Klein Modisett called on her friends, who were professional improv comics, to visit her mom and watched her mother laugh and become more alive than she had been in months. The comedic companions program has turned into workshops to train memory care staff in laughter medicine and online group laughter sessions.

"Whether you make a silly face or two, turn a napkin into a puppet, or tell a funny joke you think a loved one with dementia may remember, whatever helps you engage and connect with your loved one while also helping you keep your sanity is smart health practice," said Klein Modisett. "We have to find the absurdity in life and laughter is one of those tools that helps us do that."

Becoming Ruth: Find Your Tribe

One of my favorite Old Testament stories is the Book of Ruth, maybe because it reminds me of my maternal grandmother who also happened to be named Ruth[47]. My grandparents met as teenagers and fell madly in love marrying without the consent and blessing of my grandmother's parents. Her parents rejected my grandfather because he played a violin in an orchestra performing at dance halls which they felt was unbecoming a suitor of their daughter and they were distraught he was of a different faith.[48] But marry they did right before the Great Depression. Difficult times brought them across the country to California and while my grandmother made a few trips back to her home town, she never returned to her people instead making her life with my grandfather in a new place. My favorite passage from the Book of Ruth is, "For whither thou goest, I will go; and where thou lodgest, I will lodge: thy people shall be my people, and thy God my God." (1:16)

We know human survival requires mutual cooperation, support and interaction among a group of people. In the 1960s, South African

---

[47] Ruth in Hebrew means "friend."
[48] Despite both my grandparents having Christian backgrounds they were of different branches of the faith (my Grandfather was First Christian and my Grandmother was Methodist. In those days, this was considered a "mixed marriage" and was discouraged.)

anti-apartheid activist, Nelson Mandela, began his 27-year prison sentence where his only "crimes" were fighting for freedom and a free society. During his oppressive imprisonment he was able to survive by forming a tribe of like-minded incarcerated activists. Gay McDougall, director of the Southern African Project of the Lawyers' Committee for Civil Rights Under Law, wrote about Mandela's sense of community to maintain his sanity and his spiritual belief in his eventual freedom.

"One of the things that was extraordinary about him [Mandela] is his sense that being in a group — a collective — of people committed to the same principles, along with making collective decisions about the way forward, is an essential element in movement-building and survival in circumstances that are harsh and oppressive," McDougall said in an interview with PBS Newshour.

After being released from prison in 1990, Mandela negotiated the end to apartheid in South Africa and eventually became his country's first African American and the first democratically-elected president from 1994-1999. Without his tribe in prison, Mandela – who lived to age 95 despite his harsh treatment during his incarceration – may not have survived to eventually change the course of his country's history forever.

Countries, companies and families require the social glue of tribes to remain stable and successful. Over time, the early bonds of existence and procreation of our hunter-gatherer forebearers have become more tribal in nature. From the perspective of personal wellness, being part of a tribe gives you a sense of security, comfort and belonging critical for physical but especially mental health.

When we talk about tribes today, people have a tendency to apply political and ideological aspects to this word rendering it to have a negative connotation. But I want to stay focused on the "social equals survival" aspect of tribes. Many of us gravitate towards others who are like us: who speak our language, who have similar cultural, ethnic or religious practices, who have similar socioeconomic backgrounds. At our core, whether we like it or not, humans are tribal. Or as the saying goes, "birds of a feather flock together."

But today, tribes are more nuanced and diverse than in earlier times. While you may step outside your religious tribe or pursue relationships with people of different cultures, race and social status, our modern tribes consist of smaller groups who have similar interests such as caregivers, music lovers, travel enthusiasts, residents in our community, HGTV or MLB fans and other life pursuits. And while our evolutionary instinct is to stick with our tribe, groupthink erodes innovation that comes from divergent perspectives. Homogeneity may be more harmful than good – this is nature showing you once again, balance is better.

Despite how many LinkedIn or Facebook connections you have, one U.S. study found when it comes to personal networks, most people can count an average 291 contacts as those they feel some level of relationship. The difference being the 291 number reflects people you know, have interacted with personally and to whom you are connected.

When French historian and philosopher, Alexis de Tocqueville, traveled the U.S. in the 1830s to write his insightful findings on our new nation, he was impressed with the social capital that was at the root of American life. In his seminal book, *Democracy in America*, he observed, "Americans of all ages, all stations in life, and all types of disposition . . . are forever forming associations."

But at its essence, tribes start with kin – our families – and grow from there. What matters in finding your tribe is it provides a protective factor through social engagement. By cultivating a sense of belonging you build your resiliency and skills for coping with challenges in life.

This need for social connection is why it is imperative for family caregivers to not abandon the ties that bind. Having a chat or coffee with a friend gives you renewed perspective on the challenges you may be facing in caregiving. Seeking support groups who understand your daily duties as a caregiver is similar to the bonds formed between military units. You understand each other, you experience the same difficulties and have a connection to those who have gone through the same experiences. If you are a caregiver and you isolate yourself from the comfort, nurturing and trust you need from these social connections, you will begin to suffer burnout and emotional health distress. And family bonds can be chosen families of friends not related by blood, but they would shed blood for you and this is the social glue that lets you survive and thrive.

> Health is as much *biography* as it is *biology*.

Younger generations are seeking these connections and tribes through the growing trend in social wellness clubs. Rather than a spa day or resort getaway for personal relaxation and stress relief, the trend is to seek more of the social aspect of wellness. Experts are analyzing this trend as a reaction to the isolation felt during the pandemic but systemic loneliness has been increasing for years. The Global Wellness Institute (GWI) 2023 report identifies the backlash to the consumerism of wellness as well as the need to connect. During a 2023 presentation, Beth McGroarty, head researcher for GWI reports, said, "We have gone from buying to belonging, from Goop to group, from Soul Cycle to social circle and from ego to empathy."

Even Soul Cycle founders are spinning a new business venture from social wellness. Their new startup is called Peoplehood where you ditch the bikes for relational fitness through 60-minute guided group conversations called "Gathers" to encourage active listening on a variety of life topics. Launched in 2023, think of it like talk therapy instead of sweat therapy.

The Grandmother Hypothesis

Scientists have long been searching for answers on why women live longer than men. There is an interesting clue from our ancient tribal natures called the *grandmother hypothesis* that may hold the answer. In the 1960s researchers found the genetic makeup of humans is to have older women in a tribe care for the younger children while younger adult women work (cook, clean, etc.) and have more children. This allowed the tribe to survive since the average woman before the 20th century bore between 5-8 children. But it is more than that. Scientists also believe post-menopausal women live 3-4 years longer than men because these grandmothers had a role and purpose in the tribe beyond reproduction. Conversely, older men could no longer reproduce nor serve as warriors to defend the tribe, thus their role and value diminished and they died before older women.

I benefitted from a grandmother who was my caregiver. While we only lived with my maternal grandparents for two years after my parents divorced, when I was ages six to eight, I cherish that time with my grandmother laughing and reading stories, having her make her famous cinnamon toast and watching "The Brady Bunch" and "The Lawrence Welk Show."

Many of today's young mothers would like to rely on their mothers or mothers-in-law to help out with babysitting while they go back to work. But caregivers face two challenges: mom may not live close enough to help and the other challenge is women are having children later in life. It is one thing for a 55-year-old or even 70-year-old grandmother to help out with grandchildren but the older you are as a mother means your mother may now be needing care instead of contributing to the care of your children. This is the classic Sandwich Generation caregiver – caring for two generations, both young and old, simultaneously.

Which brings us back to Ruth. After losing her husband, Ruth never returned to her family, but stayed as a caregiver for her mother-in-law, Naomi. Her story is one of loyalty, faithfulness, sacrifice but also coping, surviving and finding your tribe. Ruth's choice led to the bloodline that would beget King David and Jesus. Ruth teaches us in finding your tribe you can also find your purpose.

Intellectual Wellness

Brain training helped make Brady a GOAT

Critics of NFL quarterback Tom Brady highlight what he lacked: muscular build, mobility, "big arm," and swift foot work of other notable QBs. They point out he did not start his career as a sought-after talent. Instead, every NFL team passed over him in 4-6 rounds of the NFL draft (he finally went in the 199th pick.) However, Brady is known as one of football's "greatest of all time" (GOAT) because there is no one of his era who surpassed his mental agility and strength: his swift decision-making, his surgical accuracy to get the ball into a receiver's hands, his leadership skills on and off the field and his emotional intelligence.

Retiring at 45, Brady played twice as long as other players who peak in their 20s. What was his secret? Brady operated at his *peak performance* level similar to the *peak experiences* described by Abraham Maslow in his motivational theory. With seven Super Bowl rings, Brady surpassed other NFL players because he had mastered the flow theory of energy, effort and enjoyment that was about his love of the game.

But he is also a disciplined machine, helping himself overcome some of the typical physical challenges of age, including decreased cardiovascular performance and slower processing speeds of the body and brain. He did this by embracing the principles of neuroplasticity and training his brain as much as he honed his physical strength. As he approached age 40, Brady underwent daily cognitive training with a suite of scientifically developed brain exercises from brainHQ. This brain workout is a cross-training regimen for different areas of the brain to maximize spatial perception, reaction time and in Brady's words helped him "stay sharp." Rather than rely on what made him special in the first place, Brady decided to double-down and continue to hone his cognitive gifts that gave a him a competitive edge.

For Brady, the ability to continue to play the game, meant he had to embrace a new game - brain training. Brady showed brain health is not about prevention but about potential and what is to be gained, making Tom Brady a classic case study in Intellectual Wellness.

Cross-Train Your Brain

In my Me Time Monday workshops, Intellectual Wellness is the one element of the 7 Wellness Elements few people grasp immediately. They often believe it is about boosting your IQ or taking classes for higher achievement. And while lifelong learning is a component of Intellectual Wellness, it is really about brain health and wellness for your mind. Intellectual Wellness is defined as a person who places high value on things of interest, who seeks knowledge, who finds beauty and who uses facts to make decisions. Intellectual Wellness is about using your top-down brain processing of the new brain.

In this section, I will touch upon ways to enhance your Intellectual Wellness, including how to create a brain training program, how to use daydreaming to build resiliency and how much your work and choice of a job or career is dictating not just your Intellectual Wellness but your Emotional, Environmental and Social Wellness.

Most people use the terms "brain" and "mind" interchangeably as they are two sides of the same coin. However, we think of the brain as the physical organ made up of blood vessels, gray matter and white matter, and neurons with a distinct shape, placement and function in the body. The mind is more about the phenomena of vibrational energy we learned about in Emotional Wellness. The mind is about emotions, thinking, memory, reasoning – it is about what manifests from the function of the brain.

The key driver of Intellectual Wellness is curiosity. From the earliest beginnings as humans, what helped Homo sapiens out-survive Neanderthals 40,000 years ago is Homo sapiens had wanderlust. They traveled outside their origins in Sub-Saharan Africa to explore what today we know as Australia as well as most of Europe and Asia. They built trade networks, adapted to different climes, interbred with different species and explored different food sources among other factors that helped our direct human ancestors remain on Earth. Neanderthals, like the dinosaurs before them, simply stayed put and became extinct. Anthropologists have also found the other advantage of being curious and exploring our environs is it helped our brain size grow over time based on the social influences we encountered of collaborative work, exchanging food and other resources, creating better tools to hunt with and finding ways to protect ourselves from predators.

Our innate curiosity as a species is what has helped us survive and thrive. We want to know what is across the next land bridge or over the next mountain. Our curiosity has taken us to the moon, Mars and the depths of marine life on the ocean floor. Curiosity is the characteristic that drives all innovation and is also a key aspect of happiness and joy.

In gerontology we focus on two types of intelligence: crystallized and fluid. Just as they sound, crystallized intelligence is hardwired knowledge. This type of intelligence is based on the evolution of your ancient brain that still taps into those early human behaviors of finding food, creating a safe place to sleep and reproducing future generations. Crystallized intelligence is also about your modern-day, personal, cumulative experiences – often based on trial and error – that become embedded in your brain such as how to ride a bike, remembering how to brush your teeth, knowing where you live and recalling historical events. Crystallized intelligence does not deteriorate with age but remains stable, although you may have slower recall later in life. When you adopt habit-stacking you use your crystallized intelligence.

Fluid intelligence is more about the ebb and flow of your brain power — the side of the brain referred to as the new brain that optimizes rationality, decision-making, emotions and is involved in complex problem-solving. It is typically associated with the speed of decision-making and flexibility in figuring out problems that are not based on past experience but may be completely new. Examples of fluid intelligence may be figuring out an alternative route to work from your daily routine, navigating the health care system when caring for an older loved one, or having a philosophical debate with a friend. As opposed to crystallized intelligence, you will peak and then experience a decline with age when it comes to fluid intelligence.

There is a great debate on when intelligence begins to decline. As noted, crystallized intelligence remains stable through most if not all of your life. But when it comes to fluid intelligence, some scientists believe the decline begins in your 20s while other studies have shown it peaks and then descends after 40. More recent research shows the declines do not really start happening until after age 60.[49] However, with brain health exercises you can control the decline to slow, halt and even reverse it if you learn to cross-train your brain.

Brain Training *Not* Brain Games

As scientists have produced more research on how the brain works, the old notion the brain could *not* regenerate itself is debunked. Similar to how the liver can regenerate itself after damage (regrowing to a normal size

---

[49] This is a great example of how scientists rarely agree and how findings change with new research.

even after up to 90% of it has been removed) you can grow new neuronal connections to improve cognitive function. Some people believe the brain is a muscle but it is actually an organ, like the liver, and has the ability to control the muscles and other bodily functions as well as the cognitive and emotional actions of the body. While both the brain and liver are not invincible, this unique ability to repair some damage and strengthen the ability to perform physical activities is the remarkable new discovery in brain plasticity. These advancements in neuroplasticity allow stroke patients to build new neurons to recover some function or for those who are blind or deaf to strengthen neurons that enhance other senses.

Many believe by playing sudoku or doing crossword puzzles you can attain brain plasticity. But brain science says "no." In fact, one brain game company had to pay $2 million in fines because of false advertising claims it improved brain function when all it did was enhance rote memorization of its game rather than affect change in overall brain performance.

Only a handful of credible companies, such as Posit Science, creators of the brainHQ exercises, can claim to improve brain performance. Co-founded by tech entrepreneur, Jeff Zimman, and leading neuroscientists, Mark Merzenich and Henry Mahncke, pioneers in brain plasticity research with more than 200 evidenced-based peer-reviewed studies, brainHQ focuses on speed and accuracy of cognitive function.

"If we were to wind back the clock to 1970 and ask any neuroscientist about the brain, they would have said it is like a computer chip – it has wires and electricity and processes information but we all know computer chips wear out after a while and if they get damaged you cannot fix them," said Mahncke during my podcast interview with him. "This was everyone's view of the adult brain – it is hardwired, wears out when you get old, if you break it, too bad, you're out of luck."

But Merzenich and Mahncke were early advocates for viewing the brain as a constantly adapting biological system, rewiring itself all the time. The key is in finding solutions that offer cross-training brain exercises in a similar way that we optimize our physical workouts through cross-training efforts. By mixing up brain exercises into a full suite of activities, you improve memory, decrease depression, enhance self-confidence and can even enhance driving skills.

To understand how to build a better brain, Mahncke explains we first have to understand what happens in the brain as we get older.

"As it turns out, the brain gets noisier as we age," said Mahncke. "It's almost like listening to an old radio that kind of got off the signal a bit and became full of static or trying to have a conversation in a really noisy restaurant but it's hard to pay attention with all the disruption."

Mahncke clarifies by "older" he means age 27 because this is the age when the static actually slows down your brain and makes memory and attention harder. What brainHQ exercises will do is eliminate static noise and make brain processing sharp and fast through training.

Just as we improve our performance levels in physical exercise – such as being able to lift heavier weights or do more reps, walking more steps, improving breathing and heart rates through yoga and meditation – brain training applies the same principles. You want to find programs that consistently ask you to try new exercises and guide you to go to the next level of the brain exercise or perform the exercises faster. Only then will you truly achieve brain plasticity and better brain health. The good news about brain training is it only takes a few minutes a day not 45-60 minutes to accomplish your goals. Most of the individual brainHQ exercises can be completed in 7-10 minutes.

> Fitness includes both a "neck down"
> workout and "neck up" exercises.

While we know there is no science behind sudoku brain puzzle games or apps such as Words With Friends to show improved brain performance, there is a health trend called "gamification" designed to make health exercises entertaining similar to video games. Gamification in health is the concept of advancing to new levels of the game and perhaps having to play the game faster, which sounds similar to the principles of the brainHQ exercises, but is it?

When I posed this question to Mahncke, he responded, "I play a lot of video games with my daughter and I see there are good things that come from video games such as a strong sense of progress and mastery. In fact, brain training should incorporate this humanistic sense of immediate progress and mastery. But this whole field took a wrong turn which it is only now recovering from because 5-6 years ago people thought 'games are fun so let's make all our apps into games and people will play them as much as they play Wordle or Pac-Man.'"

Mahncke said this was a wrong turn for neuroscience because it changed the motivation. If you want someone to do a brain training program but you make it into a game, in the end they will play the game for fun and not necessarily for the reasons that improve their brain performance. And that can end up meaning they do not use the program in the ways it was intended. If you are so focused on how to earn stars or points, then your focus becomes about that achievement and not brain health.

"We want to encourage and motivate people to adopt brain training but not have it distract from the underlying reason they are doing this," said Mahncke. "Brain exercises can be fun and engaging so we have taken the best part of video gaming to improve health."

Another area of brain training is music making. While music helps you recall memories, change the way you think and influences the way you behave – it is also a full brain workout. As opposed to just passive listening, making music engages all regions of the brain. Johns Hopkins medical researchers asked jazz and hip hop artists to play music while getting a functional MRI that showed the musicians' brains lit up like fireworks going off. Music making is one of the best brain exercises and ultimate cross trainer to build better brain function and health. One study found musicians have a 64% less risk of developing Alzheimer's than non-musicians – meaning music making can be neuroprotective.[50]

We go to the gym for physical (and social) benefit, but your fitness routine needs to focus as much on the neck up as the neck down. One of the new trends in brain health is *cerebral gymnastics*. The principle of this neuro version of Simone Biles is to work out all areas of the brain associated with the five senses.

Following is one of my favorite brain health wellness hacks that is part of a cerebral gymnastics routine from the Me Time Monday workshop. It can be done in 5 minutes sitting at your desk:

o   1 minute: Look at 5 objects near you. Notice colors, shapes, textures
o   1 minute: Touch 4 things – enjoy the tactile feeling of the objects

---

[50] You will read more about musical health in Spiritual Wellness.

- o 1 minute: Listen to 3 sounds – are they high or low pitch? Is it a nature sound like a bird chirping or a child laughing, music or technology such as a car traveling down the street?
- o 1 minute: Smell 2 things. Are they sweet, fresh, floral, woodsy?
- o 1 minute: Taste something – feel the texture on your tongue, close your eyes and focus. Savor the flavor

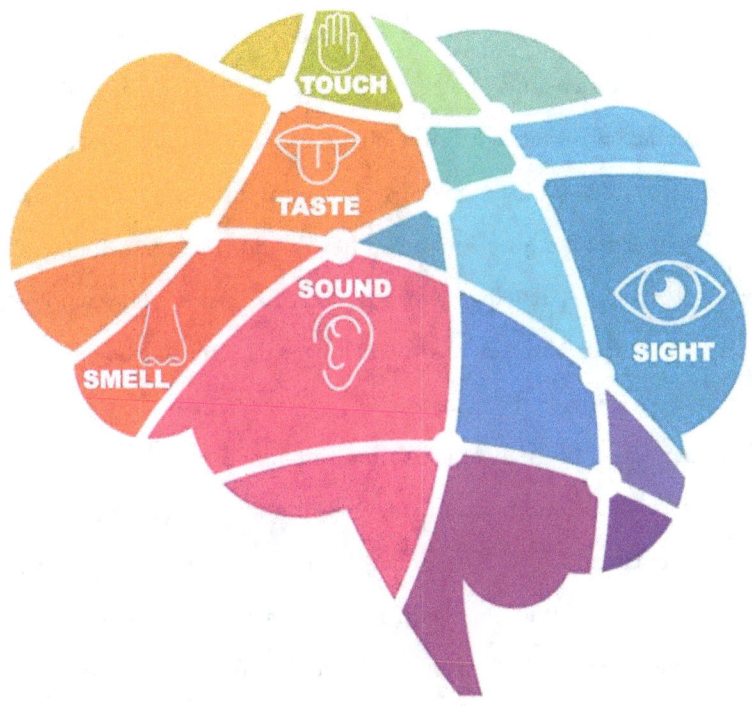

Figure 19: 5 Sensory Areas of the Brain

Brain Health School: Reading and Learning

Other ways to work out the brain include reading fiction. As opposed to non-fiction books (like this book!) where you can skip to chapters or sections, the brain has to engage the hippocampus (memory region) to follow characters and storylines. Neuropsychiatrist, Richard Restak, observed people with early stage dementia stopped reading fiction novels as the disease progresses because they are not retaining the storyline and character development due to short-term memory loss.

Other research, particularly in the area of Theory of Mind (ToM), shows reading fiction fine tunes your empathy and ability to practice active listening, especially of other's mental state because you have developed the capacity to understand other's beliefs and desires through following fictional characters. One study found 30 minutes of reading lowered blood pressure, heart rate and feelings of psychological distress as effectively as yoga did. Other research on long-term health and retirement followed a cohort of 3,635 adult participants for a period of 12 years. Those who read books survived approximately two years longer than those who either did not read or who only read magazines.[51]

Another aspect of Intellectual Wellness is combining lifelong learning in a socially connected environment. Two innovative companies, U.S.-based Get Set Up and U.K.-based The Joy Club, provide online platforms for people over age 50 to engage in lifelong learning and social fitness. These lifelong learning platforms for older adults offer hundreds of classes including how to speak another language, perfect your culinary skills or become an expert bird watcher or stargazer. But it is also where the social connections are as vital as the curriculum.

For younger generations, brain health has more to do with mental and emotional health than concerns about dementia, cognitive decline or finding

---

[51] That is good news for bibliophiles like me (I'm actually bordering on bibliomania). I do love reading, collecting and displaying books (they are in every room of my home) and it is also why as a writer and entrepreneur I define myself as an "authorpreneur."

your flow. One study found 42% of Gen Z (also known as iGen comprised of mostly teens and early 20s) had been diagnosed with a mental health condition in 2022. In January, 2023, the hashtag #frontallobe had 27 million views on Tik Tok – the social media hub for Gen Z – and 5,000 different posts on Instagram. And a Forbes Health/One Poll survey of 1,005 adults found 50% of people between the ages of 18-25 had a 2023 New Year's resolution to improve their mental health more than they wanted to lose weight.

Curiosity drives all innovation and creates joy.

We know the frontal lobes control executive functioning and impulse control and are the last area of the brain to develop typically in your early 20s. A post-pandemic study found the MRIs of teen brains had accelerated aging due to the stress of lockdowns and social distancing. Not only could this lead to later life higher risk of cardiovascular disease, Alzheimer's and diabetes but also mental illness. Young adults are taking their brains into their own hands and are seeking supplements and exercises that will keep their brains healthy for a lifetime. In addition, Gen Z/iGen are also seeking tech-enabled devices such as Frenz, a brain-band that monitors brain activity throughout the day. The visor-shaped device uses artificial intelligence (AI) to collect data on the wearer to provide feedback on a person's levels of concentration, energy, and sleep, as well as their heart rate.

Your Brain and Alzheimer's

When it comes to brain health for many older adults, the question is what is normal cognitive decline versus Alzheimer's disease and can we prevent dementia?

So much of my work in caregiving over the last two decades, including being a board member for the local Alzheimer's Association chapter and consulting for the UsAgainstAlzheimer's network, has focused on brain health and particularly the impact of dementia and Alzheimer's on families. In my workshops I often have family caregivers of those with dementia and Alzheimer's and it is worth a pause here on Intellectual Wellness to address this neurodegenerative disease.

Alzheimer's attacks indiscriminately and has nothing to do with intelligence levels. However, there are brain training exercises and activities that may help prevent or slow the decline of dementia as well as mild cognitive impairment (MCI), a type of dementia that can become a risk factor for Alzheimer's.

In the 1970s President Nixon declared war on cancer, which was the biggest health scare for most Americans at the time. Today, the new fear factor in growing older is Alzheimer's disease (AD). Since dementia and Alzheimer's are terms that often get used interchangeably, think of them like cancer (the category of diseases defined as the division and growth of abnormal cells) and then there are sub-categories of specific cancers such as breast, lung, bone, brain and blood (also known as lymphoma, leukemia or myeloma). Dementia is the category of diseases that are neurodegenerative – meaning they get progressively worse – and affect cognition such as memory, behavior and reasoning. Within this category of dementia diseases, Alzheimer's accounts for 70% of all dementia cases but there is also vascular dementia, frontotemporal dementia, Lewy Body dementia, Huntington's disease and others. As the most widely known and diagnosed of dementias, Alzheimer's is a neurodegenerative disease that causes significant changes in the brain and impacts memory, communication and behavior and in the end stages significantly impairs quality of life.

According to the Alzheimer's Association's 2023 report, an estimated 6.7. million Americans over age 65 have AD, a number projected to double by 2050. Women are disproportionately affected by AD with two-thirds of all Alzheimer's cases being women and most family caregivers being female – typically an adult daughter, sister or granddaughter. After age 60, women are twice as likely to develop Alzheimer's as they are to be diagnosed with breast cancer. In fact, women have a one in six chance of developing AD compared to a one in 11 chance for men.

One question is are the brains of males versus females different and how does that relate to Alzheimer's risk? The answer is yes but in subtle ways. For instance, male brains are 10% larger than women's (note: this does not impact intelligence). While male brains have less gray matter, they use it more than females to optimize their task-focused abilities. Women tap into more of their white matter letting them excel at language and multi-tasking. In fact, it is this advantage in language skills that may mask Alzheimer's in women allowing them to score better on verbal memory tests despite having the disease which may delay their diagnosis until later in life. One study found women's brains have more tau proteins that become tau tangles, a classic hallmark of Alzheimer's.

However, women's brains have higher emotional intelligence than men's (although scientists believe this is innate for women, men can level the playing field with training). Also, male and female brains process neurochemicals differently which may point to why women have more depression and anxiety while males have more autism and schizophrenia. One study found measuring brain metabolism – which is the rate of glucose and oxygen-powered energy and activities – showed the brains of adult women consistently appear about three years younger than men's brains do. This may be why females live longer. In addition, women metabolize glucose more efficiently which may give women the ability to compensate for dementia damage and retain some cognitive function longer.

The female factor of the disease is a key area of focus for Dr. Art Toga, head of the USC Mark and Mary Stevens Neuroimaging and Infomatics Institute, with whom I had the honor of working. Dr. Toga is one of the most highly funded researchers by the National Institute on Aging (NIA) receiving a grant along with his colleague and collaborator, Dr. Paul Thompson, for $23 million to oversee the world's largest brain mapping research project. In the same way Gerardus Mercator, a 16th-century Flemish cartographer, became the first to create a map of the world, Toga and Thompson's project will pioneer the mapping of the human brain to unlock insights into why Alzheimer's, Parkinson's, autism and mental health issues affect some and not others. They achieve this through a proprietary mathematical computing program analyzing all the biomarkers and changes in billions of brain scans. It is part of the promise of this Big Data analysis to unlock the secrets leading to prevention, treatment and cures for diseases affecting the brain.

In a 2017 article I wrote about Dr. Toga's work, he explained, "We [at USC] act as the hub of these global efforts to combine data that comes from centers and projects around the world, so we can better understand the disease process through biomarkers that chart its progression — and look for opportunities for therapeutic interventions. This is a global cooperation among scientists and clinicians around the world because it really is a grand challenge for us as a species that we need to solve."

Toga's passion for finding clues in billions of brain scans is not just professional but personal. His lost his mother, grandmother and aunt to Alzheimer's and has three daughters. For the women in his family, he is dedicated to finding the biomarkers and links to unlocking why women are most affected by this disease.

In addition to mapping the human brain and analyzing brain scans, other diagnostics are improving for Alzheimer's. Recently news of blood tests that can look for certain biomarkers that lead to dementia, or even getting an annual comprehensive eye exam that can look at the retina to see early signs of Alzheimer's (as well as diabetes) are improving our ability to detect dementia earlier when some drug therapies are more effective.

Today, Alzheimer's remains the only disease in the Top 10 causes of death with no proven preventive measures, no long-term effective treatments and no cure. While aging is a risk factor for developing the disease,[52] early on-set Alzheimer's (only 5% of all cases) affects a special allele on the DNA strand – APOE-e4 – and is seen to be more genetically tied than older onset AD. Those with early onset have symptoms before age 65, and even people in their 30s, 40s and 50s can be diagnosed, meaning age is not a factor. Since early onset has a genetic link, a grandparent, parent or other relative with early onset increases your risk factor.

---

[52] Since women live longer than men this is one hypothesis why more women have AD.

The fear of dementia has sparked recent news headlines such as actor Bruce Willis who was originally diagnosed with aphasia[53] in 2022 but received a diagnosis of frontotemporal dementia (FTD) a year later; or former Morgan Stanley CEO, John Mack, who announced he has mild cognitive impairment (MCI). As well, we have seen a parade of famous names such as former President Ronald Reagan, former Supreme Court Justice Sandra Day O'Connor, Sean Connery (the original James Bond), actor Omar Sharif and lifestyle guru B. Smith – all who had Alzheimer's.

When I appeared on "The Doctors" TV program as a gerontologist specializing in Alzheimer's and family caregiving, I used a neuroscience + computer metaphor to explain the confusion so many have about this disease. Essentially, our brains, as stated earlier, are like the world's largest filing cabinet or computer storage. Everything we learn, every piece of information, every person, every situation, every memory gets stored in our brains. Now, some of these memories are not imprinted as strongly or embedded to last, our brains sort this out during our sleep cycles transferring short term memory (hippocampus) to our long-term memory area of the brain (neocortex). After living for decades, you can imagine how many files are stored in your brain. Also, as we age, we do not move quite as fast as when we were 12 or 20 so the ability to sift through a ton of files in your brain to remember a grandchild's name or a long forgotten trivial factoid, takes more time. This is normal cognitive aging.

However, when someone has Alzheimer's, it is not a matter of waiting a bit longer to retrieve the file, the file does not exist. The minute someone with Alzheimer's asks a question (What time is it?), the memory is not stored, it is deleted. This is why within the span of 1-5 minutes your mom

---

[53] Aphasia is a language disorder that can be caused by brain injury but is not necessarily dementia.

may ask you 10 times what time it is – she simply has no memory she just asked you that question.

There are also two scientific conundrums that can happen with Alzheimer's patients that are confusing to family caregivers: *cognitive reserve compensation* and *terminal lucidity*.[54] For some, cognitive reserve (CR) can overcome the more serious declines associated with Alzheimer's by staying active, attaining higher education, being employed or working longer (including volunteerism). These activities can compensate for typical decline in cognitive function as opposed to those less active and engaged. Another surprising paradox of Alzheimer's is terminal lucidity or what some call "the rally." Typically happening in the end stage of the disease, the person suddenly has clarity and regained memory to a point of almost seeming to return to their pre-Alzheimer's status. However, this is typically a short period of maybe a few days or weeks that happen before death. While families are hopeful this means a reversal of the disease, it is a sign of impending loss of your loved one.

A scientific explanation of Alzheimer's begins with a healthy brain that has 100 billion neurons connecting via neurotransmitters and 100 trillion synapses as well as 400 miles of blood vessels. This intricate neuronal circuitry allows memories, language, emotions, decision-making, motor skills and more. In Alzheimer's disease, amyloid beta (Aβ) plaque accumulates outside of the neurons and protein tau tangles happen inside the neurons, negatively impacting the neurons' ability to communicate, thus, contributing to cellular atrophy and brain death. As well, the toxic Aβ and tau tangles activate the brain's microglia immune system that are unable to clear toxic proteins that have permeated the blood-brain barrier via leaky blood vessels weakened by hypertension (think of a 400-mile highway with

---

[54] Terminal lucidity is also known as paradoxical lucidity.

potholes and sink holes). This creates chronic inflammation that cause dying cells because the brain is unable to metabolize glucose needed for energy.

The glucose connection is why some researchers call Alzheimer's a metabolic disease. Research on oxidative stress in the brain caused by starvation of glucose as well as insulin resistance (IR) – which 80% of AD patients have – point to risks for Alzheimer's and why some call it Type 3 diabetes. It also is a possible link to why African Americans have twice the risk and Latinos 1.5 times the risk as Whites for Alzheimer's since those populations also typically have higher rates of diabesity.

In 2020, The Lancet Commission reported 40% of worldwide dementia cases could be prevented or delayed if people adhered to 12 lifestyle factors including: Maintaining a 120 systolic blood pressure reading (top number in a 120/80 reading); move more regularly (daily walking/steps); reduce obesity and maintain a healthy weight; address depression; avoid social isolation and feelings of loneliness; correct hearing loss; avoid smoking and drinking, attain good sleep and higher education, reduce exposure to air pollution and second-hand smoke. Some studies have shown by adopting healthier lifestyle choices above and performing brain exercises you can see positive changes in brain scans as quickly as 2-8 weeks.

You probably get an annual doctor check-up for physical health and you need to do the same for your brain health. Scientists now reject that declines in cognitive performance are normal aging. You can control and even reverse the decline that starts at age 27. It is never too early to start thinking about brain exercises and to take a free brain health assessment that can be found online at sites such as MyBrainGuide.org.

chapter 24

Through the Looking Glass: Daydreams Build Resilience

In a Wonderland they lie,

Dreaming as the days go by,

Dreaming as the summers die:

Ever drifting down the stream,

Lingering in the golden gleam,

Life, what is it but a dream?

- Lewis Carroll - *Through the Looking Glass and What Alice Found There*

This quote is painted on one of my favorite pieces of furniture – my grandmother's childhood chest of drawers where I now keep my PJs, socks, sleep masks and my dream journal. It also reminds me of my childhood as the *Alice in Wonderland* books were my favorite stories growing up and I would spend hours daydreaming in my grandparent's pool floating under the summer sun.

As an adult, I have gained newfound insights and a whole new perspective into how modern problems are seen through Carroll's looking glass. What resonated about Alice's tale is despite all the confusing worlds in which she finds herself, she is resilient.

Resiliency is defined as how to optimize your current state. Most psychologists agree people who are more resilient embrace optimism and hope, accept difficult situations, are solution-oriented, do not prescribe to the victim mentality, curate a success network, plan for a positive future, and take time for self-reflection. The greatest teacher of resilience is failure. Only then can you learn to survive and flourish.

The trend in today's participation trophies, rather than accepting winners and losers, is just one example of how we have made children *less* resilient. The only way to become resilient is to face bad or negative events because it helps build strengths you did not know you had. Coping with lifestyle stress helps build toughness that is empowering. When life is too easy and there are no disappointments, you are living in a gray world devoid of the essential roller coaster of human emotions needed to become brave, courageous and determined. As a society, we love underdogs because when they win you can relate to the sweet feeling of overcoming seemingly insurmountable hurdles. Also, believing things are inevitable takes away your internal locus of control giving all the power to external factors.[55]

Many psychologists, philosophers and neuroscientists have probed the themes of Lewis Carroll's *literary nonsense* genre of stories but the big reveal for me is you find Alice was only dreaming of these nonsensical *fantasy*

---

[55] This was covered in-depth in Emotional Wellness.

worlds in order to make sense of an even more nonsensical *real* world. Daydreaming to deal with reality and build her reservoir of resiliency becomes Alice's superpower.

I often find Alice's journey to be similar to family caregiving. Your world is turned upside down and inside out while everything is backwards. There are times you wish you could drink a potion shrinking you to a size where you almost disappear. While Alice travels on her journey alone, she meets a lot of crazy characters all of whom she learns from along the way. In the end it is about Alice finding her way back home. These are the gifts caregivers find on their journey.

Alice becomes wise and strong on her journey mostly because she remains curious ("curiouser and curiouser"). She discovers many insights for real life: she finds you cannot change the past but you can learn from it; doing things for others is a worthy pursuit; friends cannot be neglected; everything changes no matter what you do to keep it the same and these unforeseen journeys help you discover who you are – it is a path to identity. These are themes many caregivers face, even though navigating a fragmented health care system makes you feel more like the Cheshire cat who famously said, "Everyone is mad here."

When it comes to how daydreams may help or hurt your health, there are, as always, differing camps of experts. But the scientific literature tilts toward the more positive aspect of daydreaming as it relates to your Intellectual Wellness. While you think of daydream moments, studies have shown daydreams actually occupy up to one-half of all your waking hours.

But do not confuse daydreams from the dreams you have during sleep – they are very different. Your dreams while you sleep are often confusing and have you jumping from one bizarre or unexplainable scene to the next. Night dreaming tends be illogical because they come from your subconscious mind and thus are not interpreted literally. In night dreams you are an observer where you are emotionally distant from what is happening. In daydreams, you experience them firsthand with all five senses even if it is coming from memory and being forecasted into your future. Daydreams can often include smells or tastes or scenes from your past to help create connected memories into your future (think of Proust and his madeleines).

Daydreams are empowering because they are 100% of your own making. Daydreams are movies in your mind where you are the actor, director, producer, screenwriter and audience all in one. The same kind of creativity that goes into moviemaking is at work when you daydream. You are thinking for pleasure similar to when you escape into a theater to watch a movie. Daydreams help inspire innovative thinking.

Daydreams are mental floss.

In years past, teachers and parents scolded children for staring into a faraway vista and following their own thoughts. "Get your head out of the clouds and focus!" was the old refrain. But today we know daydreaming increases your creativity and problem-solving skills, improves your sense of self-identity and resiliency and makes you more empathetic and flexible in your thinking.

When you engage in daydreams to alleviate stress or to problem-solve it is what gerontologists call Positive Constructive Daydreaming (PCD). Sometimes when you daydream unintentionally you are really ruminating by allowing toxic memories to invade and disrupt your thinking. Scientists have tracked daydreaming in several studies and found not only does the content of your daydreams matter but you also need to be *free-moving* to avoid the continual worry that causes negative effects such as depression or increased anxiety. Daydreams are your mental floss.

When you free-move your mind typically goes to a playful place or positive fantasy life to boost your mood. It also allows you to not be anchored in your past but to float freely into a future of more happiness and hopefulness. In the animal kingdom, scientists have found humans, unlike most other animals, can focus on things that may happen in the future as much as the things happening in the present. This gives you an enormous advantage to create your own happiness.

Neuroscientists believe since daydreams involve your past and current lives as well as your fantasy future life, the brain is performing complex thinking. Thus, daydreams become another way to increase your neuroplasticity. For caregivers, the ability to use daydreams allows you to creatively think through complex emotional problems without feeling pressured to solve the problem RIGHT NOW. It also gives you a welcome escape to then refocus your energies on the present.

When you allow your brain to rest from the left-sided analytical, decision-making area of the brain and instead flex the right side of the brain where creativity resides, you are helping yourself to unplug from current stressors and avoid building up to the point of burnout. Other studies have found you become more flexible and more empathetic because you daydream about alternative scenarios and solutions that foster more flexibility that helps you with stress.

This phenomenon is called *elastic thinking*, a term coined by physicist and author, Leonard Mlodinow. Most of the innovations of the world, whether in business or science or art, come from elastic thinking. Elastic thinkers are the phenomenal dreamers who change our world: Walt Disney, Elon Musk, Madame Curie and Oprah Winfrey. This concept requires the capacity to let go of comfortable ideas, become accustomed to ambiguity and rely on both imagination and logic to generate curiosity and creative solutions.

Just as our ancient ancestors survived because they had a propensity for wanderlust, it is important to allow your modern brain to wander now and then to ensure your survival. Daydreams help you disconnect from the constant bombardment of technology tools and go back to focused creativity. By shifting your mind into neutral and blocking the intrusions on your free-moving, you become less anxious, more empowered, more resilient and ultimately happier.

To master daydreaming and elastic thinking, remember Alice. She taught us to never let go of the wonderment of childhood that is inside all of us. For it is this child-like curiosity that fuels your creativity and resilience in life.

chapter 25

Life-Work Balance: New Social Contracts at Work

In 1962, John Glenn was the first astronaut sent by NASA to orbit the Earth. Thirty-six years later, at age 77, he put on his space suit again as the oldest person in outer space, this time on the space shuttle Discovery. His fellow space travelers were only 1-2 years old when he was circling the Earth the first time. In fact, in 1969 there were half as many people over age 65 then (14 million) as there were in 1998 when Glenn ventured back into space (28 million).

When he was asked about his pending space trip 30 years after his first adventure, Glenn remarked, "Old people have dreams too!" In the same way he inspired the American space program in the '60s, he once again led the way for older Americans to think if John Glenn can go back into space, then they too could pursue their lifelong passions.

At age 77, John Glenn would not be a traditional new hire within a typical workplace. Many recruiters today would erroneously feel his age, experience level and probable health issues as well as perceived lack of adeptness with current technology make him an expensive hire and culturally unfit. But as those who saw Nancy Meyer's movie, "The Intern," know this ageist notion could not be more wrong. The Discovery space shuttle crew learned Glenn's experience far outweighed any concerns about his age. And the intergenerational cooperation brought the best of both worlds to the mission – the wisdom, patience and experience of Glenn matched with the technological innovation and energy of younger crew members.

In many ways, employers are stuck in the same time machine as Glenn's first global orbit - a "Mad Men" 1960s mindset where hiring anyone over age 50, let alone 60, 70 or 80, is rare. While some members of the C-suite are aging boomers or silent generation such as Warren Buffett – who at age 92 was born well before Amazon, Apple, Home Depot, Nike, Starbucks and Verizon even existed – the average age of a Fortune 500 CEO is 50. Workplaces seem to be youth-focused adapting to entice younger generation workers with perks such as Google's ping pong table and foosball game, Thrive Global's nap rooms or something as private as Apple and Meta paying for freezing the eggs of its female employees. I remember my parents warning me "there is no free lunch in life." Yet it is the free lunches *and* dinners Twitter's thousands of employees love most about their jobs according to Glassdoor.[56]

We are piling on the benefits to attract younger employees yet not addressing some basic human needs that are extremely valuable for American workers of all ages. The unsubtle subtext of all this employer-sponsored "fun and play" is to encourage employees to build their lives around work rather than have work simply be the financial fuel for more meaningful lives away from work. And despite employers offering all this hedonic excess, Jon Clifton, CEO of Gallup, shared in his book, *Blind Spot – The Global Rise*

---

[56] As I am writing this our economy is facing tough challenges with many layoffs at top tech and media employers including: Amazon, Apple, CBS and Meta; Elon Musk bought and is transforming Twitter while laying off thousands of workers; and financial services were rocked by the implosion of Silicon Valley Bank and First Republic Bank.

of Unhappiness and How Leaders Missed It, only 1 in 5 employees are thriving at work while 62% are indifferent and 18% are just downright miserable.

Employers need to focus less on the extrinsic benefits and more on the intrinsic values of its workforce. Currently, employers are stuck in hedonic adaptation that addresses momentary desire but not a meaningful life. Most employees would give up the rock-climbing wall in the lobby and even the free massage for more recognition and support from supervisors and leadership according to a 2019 Deloitte report. Employees want eudemonic benefits for more meaningful lives.

One area for employers to start is with the data that rocked human resource departments in 2019 from the Harvard Business School report, "The Caring Company." Most employers believe they are offering adequate support to caregiving employees, whereas these caregiving employees felt what they really needed was not available. For instance, 7 in 10 employees described referral services for caregivers as "very important" in terms of company loyalty yet only 38% of employers felt these services were effective in employee retention rates. Employers would do well to drop the roof-top putting greens and provide more help educating employees on family caregiving planning, financial wellness and connecting them to care resources. It is about needs versus niceties.

When I participated on a task force about caregiving employees in the workplace for the National Alliance Caregiving, the report highlighted 1 in 3 employees are caring for a loved one with 1 in 6 of those employees caring for someone over age 50. It also predicted that as demands on caregiving employees increase with our growing aging society, the talent pool will shrink for employers. Most caregiving employees want to continue to work but need flexibility. They also know culture plays a big role with most saying if a supervisor or C-suite executive has been a caregiver, the support at work is better.

The Harvard report also showed one-third of employees – more than half of which are senior management and senior executive level – are leaving their jobs to care for older loved ones typically at a time when they are at their highest earning potential and value to the company given their experience and expertise. The result is a loss of income and benefits for employees and a loss of talent, mentorship and continuity for employers.

This caregiving workplace dilemma also ties into mental and emotional health in the workplace as one of the biggest issues today. The American Psychological Association published a "2022 Work and Well-Being Survey" showing 81% of respondents indicated an employers' support for mental health will be an important consideration when they look for work in the future. This benefit trend was growing in 2020 when the Society of Human Resources Management Employee Benefits Survey showed 25% of human resource executives reported their organizations increased mental health benefits and programs since 2019.

Analyst firm CB Insights reports 81% of U.S. businesses with 50 or more employees have some form of wellness program representing a $48 billion workplace wellness market. But wellness only works if employees are using the benefits. Despite innovative wellness approaches, a 2022 survey among 10,000 employees found less than a quarter of employees (23%) in the United States and the United Kingdom use employer-sponsored stress management programs, and only 15% reported being aware of them.

This gap in availability versus usability is significant and leads one to wonder: Is the communication faulty or are the solutions from employers not meeting employee needs? Gallup's Clifton advises one of the most important things employers can do for employees is meet their emotional needs. So where is the disconnect?

The New Social Contract at Work: Care, Time, Trust

Most of the work I have done over the last 15-20 years has been with employers looking for ways to support employees in the workplace, especially those challenged with caregiving duties. A few years ago, I completed a master's credential in "Shaping the Jobs of the Future" from MIT Sloan School of Management. The focus of this education was on social contracts at work. Part of this social contract is providing the right training for all levels of the organization and communicating effectively that requires empathy and active listening.

Estimates show you spend 90,000 - 155,704 hours of your life at work – one-third of your life and 50% of your waking hours – the most time-consuming activity second only to sleeping. Essentially, you spend more wake time at the office than in your home or with your family and friends. It is not too hard to see why work has such influence on your physical, emotional and social health not to mention financial and intellectual health. And while some companies began to address the health issues of employees such as Headspace Health being adopted by many EAPs (employee assistance programs), IBM buying FitBits for all employees to encourage walking meetings or Silicon Valley companies providing stand-to-sit desks and airline-style recliner office chairs – recognizing that white collar office employees spend more time sitting than nursing home residents – the three areas employers were not focusing on when it comes to brainstorming employee benefits are your environmental, social and spiritual health.

The concept of social contracts in the workplace is to understand internal needs (employee and capital investment) before you can address external solutions (customer service, production or service delivery). According to my MIT professor, Tom Kochan, who co-authored *Shaping the Future of Work*, the premise is, "The key reason for the challenges the workforce of today and tomorrow face is that the rapid pace of globalization, technology and demographics has outpaced many public policies, business strategies and organizational practices designed in an earlier era."

What is important about social contracts at work is both sides – employers *and* employees – have a responsibility to come together to optimize work practices and environments for a new age. Many employers are wanting to entice workers back to the office. One of the simple ways to do this is to reframe how you talk about your life versus your work. Everyone uses "work-life" benefits but if an employer wants an employee to know they understand your life outside of work, flip this to "life-work" balance or just "life balance." To engender productive, happy employees, you need to *hear* them and *know* them and this means being in tune with life's challenges and priorities outside the office. Employee resource groups (ERGs) are helping with this effort because many groups are caregiving-related and can deliver the concerns and issues to HR departments in ways surveys will never uncover.

Caregiving, as mentioned earlier, now defines any employee responsible for the care of a loved one from a child to a spouse or an older parent or grandparent. Caregiving can be a leading source of burnout and declining emotional health not only because caregivers are time impoverished but also because of the lack of value placed on caregiving.

Some work-life benefits companies reported an exponential increase in services such as back-up emergency care, particularly during the pandemic.

I have consulted for Care.com. that offers comprehensive senior care and child care services to employers including a Leave Coach option to help with employee transitions in Family and Medical Leave Act (FMLA) situations and backup care services. In 2018, a client of Care.com, Starbucks, announced 10 subsidized backup care days provided annually for its 180,000 employees to help in emergency situations when an employee cannot be in two places at once and needs on demand help with older parents or children. This is how to listen to and understand your workforce needs.

The other area where innovation in workplace behavior can make a difference is to be mindful of valuing an employee's time. For instance, all meetings should be either 20-25 minutes or 50-55 minutes instead of 30 minutes and 60 minutes. This allows employees 5-10 minutes back to themselves to do some breathing exercises, walk outside for a couple of minutes, make a quick personal phone call or just get a quick bathroom break. When employees are running from one meeting to the next, they are not being allowed time to decompress and dissect what they just learned or heard from the previous meeting. Giving employees the gift of time – even in short breaks – is a valuable psychological and relational message that says, "We understand you have a life and need a few minutes to focus on yourself."

As an employee, you have to learn how to set boundaries even if your employer or supervisor does not understand the meaning of the word. Some enlightened employers, including Volkswagen, are analyzing the global trend in "right to disconnect" laws that ban employers from requiring employees to respond to emails, texts or phone calls during non-work hours. Some countries, including France, Portugal and Canada already have these laws in place.

While not a law in the U.S., American workers did adopt a "quiet quitting" posture post-pandemic essentially identifying their job as limited to required work hours and nothing more. This movement creates a transactional relationship with an employer instead of a relational one. While in Emotional Wellness I examined *toxic positivity,* quiet quitting became a reflection of the *toxic productivity* where employees signaled that work hours required equals work pay. Period. No pro bono, free overtime or life intrusions from the boss or colleagues. The employer perspective on this is to trust their employees to not be shopping on Amazon, watching funny cat videos on YouTube or posting TikTok videos during work hours. This is the reciprocity of the social contract at work that has to be forged between employers and employees.

This is also an area where Me Time Monday can help. Try scheduling 7-15 minute breaks during your days – especially on the days when there are a lot of meetings or stressful deadlines. Block this time on your calendar as a Me Time Monday break. This makes Me Time as important as any other meeting you have and is a visual reminder when you open your calendar that you need those mental moment breaks to stay energetic and positive during the day.

By training yourself to value your Me Time to be as important as your work meetings, you start to discipline yourself as a caregiver as well. It is not always easy to have boundaries when you start caring for a loved one, but it is essential to find your Me Time when caregiving just as when you are working for an employer.

One of the upsides for employees who have experience caregiving are the soft skills that are becoming so valuable to employers. For instance, being able to multitask, having more patience and empathy, knowing how to research difficult topics are all beneficial skills caregivers should use in any job interview or promotion requests.

Another potential benefit essential for caregiving employees is the flexibility of work from home (WFH). During the pandemic, the ability to avoid traffic, crowded subways and train stations gave workers more flexibility and precious time back. One estimate showed employees were able to recoup nine days back a year[57] to focus on other activities including more time for self-care. The downside of work from home or remote work is work days become blursdays with many employees spending longer hours rather than regular 9-to-5 routine hours answering emails and completing a "day's" work.

> The emotional intelligence of employers is as important as the emotional intelligence of its employees.

Besides blursdays there is another downside to WFH every day. The disconnect from fellow employees posed more emotional health challenges and what psychologists termed *workplace loneliness*. Most people are used to having confidantes at work and the remoteness of not being in the office made some people feel even more disconnected. One 2019 study found workplace social connections are shown to not only increase job performance but reduce mental health issues such as depression. This is where social health is critical for HR departments to acknowledge. This is not about the annual BBQ or company-directed social activities, this is about spontaneous relationships that form between colleagues and become vital to emotional well-being.

Gallup research found employees who are not thriving in their lives have a 61% higher rate of burnout as well as two times the rate of daily sadness and anger compared to employees who are thriving. The research also found only 3 in 10 employees report having a best friend at work who can help with burnout and bond them to the employer tribe. These surveys

---

[57] Based on a 2018 average 27 minutes a day commute.

are driving the new corporate wellness retreats and push to get back to the office at least a few days a week.

The best run organizations understand the complexities of caregiving and how there is no one-size-fits-all solution for employees. Some may need WFH flexibility and support, while others need to be in the office for workplace friendships but then will also need backup care. And all employees state in survey after survey they want more information and coaching on caregiving.

The emotional intelligence of companies is as important as the emotional intelligence of employees. While most caregivers in the workplace are going to trend older – age 45 and above – caregivers are represented in five generations and every age group at work. It is also important to note that older workers over age 50 can be workplace and caregiving mentors to younger gen workers. This is another silver lining (pardon the pun) for older workers as employers are beginning to change their views on age 50+ employees. Not only do older employees have more experience and can provide essential mentoring to newer employees but they are more reliable and not prone to job-hopping. Even though these employees may be in the sweet spot of caregiving for older parents and younger children, their value outweighs any lifestyle challenges for employers. AARP reported companies who committed to have age-friendly workplaces rose 122% from 2022 to 2021. Ultimately what employees are seeking is a *flex and control* model. Provide flexibility, especially for caregiving employees, and give employees some control over their environment and work lives. And both employees and employers need to respect each other's time. It is about care, time, trust.

From Cubical Farms to Green Space and God

As employers look to the future, there are three areas where corporate cultures are evolving to more authentically connect with the workforce and meet recruitment and retention goals: caregiving services that make a difference, improving mental health through biophilic design[58] and a faith-based twist on diversity, equity and inclusion (DEI).

When it comes to environmental health and your office space, rather than thinking about activities such as a rock-climbing wall as a benefit, employers would be wise to consider environmental makeovers as an enticement for workers of all ages and stages of life. This is not about LEED buildings or sustainable, eco-friendly design. I leave that to the architects and builders. Instead my work with employers on environmental design for employee wellness uses the principles from the WELL Building Standards® that embrace biophilic interior and exterior design (greenery, air, lighting), color psychology and soundscaping to optimize multisensory responses. These immersive without being intrusive environments are based on the *nature effect* and are set to be the next decade's biggest movement in workplace design.

As you have read, we began human life on the open savanna and remained an agricultural and outdoors society until the 1800s when factories and offices moved us inside. This deviation from our hundreds of thousands of years of being free to wander in the open spaces, in sunlight and fresh air is still affecting us. You spend 90-95% of your time indoors and this makes your office (and sometimes even your home) a place of confinement. Most animals, including humans, do not do well when trapped. Thus, being indoors for too

---

[58] You will learn more about biophilic design (which means "love of nature") in Environmental Wellness.

long creates anxiety and affects your mood even leading to depression. By understanding this connection to the ancient brain, you are starting to tap into what might be making you feel your emotional and mental health is declining.

To counter this, employers should optimize the psychological connections and relationships we have with spaces and places. Is it a welcoming environment or does your workplace design create a visceral disconnect for employees? By incorporating more biophilic design and sensemaking activities into the office employers create a place that employees seek rather than want to retreat from. According to the International WELL Building Institute "2023 Workforce Well-Being Poll," employees want more daylight, more thermal control for comfortable office temperatures, more access to nature and outdoor settings and more comfortable and healthful workstations. In return, research shows employers benefit because these types of perks enhance workplace performance and productivity and create allegiance from loyal employees.

Many employers are starting to embrace biophilia almost by accident because they are focused on sustainability. Two great examples are the Etsy headquarters in New York and the Spheres, Amazon's headquarters in Seattle with 40,000 different trees and plants. Yet, purposeful wellness infrastructure is trending. Twenty years ago, an innovative biophilic-designed space called Highline was built on an abandoned railway line along the Hudson River in Manhattan. Today, Highline is a premier wellness destination for local workers and visitors to exercise, socialize and take in nature's beauty in the heart of New York City's Meatpacking district and Chelsea area.

Employers can design workspaces with greenhouses, greenscaping, garden rooms or views outside onto lush greenery. Employees can meet in these lush spaces instead of stark, gray, windowless conference rooms. This not only sparks creativity but makes employees feel more healthful. One checklist item is to have office layouts ensure everyone has a view or plant life. If every cubicle cannot be near a window at least ensure the internal cubicles have sight lines to greenery, fountains, aquariums, etc. Adopting living walls in interior design is one of the best ways to oxygenate a stuffy office and enhance air quality (smell) as well as bring the emotional health benefit into the workplace of gazing up at green plant life (sight).

One study took employees and gave them an office in three different environments: 1) Views of trees but no plants in the office; 2) Views of trees and a plant in the office; 3) No windows but an office filled with plants. Interestingly, 69% of those with no views but multiple plants reported feeling happier and content over 60% reporting the same who had a view but no plants. One study found enhanced indoor environmental quality improves cognitive function by at least 61%. And do not try to fake it – studies show nature scenes displayed on large screens or monitors have the same negligible effect on mental health as staring at a blank wall.

In addition to greenery there is also office layout and office furniture design. For instance, all conference room tables should be round. You are happier when you see round or curved objects because your brain translates that they pose less of a threat to your body (sharp corners or spiky edges). The round table also alleviates the hierarchical structure and encourages more collaboration and equal voices being heard.

Also, pay attention to lighting. Fluorescent lights of yesteryear were bad but the LED lighting of today will literally make you lose your mind. Most doctors agree the majority of office lighting is detrimental to mental health and can cause headaches and migraines that can impact your quality of life. Many office workers find themselves suffering from SAD – seasonal affective disorder – that normally affects people living in places where there is less sunlight (think Portland, Oregon or Alaska). The way to alleviate SAD, also known as *light hunger,* is through light therapy lamps that mimic outdoor light and boost serotonin for improved mood. In the office environment design the goal is not to illuminate the entire office floor to excessive brightness but simulate soft sunlight across the floor plan. For near-work on computers, ensure each desk has adjustable task lighting that can become brighter or softer according to the worker's preferences and visual acuity.

The most sophisticated offices now use lighting systems that mimic circadian rhythms – brighter blue light at Noon easing into soft pinky-orange hues in the afternoon. Also, employees should use blue-light blocking filters or eyeglasses to help with screen glare and every 20 minutes take a break for 20 seconds to two minutes and walk outside or stare into a far-off vista to exercise your brain and eye muscles that are becoming fatigued by staring at an artificially lit screen. And, try to balance each workstation's plastic and metal technology tools with wooden pencil holders or canvas file bins, or other natural elements.

One interesting aspect of employer building design that deviates from home design is the concept of open-floor plans. While open space in the home fosters comfort and safety, in the workplace it has the opposite effect. Workplace open floor plans – also known as *cubicle farms* – actually attacks an individual employee's emotional wellness because it creates a sense of containment and confinement much like factory assembly lines with desks lined up perfectly in a grid format rather than a wide-open savanna. In West Germany after World War II, office landscaping, known as *Bürolandschaft*, was modeled after American open space grid design but European workers quickly rejected these plans in favor of the older design of private offices. However, the U.K. and the U.S. maintained the "rats in maze boxes" design to detrimental effects.

Despite Robert Propst of Herman Miller creating the Action Office for flexible design based on individual needs and preferences, companies conformed his vision to squeeze as many workers into the space resulting in the cubicle farms we still have today. A 2014 survey found 70% of American workers spend their days in open floor plan office spaces which Propst called "monolithic insanity." He was right about the emotional fall-out of the design. One study found the open space grid created tension and conflict among employees resulting in higher blood pressure for some while others simply resigned. Researchers found employees lose 86 minutes a day in focus and productivity due to the disturbances of open office spaces while another study showed office workers who are interrupted once every 11 minutes, take up to 23 minutes to get back to what they were doing before being interrupted.

One way to make cubicle farm layouts more neuro-friendly is if they are laid out on curving pathways or a hub and spoke design not a grid layout. The hub and spoke is used in Paris (with the hub being the Arc de Triomphe) and at Disneyland theme parks (the fountains in front of the castles are the hub with different worlds found along different paths). These circular and curved pathways trigger your ancient brain to feel secure and allows for more creative thinking – you want to explore and seek what is around the next bend or corner. And the higher the ceilings the better to help workers overcome the anxiety of feeling trapped. Taller ceilings also ignite the frontal cortex of your brain where creativity resides. These types of neuroaesthetic and multisensory office designs will go a long way to lure employees back into the workplace to feel more emotionally comforted and secure.

ME TIME MONDAY

Office spaces with nature views, curved pathways and greenery improve employee mental health.

And it is not just about higher ceilings but also higher powers that are trending in America's workplaces. According to the 2023 Global Wellness Institute (GWI) Trends Report, more companies are embracing the full identities of their employees as part of their diversity, equity and inclusion (DEI) mission and recognizing religion (or SBNR[59]) as part of that identity. This faith-friendly work movement has led some companies to create affinity groups around different beliefs just as they do around women, people of color, LGBTQAI+ and caregiving. For instance, Intel has seven different faiths/beliefs employee resource groups (ERGs) including smaller religions such as Bahá'í; Google's long-running "no religion in the workplace" policy has been replaced with Inter Belief Network to allow sub-groups for Christianity, Buddhism and other beliefs; and Salesforce has its Faithforce.

A 2016 report on the socio-economic value of religion to American society and workplaces found it to be $4.8 trillion annually. But even more importantly, 80% of the scientific studies done on religion and health are focused on improved mental health. We know from years of research religion aids longevity by providing connectedness, hope, optimism and resiliency to help decrease stress. With burnout and mental health huge workplace challenges, employers are finding faith-friendly workplaces help address these issues.

It is tricky for HR departments to foster religious identities among workers without disrupting collegial harmony and tolerance. But this faith-at-work movement has legs. The nonprofit Religious Freedom and Business

---

[59] SBNR is an acronym for "spiritual but not religious."

Foundation (RFBF) supports the use of ERGs for religious identity at work and has developed "The Corporate Religious Equity, Diversity & Inclusion (REDI) Index," a benchmarking measure of a company's commitment to include religion as part of its overall diversity initiatives. In their 2023 Index Report, Intel was the most faith-friendly corporate workplace among the 500 largest companies in America with American Airlines, Equinix, PayPal, Salesforce, Dell Technologies, AIG, Tyson Foods, Texas Instruments and Google rounding out the Top 10.

The social contract at work is a blend of integrating employee voices into policies and benefits and focusing on eudemonic not hedonic desires. Caregiving support, valuing employee faith and diverse lives outside of work and creating biophilic-designed office environments to maximize emotional and physical health are the benefits of coming back to the office and a glimpse into the office of the future.

Environmental Wellness

Central Park brings biophilic design to New York City

In the mid-1800s we see all health break loose in America at the same time as the Industrial Revolution was transforming communities. The move from farms to urban cities for work, the introduction of technology such as electric lighting, noise and pollution from factories and crowded housing, and a 60+ hour workweek kept people inside rather than outside in fresh air. This dangerously disconnected the populace from nature and damage to body, mind and soul had begun.

In 1859, Frederick Law Olmsted, a biophilic design advocate[60] who believed health was connected to being outdoors in nature settings, was contracted by the city of New York to address the public health crisis afflicting the metropolis. Cramped living quarters, especially in the poorer areas of Manhattan such as the Lower East Side tenements, along with poor city sanitation (did we learn nothing from the ancient Romans?!) helped fuel epidemics such as typhus, typhoid fever, dysentery, tuberculosis and cholera. It was also during this time wealthy Knickerbockers wanted a public space similar to the envied gardens of European meccas such as London and Paris. Money, public health and a man with a biophilic design plan had the solution.

Olmsted devised the "Greensward Plan" or as we know it, Central Park. It became the first landscaped public park in America with 270,000 trees, rolling meadows for sheep grazing, a lake and boats, curved pathways for walking and carriage rides in stark contrast to the claustrophobic grid lines of the city's fast developing concrete jungle. Housed on 843 acres in central Manhattan, the effort became known as "the poor man's lung" or the more politically correct "lungs of the city" as the purpose was to coax all strata of society into fresh air oxygenated by the forest design.

By 1865, Central Park welcomed more than 7 million visitors a year – almost one-quarter of the entire population of the country at that time. America's love for biophilic design had begun.

---

[60] The term "biophilic design" would not be coined until the 1980s with E.O. Wilson's research but the essence of nature design found a champion in Olmstead.

Biophilic Design: Your Brain on Nature

We are so focused on our physical, emotional and social needs for wellness (Meditate more! Be grateful! Move your body! Make time for friends!) we forgot how much joy can be created by our environments.

As I have shared, our most ancient emotions and health are tied to nature and our ancestors living on the African savanna with natural light and dark cycles, fresh air from the photosynthesis of trees and abundant, colorful flora and fauna to comfort our concern about food and water sources. In our modern lives where we spend 90-95% of our time indoors, we need to adopt biophilic design into our living environments to replicate these feelings of security and sanctuary.

Biophilia is a Greek work that means "life, nature" (bio) and "love" (philia) – essentially love of nature, love of life. While in the Physical Wellness section I explored ways to optimize a nutritious, balanced diet, biophilia is your recipe for a balanced "design diet" to feed your five senses in your living environment. Through biophilic design, you optimize the integration of sensemaking which is multisensory health and wellness that is regenerative. In the 1980s, famed Harvard University biologist, naturalist and evolutionary psychologist, E.O. Wilson, created the *biophilia hypothesis* showing how humans have a genetic and instinctive connection to nature. Biophilic design, the seminal nature-based design aesthetic, is a *bottom-up* process taking sensory information and assembling and integrating it into action needed to sustain health. After the death of her husband, Gretel Ehrlich, author of *The Solace of Open Spaces,* moved from New York City to Wyoming, a place she and her husband had lived. She found comfort and emotional well-being in a natural setting among the vast mountain ranges and high plains open air landscape. "Everything in nature invites us constantly to be what we are," Ehrlich wrote of her experience.

It is why those who are confined, such as in prison or even in nursing homes, express anxiety and depression and why open floor plans in home design are so desirable. As I touched upon in Intellectual Wellness regarding office space design, we will explore more biophilic design in this chapter, specifically as it reinforces life and living in your home environment as well as your neighborhood.

....

Biophilic Design in Your Home

"If you have a garden and a library, you have everything you need."
--Cicero (106-43 BC)

....

In 2020 as we all spent much more time at home, I was inspired to create the Snug Home. Originally a blog about the intersection of universal design and biophilic design principles, my writing turned into a consulting service to help family caregivers both optimize their older loved one's home to live there as long, as safely and as independently at possible but also to incorporate biophilic design and multisensory design into the home to promote wellness and spark joy. Many of my clients were family caregivers who initially wanted help in transforming their parent's home but they also had me create plans for their homes proving biophilic design is ageless. What I learned is you spend a lot of time focused on well-being of the mind and health of the body but you may also overlook the important influence your living environment has on you.

In the longevity economy, we talk about universal design, a concept that means ageless design that works for those whether age 8 or 88. Most of these home modifications are about accessibility and safety including: roll-out or pull-down shelves, safety grab bars in the bath (where 80% of falls at home happen for all ages), contrasting colors and textures on stair treads and rise or to distinguish cabinetry from counters, automated window coverings and counter heights. These are all classic elements of universal design where specialists – Certified Aging in Place Specialists (CAPS) through the National Home Builders Association, Senior Home Safety Specialists through AgeSafe America and other American Disability Act (ADA) service providers – will help in identifying the accessibility and adaptability needs of the home dweller and properly install the solutions.

What is missing from universal design is the wellness aspect that is more about your emotional health and multisensory integration – what I call a sanctuary for your five senses. Instead of just focusing on physical ability, I combined universal design with biophilic design based on the WELL Building Standards® to create what I call the Well Home Design for Life Plan.[61] The core wellness elements of my Well Home Design for Life plans begin with biophilic design based on nature elements: Earth (natural woods and

---

[61] You will read more about this in Financial Wellness.

greenery), Wind (air care, breezeways and windows), Fire (warmth sources you can see clearly) and Water (fountains, aquariums, hydrotherapy). By integrating these nature elements with your five senses to see, smell, hear, touch or taste, you soothe your ancient brain. These biophilic elements are incorporated into your multisensory design with sound, scent, light and temperature.

You may feel biophilic design appears similar to Chinese feng shui design.[62] Both design philosophies focus on creating optimal living environments for holistic health through balance in design to help you not just survive but flourish. However, biophilic design is less concerned with where you place things for energy flow and in what type of pairings for future prosperity, it is simply ensuring nature and sensemaking objects and design inhabit every room of your home in some way.

Think of biophilic design as a cleanse for your home. One way to test your home for biophilic design readiness is to walk into each room and try to identify all five senses in each room: what you can see, hear, touch and smell/taste that connects you to nature. It might be a cashmere or cotton throw over a metal chair (touch), a scented candle evoking the aroma of firewood, the seashore or citrus (smell), a piece of driftwood or a cedar pen holder on your desk (sight, touch) or floating shelves made of natural wood (sight), the sounds of a fountain outside through a window (sight, sound), a potted plant in your home office (sight, smell), breezy drapes (touch, sight, smell), a large natural light window (sight) or a clear bowl of colorful mandarins on your kitchen counter (sight and taste). This sensemaking is also important for your older loved one's home because biophilic design is a reminder of life and living that boosts emotional health of all ages.

---

[62] Feng shui means "wind-water."

What is important to note is biophilic design is not an interior design style such as Modern, Farmhouse, Japandi, Coastal, Traditional or Eclectic. It is a *design principle* that can be incorporated into any of these personal styles for improved wellness. A natural wood shelf above a Mid-Century Modern fireplace, a living wall of greenery in a Japandi minimalist entryway, herb pots on a window sill in a Farmhouse kitchen, a lighted water fountain in an Eclectic backyard, a seashell ceiling fan in a Coastal bedroom, an elevated fireplace in a Traditional living room.[63]

In addition to the nature elements, there are also natural patterns in biophilic design such as curves or fractals that mimic plant life or curving pathways in nature. For instance, curved counters, tables and couches all message "safety" to the brain whereas spiky, angular, square or rectangular objects pose threats. Curvilinear design and furniture, such as kitchen, dining or living room tables, encourage both collaboration and agreement for those sitting at a round table but the shape also sparks joy and playfulness while also ensuring pointy edges of coffee tables or counters are eliminated to avoid harmful bruising that can happen based on balance issues for both younger toddlers and older adults.

Biophilic design is a cleanse for your home.

Fractals also embrace the nature aspect of biophilic design. These are essentially never-ending designs that repeat themselves such as the leaves of a fern, petals on a rose, rolling clouds, endless coastlines, honeycomb in a beehive or mountain ranges. You yearn for fractals in your

---

[63] Check out my Snug Home blog online at CaregivingClub.com for visual examples.

environmental designs because you are genetically encoded from ancient Homo sapiens who were successful at seeking and finding these patterns in their surroundings that meant survival. The repeating patterns trigger in your ancient brain recognition of nourishment and comfort sources. You can use fractals in wallpaper design, framed images, objets d'art items on shelving or views through a magnificent window where you gaze upon the real thing: ferns, coastlines, mountains or clouds.

Bringing the forest into the home in small or big ways or at least having a view of trees, flowers and bushes from windows in most rooms is an essential principle of biophilic design based on human evolution. Third century Egyptians knew nature views were healing and had potted plants which were discovered in the fossils found in the ruins of Pompeii.

One of the most frequently cited researchers in evidence-based healthcare biophilic design, Roger Ulrich, conducted a seminal study in the '70s and '80s demonstrating the healing power of nature views in a hospital setting. Ulrich had one group of hospital surgical patients placed in rooms with a nature view onto trees and plants; the other group had windows facing a brick wall. The group with a nature view were discharged from the hospital twice as fast and needed one-half the medications than the brick wall group. What Ulrich projected is the use of biophilic design could reduce health care costs by $89 million (adjusted for 2023 dollars this is $253 million). Several studies show people feel happier and calmer after just 10-20 minutes in a room with plants while researchers found depression and anxiety were lowered for those who had houseplants. They concluded plants are restorative. The greener the plant color the better and five plants is optimal to enhance your mood.

However, true biophilic design uses multisensory elements to amplify each other for increased well-being. While the visual of greenery is important, another key aspect of biophilic home design is in the smells and air quality of your home called *air care*.

In the U.S., 90% of all households and most of commercial, government and corporate buildings have some type of air conditioning. When you think about all the time you spend indoors air care becomes vitally important to wellness. Starting with your home, a National Air Duct Cleaners Association report a few years ago showed the average home collects 40 pounds of dust laced with 45 different toxins including dead skin cells and dust mite droppings. In addition, the EPA estimates there are 2-5 times the air pollutants indoors than outside. The use of HEPA filters, ionic air purifiers, humidifiers, dealing with dust and maintaining home cleanliness helps. In addition, paint manufacturers such as Sherwin Williams offer bacteria and odor-resistant paints to help promote better air care.

Plants, however, may be your best defense. A groundbreaking Clean Air Study conducted by NASA in 1989 showed certain indoor plants can help reduce indoor air pollutants and reduce carbon dioxide levels, including removal of harmful elements known as VOCs (volatile organic compounds) such as benzene and formaldehyde. These are significant contributors to childhood asthma and increased rates of asthma in older adults. About 7% of people over 65 are often incorrectly diagnosed with COPD based on inflammation and lowered immunity, when they actually have asthma. The indoor plants with the most pollutant fighting strength are: English ivy (can reduce airborne mold in hours), peace lily, areca and bamboo palms (absorb pollutants and moisturize air to help with sinus problems), aloe vera plants (release oxygen all night and fight benzene) and spider plants.

Open floor plans are also key for biophilic design. The wide and long sightlines in activity areas, such as living rooms, dining rooms and kitchens where you spend most of your active time at home, create calm mirroring how our ancestors felt on those Ethiopian plains able to see predators and prey. This sense of calm is still imprinted on your ancient brain and scientists call it *refuge theory*. Compartmentalized rooms in a home as well as clutter defeat this openness and you become stressed. You seek the opposite of open floor design when sleeping because your ancient brain wants the security of a cave-like environment in your bedroom as well as a sanctuary space, such as a cozy reading nook, to retreat to for reduced stress. These snug spaces create psychological comfort while at rest.

For home offices, biophilic design will improve your well-being because the technology you use in your job has alienated you from the nature you need. Having a window to gaze out of onto greenery or flowers will not only rest your weary eyes from staring at a digital screen but help to kick-start the parasympathetic nervous system to calm your stress. Also, having tactile natural elements counter-balance all the plastic, steel and digital tools – a block of wood; a little sandbox to trace patterns; a comfortable cotton, faux fur or cashmere throw for cold days; a desk fan to feel a light breeze on your face for hotter days. And aromatherapy is important in any room where you spend a good amount of time. Use a candle or room scent to evoke pleasant memories as well as alertness and creativity such as mint, jasmine, bergamot, eucalyptus fragrances or my favorite, a coastal sea salt scent mixed with tuberose and pine.[64] Studies have found the fresher a room smells, the larger, brighter and cleaner it appears via multisensory interplay in your brain.

---

[64] You will read about color psychology later in this chapter and sensory wellness of sound and music in Spiritual Wellness.

Biophilic Design in Your Neighborhood

"Healing . . . is not a science, but the intuitive art of wooing Nature."
— W.H. Auden, *The Art of Healing*

While your home sanctuary is under your control when it comes to creating a biophilic designed oasis that will promote wellness, where you choose to live – your neighborhood and community – are equally important. Whether you call it cabin fever or cave syndrome, you cannot stay locked up forever and therefore experiencing biophilia in your home town is beneficial to your well-being. It takes you from an environment dominated by digital devices and artificial lighting to environments where you actually are immersed in a multisensory nature habitat. You go from passive to active participant in nature.

One study pinpointed the magic number of 120 minutes (two hours) being in nature over the course of one week will boost your health and well-being. If you break this down over the seven days of Me Time Monday you are spending 17 minutes a day outside where there are trees, fresh air, nature sounds and smells (or break it down even further and spend 8 minutes twice a day or 6 minutes three times a day), that is all it takes to boost your wellness score. First of all, the regenerative feeling of sunshine and the vitamin D you absorb by being outside is extremely important for it promotes the release of serotonin to brighten your mood. Also, as discussed, sunshine helps support bone strength, enhances your immune system and reduces your stress.

But as discussed, it is about more than sunshine, our brains crave being in nature and this stimulates healthier living. Researchers at the Brigham and Women's Hospital and Harvard T.H. Chan School of Public Health studied the life expectancy and mental health of 100,000 women. They discovered women who lived near green spaces had a 12% lower mortality rate than those living in locations with less trees and greenery. The scientists concluded green spaces provided more opportunities for participants to socialize outdoors that benefitted their mental health. Other studies have shown biophilic design promotes better physical and mental health in children by reducing oxidative stress, the imbalance between free radicals and antioxidants in the body tied to accelerated aging and chronic illness. Living in a community, whether a home town or senior living community, with nature views can also lower Alzheimer's risk in adults over age 60.

Humans have an instinctive connection to nature.

According to the Global Wellness Institute Trends Report 2022, there is also a growing desire to get our hands in the dirt – whether it is gardening or farming, there is something soothing about planting things in soil. Over the last few years in the U.S., there is a growing trend of agrihoods, an organic farm-style living movement that harkens back to America's beginnings in the 1700s and 1800s. According to the Urban Land Institute, there are currently 150 agrihoods across the U.S.

One of these agrihoods is Serenbe, a 750-resident, 1,400-acre biophilic-designed community located approximately 30 miles outside Atlanta nestled in the forest of the Chattahoochee Hills. Originally a B&B vacation destination, the community includes a rustic-chic farmhouse restaurant, a 25-acre organic farm where residents enjoy a community garden and an on-site farmer's market, year-round cultural events including outdoor concerts, films and author lectures in the community theater and forest bathing with numerous green pathways among the trees complete with a beautiful waterfall. The increasing appeal of agrihoods, especially for stressed out city dwellers, is to escape the traffic, noise and crime of today's urban, larger cities and revert back to the living style of America's early years. This simpler life with community gardens and orchards creates a neighborhood farm to table culture enticing both younger and older adults to these nature-filled, more rural and utopian communities.

I interviewed Steve Nygren, founder of Serenbe for a PBS Next Avenue article and also on my podcast to find out why the future of communities seems to be going back to our past.

"Back in 2008 when we had the housing market crash, the first communities to step out of the recession were walkable communities and those focused on environmental or biophilic design," explained Nygren. "Suddenly people started showing up to see what Serenbe was all about."

For Nygren, making the weekend trek out to the beautiful forest area of Serenbe was a breath of fresh air – literally. For three years, Nygren and his wife and three young children made Serenbe their sanctuary from hectic city life. After purchasing the old farmhouse, running it as a B&B, then adding to the original 900 acres with homebuilding, Nygren began by designing a biophilic community modeled after the charming hamlets of the English countryside.

According to Nygren, Serenbe was not a new idea but rather bringing back old ideas of how to live based on pre-World War II models where the farm was next to where you lived, where you shopped for food and ate organically. Also, the homes have 8-10 foot front porches that encourage people to connect and communicate with neighbors walking by on the wide sidewalk. And the trees and nature are abundant.

"Moving to Serenbe full-time was a value shift for me and probably very relatable to what people felt during the recent pandemic and that is reanalyzing what was important," said Nygren. "I was on the treadmill of life going faster and faster and the scenery was all looking the same. No matter what board I was on or what we were trying to do, I looked at my young children and thought I will only have this chance once. So, I sold my company, my big house in the Atlanta and stepped off the treadmill."

Beyond just the nature settings in our communities, one of the most interesting areas of neuroscience over the last 20+ years has been in neuroarchitecture. Donald Ruggles, architect and author of *Beauty, Neuroscience and Architecture*, wrote about one of the most fundamental patterns in architecture and art throughout history which is the classic nine-square. Dominating the Renaissance period, the nine-square design is the geometric design behind the tartan fabric in Scotland, the Parthenon, the Taj Mahal, Notre Dame cathedral in Paris, Byōdō-in temple in Japan, the U.S. Capitol Building, St. Peter's Basilica in Rome and even Da Vinci's *Mona Lisa* and Gustav Klimt's *The Woman In Gold*. Most would agree when you think of these buildings and works of art, you find an aesthetic and beauty in their design that ignites your brain.

This design philosophy is about right angles with varying widths rather than a rigid nine-square. When you add neuroscience to the mix you realize why cross-culturally we find nine-square design desirable. Infants as young as one-month-old will begin to discern the patterns of a parent's face: two eyes and a mouth that appear as dark blurbs in an outline of a face. Darwin hypothesized this is how infants survived by recognizing adults – especially a mother's facial structure – to signal safety and consistent nourishment. Thus, when you glimpse upon a nine-square design, especially in residential home architecture, you see the crude outlines of a face – two windows on either side as eyes, a door as a nose, two windows below as the corners of a mouth – similar to the blurry blobs an infant's eyes sees when gazing upon a parent. This nine-square design is imprinted on your brain and makes you feel inherently safe, comforted and prone to see it as beautiful.

This visual imprint is so profound on the brain that small children when asked to draw a house most will draw an outline with two windows on the sides and one door simulating facial structure. In fact, 65% of the neuronal structure of the brain is dedicated to facial recognition that becomes the template for finding beauty in architecture, art and home design.

....

Immersive Biophilia Experience:
The Enchanted Forest

"Nature in her green, tranquil woods heals and soothes all afflictions."
-- John Muir

....

It is often said our modern world has given us amnesia about nature. What we do know is without oxygen, we cannot survive and being in nature provides this life source.[65] Scientific and environmental experts believe 2 billion years ago during the first ice age, the Earth experienced increased oxygen concentrations allowing photosynthesis, an energy source for complex

---

[65] In medical school you learn the Rule of 3s for survival: 3 weeks without food, 3 days without water, 3 minutes without oxygen.

life. This process is where green plant life including trees, use sunlight to create a food source from carbon dioxide and water. This causes the plant life to emit a green pigment called chlorophyll that removes the carbon dioxide while it creates and releases oxygen in its surroundings. This is why when you are in a forest or among abundantly green plant life, your lungs breathe in more oxygen than normal to reduce stress and boost immunity.

The next time you are tempted to try out the latest wellness fad, known as oxygen bars, you may want to instead opt for *forest bathing*. Also called *shinrin-yoku*, which in Japanese means "luxuriating in the trees," forest bathing is a type of nature hike combined with meditative quiet officially launched in 1982 in Japan as a national health program. The physical and mental benefits were so evident the Japanese government has invested $4 million into funding forest therapy research – also known as ecotherapy. Japan now has 48 official forest therapy trails all across the country visited by more than 2 million people a year. From a health perspective, forest bathing increases your Natural Killer (NK) cells – the white blood cells that attack and remove viruses and tumors from your body. Essentially, trees are lifesavers.

What is unique about forest bathing versus other types of calming exercises and meditation is it is an *immersive* experience. During physical exercise or meditation, you are concentrating on your movements or your breathing. Forest bathing is all about focusing on your environment using sensemaking: your five senses of sound, sight, smell, touch and even taste. Despite Japan's official designation of forest bathing as a public health initiative similar to Olmstead's Central Park, luxuriating in nature has been part of our evolution since our earliest beginnings on the African savanna. From ancient civilizations to the 1800s, America's nature thought leaders such as Ralph Waldo Emerson and Henry David Thoreau have led to modern day Erich Fromm and E.O. Wilson, all whom have demonstrated and shared the physical and mental well-being from immersing yourself in nature.

Beyond the stress relief and healing effects, forest bathing can also help with sleep. Dr. Qing Li, an author on forest bathing and leading global researcher in *forest medicine* at Nippon Medical School in Tokyo, conducted a study on the health benefits of shinrin-yoku. His research showed after two hours of forest bathing walks, the average sleep time of participants increased by 15% that translates into 54 more minutes of sleep per night. And, quality of sleep was better with more restful hours per night. Participants were also less anxious and scored more positively on generalized anxiety surveys.

Essentially forest bathing fulfills the new movement in wellness which is not about focusing on one sense but creating an integrated multisensory experience. During a Global Wellness Institute trends report presentation, neurobiologist Ari Peralta, explained how big global brands are tapping into the senses. "Brands are reimagining how to use combinations of sensory stimulation – also called sensory signatures – to take wellness out of the spa and into everyday life and environments such as cars, airplanes, trains, hotels, homes, shopping activities and more," shared Peralta. "One example is Nissan where the automotive maker is exploring aromatherapy and soundscapes to help babies fall asleep in car seats."

About 85% of the U.S. population lives in suburban and urban areas without easy access to traditional rural forests. According to the U.S. Forest Service, there are 154 national forests and 22 national grasslands across the country. To avoid *nature deficit disorder* (NDD) tied to anxiety and lack of resiliency, there is a forest bathing finder resource online that connects you to certified forest bathing guides, group walks and best places to experience the enchanted forests.

....

Blue Wellness and Our Love Affair with Water

"The sea, once it casts its spell, holds one in its net of wonder forever."
-- Jacques-Yves Cousteau

....

I know I am biased when it comes to coastal living. I grew up in Southern California and have never left the glittering beaches, rolling waves and tidepool treasures of this area. I feel blessed to awake every day to what I consider God's glory. I feel like the coastal vista heals me and I am not alone.[66]

Eight in 10 people in the world live 60 miles or closer to a body of water – an ocean, a sea, a lake or a river – meaning you are never far from water that can rejuvenate you. One study analyzed the health status of 48 million people in England and found those who lived closer to the coast reported good health regardless of age, gender, race, socioeconomic status or even if they lived near parks or other green spaces. Water is a tonic to body and mind, a calming and comforting effect some researchers believe is associated with your memories of floating in the womb as an infant.

This peaceful state of happiness most feel when immersed in water – the human-water connection – is what marine biologist and author, Wallace Nichols, captured in his book, *Blue Mind*. Nichols believes water is our shortcut to health and happiness. "Near water, but especially in water, our

---

[66] I wrote an article for *PBS Next Avenue* about the "Coastal Grandmother" trend with millions of Millennials and Gen Z venerating both coastal living and older women.

bodily senses – touch, pressure, temperature, motion, position, balance, weight, vibration – are truly alive," writes Nichols.

When we think about sensemaking, particularly multisensory immersive experiences, few compare to how we feel in water whether the ocean, a hot tub or a warm shower. It awakens all of our senses, especially the tactile feeling of touch. We know water plays a key role in certain religious rituals such as the Ganges in Hinduism, the Well of Zamzam in Islam, John the Baptist and the River Jordan in Christianity and Lourdes in Roman Catholicism. Even agnostics and atheists will pay more for a house or hotel room with an ocean view. Real estate agents estimate waterfront homes can command twice the price of inland homes.

Scientists believe we were able to survive as a species because we were attracted to aquatic environments with an endless source of fresh water and food and this theory continues to yield insights into brain health. Some of the fish and shellfish we ate over thousands of years contained omega 3 fatty acids that became critical for brain development.

Throughout the ages, water has been a natural healer with curative properties. Ancient Roman baths were the precursors to today's modern spas. Hydrotherapy as a solution in the 19th century wellness movement of "life reform" was advocated by Louis Kuhne, a German naturopath who shunned traditional medicine for remedies such as fresh air, vegetarian diet, abstaining from salt and sugar but especially promoting the healing power of sitz baths and cold water hydrotherapy.[67]

This connection between water and health was also taking off with wealthy Victorians in England and their American Gilded Age cousins. Resort spas and hot springs, such as Bath in England and Saratoga Springs,

---

[67] Kuhne also loved nude sunbathing excursions making him a forerunner of the American hippie subculture.

New York, attracted the likes of Jane Austen, Charles Dickens and Florence Nightingale giving rise to the popularity of the pump rooms. Known as places of healing waters and often found in the same area as the ruins of Roman baths, pump rooms became the place where stylish society sought to both bathe and drink the natural elixir but also to socialize with the "in crowd." And many early 20th century physicians prescribed coastal visits or a move to the seaside or lakeside for those suffering from tuberculosis and other respiratory diseases, right out of Thomas Mann's *The Magic Mountain*.

The health benefits of fresh ocean air and natural springs continues to this day. Research shows living by the sea enhances your sleep because negative ions in sea air accelerate your ability to absorb oxygen. One study found people slept on average 47 minutes longer after a seaside hike as opposed to those who took an inland walk of a similar length. Living along the coast or a lake area helps balance your serotonin levels to regenerate body, mind and soul. And science also finds your ability to *free-move* and have your brain practice elastic thinking is enhanced when in water. When showering you may find yourself being more creative at solving problems or inventing innovative ideas.

One study found among outdoor activities, people's happiness increased 5.2% when they were near water. Think of your childhood, is there at least one cherished memory based on water? A swimming pool, the lake at camp, fishing, water skiing, surfing, slip and slide games, water balloons, running through the sprinklers. As a child you may have resisted nightly bath time, but would you give it all back now to have a luxurious, soapy bath every night?

Figure 20: An 1890 *Harper's Weekly* article on "taking the waters" at Saratoga Springs (insert), Six Senses Place urban wellness club opening in London in 2023-2024.

In 2012 the United Nations in collaboration with Gallup created the first annual World Happiness Report that after a decade has become the Olympics of emotional health. The Nordic countries take home the gold every year in this survey. Sweden, Finland, Denmark, Iceland and Norway consistently rank year after year as among the happiest people on the planet. What is in the water in Northern Europe?

Some believe water does have something to do with it. The Nordic countries are three-quarters – or in the case of Iceland completely – surrounded by water, offering constant coastal views and sea air that may contribute to the bliss of the people in these countries.

One trend that is resurging from the '80s is flotation tank therapy made famous by William Hurt in the 1980 film, "Altered States." This liquid immersion is said to be a favorite wellness activity of Silicon Valley titans as part of the new biohacking movement. Biohacking is the latest in natural human augmentation or human enhancement (as opposed to plastic surgery and steroids) where do-it-yourself (DYI) biology is focused on improving performance while amplifying health, and wellness. Biohacking activities include intermittent fasting, *nootropics* (non-prescription supplements, drinks, foods to do things such as boost brain health) and cold water therapy.

Research has shown cold water therapy – also known as ice bathing – can reduce inflammation, soothe muscles and improve breathing and has long been used by professional athletes as part of their post-performance physical relief. Now it is being used for mental and emotional health boosts for non-athletes. The 40-50 degree shock to the body is supposed to decrease inflammation and improve mental health although physicians are concerned with people who have heart problems or other breathing health issues to not try ice bathing alone. Some scientists are even investigating cold therapy as a weight-loss breakthrough where body fat can be manipulated by cryotherapy's exposure to cold environments to burn more calories.[68]

One self-professed guru, Bill Purnell of Boston, was interviewed by *The Boston Globe* about his Facebook group called "Cold Water Transformation" where his motto is "Be bold, get cold, and never grow old." What people are now paying for the late great actress Katherine Hepburn (who lived to age 96) did for free. Every morning well into her 90s she took her morning "polar bear" dip in the 20-degree below Fahrenheit temperatures near her home on the Connecticut shore. She believed her no-nonsense, New England upbringing meant "the bitterer the medicine, the better it is for you."

Speaking of freezing and the Nordic countries, Danes are embracing a form of biohacking called winter bathing where they dive into frigid lakes to stimulate blood flow and shock the senses purported to boost happiness. Not to be outdone, in Finland, the latest wellness practice is sauna ferris

---

[68] Cryotherapy uses extreme cold in medical treatments but not water which is cold water therapy.

wheels for hot therapy fun in freezing climes (you do loops in freezing cold weather in a moving hot tub).

For those of us who are not quite ready for polar bear dips or hot-cold ferris wheel rides, using water as a healing agent still makes scientific sense. Splashing cold water on your face in the morning is a habit for most of us to awaken the senses to a new day, or reveling in a hot shower that eases aching muscles or loosens a cough deep in the lungs is the healing nature of water. Even washing your hands under sudsy water for a few minutes has been shown to increase your emotional health and is a self-care activity for caregivers feeling compassion fatigue. One study found hand washing not only is hygienic to wash away germs but it also washes away any feelings of failure and guilt and boosts your optimism.

....

Solastalgia and Mental Health

"The more high-tech our lives become, the more nature we need."
-- Richard Louv, *The Nature Principle*

....

In the 1980s I was an undergraduate at the University of Southern California majoring in journalism and political science but being a lifelong movie buff, I managed to squeeze in a minor in cinematic arts.

One of the documentaries shown in class was called "Koyaanisqatsi" (pronounced: koy·aa·nuh·skaat·see) meaning "life out of balance" in the Hopi language. I am still transfixed by this haunting documentary that is a visual commentary on modern life by avant garde filmmaker, Godfrey Reggio. The style of filmmaking used no actors nor dialogue making viewers rely on imaginative but startling timelapse photography of sprawling, kinetic city life dissolving into footage of natural landscapes in America's vast deserts, mountains and rural farm lands all set against an almost apocalyptic soundtrack by minimalist composer Philip Glass.

Filmmakers explained the use of timelapse underscored the acceleration of the deterioration of society fueled by technology. From the multi-lane, frenzied Los Angeles freeways to New York City's grid-designed streets and skyscrapers, our cities look like computer chips. But as the photography moves above into images of the Earth from space (thanks to the technology of NASA and modern satellite imagery) you do not see grids. You see swirls of white clouds and undulating, flowing blue oceans and green mountains. The timelapse of prairie lands with waving wheat fields or babbling brooks and vast coral desert skies with colorful, soft edges are juxtaposed with close-up images of stressed city dwellers.

The film actually began as a popular public service multimedia advertising campaign in Albuquerque, New Mexico with 5-10-minute film clips played on local television channels over a series of nights. Part of the success of the campaign was to reduce Ritalin as a behavior-modifying drug in many New Mexico school districts by encouraging children to spend more time outdoors in nature environments.

Eventually the campaign's success caught the attention of Francis Ford Coppola[69] who helped turn the PSA into a documentary film. Climate change activists and neoliberals have embraced the film, but the message is not political, it is philosophical. It is a visual and aural masterpiece addressing what its Hopi name says – a look at how our modern lives are out of balance. The solution is to ensure there is equilibrium between the

---

[69] Academy Award-winning screenwriter/director of "The Godfather."

technology we cannot stop and the nature that will sustain us. They must co-exist or we will cease to exist.

When asked to explain his vision for the film, Reggio advised it is not about "bad, polluting technology" versus "good nature" but that we must remain mindful of not allowing technology to be the only environment we have, we must have nature to have lives in balance. "It's not that we use technology, we live technology. Technology has become as ubiquitous as the air we breathe so we are no longer conscious of its presence," said Reggio in a YouTube trailer for the film.

This eternal struggle between progress and nature is a significant factor in mental health that has led to a new term, *solastalgia*. This state of distress can affect any age group but is mostly seen as homesickness felt by older adults even when they are in their homes. Australian environmental philosopher Glenn Albrecht coined the term to explain the unique mental anguish, anxiety, despair, and trauma associated with distressing events such as natural disasters including floods, fires, earthquakes; as well as societal change such as increased neighborhood crime, invasive urban development such as living near strip malls or highways.

The opposite of solastalgia is *soliphilia* – meaning "love of place." Family caregivers can help a loved one by identifying positive outcomes of an unexpected and traumatic change. For instance, if there was a house fire that destroyed the kitchen, focus on engaging your loved one in creating a dream kitchen they always wanted. Sometimes it is not a tragic event but a changing neighborhood or local community that may be experiencing higher crime, increased pollution and traffic and lack of natural beauty. This may be the time to have the discussion with your loved one about alternative living options that would bring a renewed lease on life and more biophilic-designed living environment.

One study conducted by researchers. Anthony Longoria and Heidi Rosetti, at the University of Texas Southwestern Medical Center found the study participant's brains changed if they lived in neighborhoods where there was violence in the community or they felt their neighbors were unwilling to help or did not hold their same values. Their brain scans showed the white matter volume (WMV) and hyperintensities (WMH) changed that can affect memory, processing speed, balance and other mobility issues.

Author and biophilia advocate, Richard Louv, writes, "The future will belong to the nature-smart—those individuals, families, businesses, and political leaders who develop a deeper understanding of the transformative power of the natural world and who balance the virtual with the real.

chapter 27

Color Psychology and Well Home Design

Anthropologists have found the earliest humans decorated rocks with dyes to create special meaning with color. At least 160,000 years ago, ochre, a natural clay earth pigment that creates a brown-red color, was used in cave drawings and painted stones used during rituals. Color meanings began as the earliest form of language and storytelling.

Today, color psychology and chromatherapy are two different aspects of how color is used in terms of emotional and social wellness as well as for the healing arts of the mind and body. While chromatherapy has been accepted by medical science, it is only over the last few years color psychology has been taken seriously by the health care industry and not relegated to pop psychology or pseudo-science.

As covered in the Me Time Monday section, you have three different rods in the retinas of your eyes that perceive colors, each of which can see at least 100 different tones and shades such as pink, a lighter shade of red, meaning the eye can see at least 1 million colors. Bevil Conway, a neuroscientist and artist who studies color and emotions at the National Eye Institute, feels our brains have their own Pantone color system. Conway explains the rods and cones in our eyes are the photoreceptors for motion, faces, places and navigation. In an interview with *Fast Company*, Conway discussed the neuroscience of colors and emotional influence, "I think it's a very powerful system and it's completely underexploited."

Kathryn Grube is an internationally noted color designer as well as top interior designer using color psychology to create spaces that energize, calm, promote sleep, healthy eating and more. Her company, Functional Color Solutions, designs for companies and industrial spaces as well as for private clients in interior home design. I spoke to her for my podcast and this book about the power of color when it comes to personalizing a wellness plan.

"First of all, color is reflected light and an organic form of nature," explained Grube. "Sunlight is all seven colors of the spectrum where the light bends and we see these individual colors reflected: red, orange, yellow, green, blue, indigo and violet, known as ROYGBIV. But color is also energy just like the energy fields around humans and other organisms. We measure this combination of light and energy in nanometers where the longest wavelength is red (700 nanometers) that when seen with the human eye creates stimulation and the shortest wavelength is violet (380 nanometers) that produces calming effects."

If you gaze upon an orange sunset or blue waters or a red apple, those objects and scenery are not those colors it is simply the light is reflected in a way that what your eye sees is transmitted to your brain and is interpreted in those colors. The sun is actually rainbow colors (ROYGBIV) that become white light, or some believe blue light that you see as white. When sunlight is reflected off a white object, you see white because your eyes absorb no color reflection. When sunlight is reflected off a solid object, it absorbs a certain amount of light and you then see that color. When it hits a black object, you see black because rather than reflect a color back to you, the black object absorbs all colors so all you see is black. About 8% of men and 1% of women have some form of color impairment, the most common is dichromatism where you cannot distinguish red from green.

Isaac Newton first identified ROYGBIV in his 1671 book, *Optiks*. He decided on seven individual colors as the most common seen by humans but also for the synergy of connecting colors to the seven days of the week, seven musical notes and seven planets in the solar system (known at that time) to show color's connection to nature elements.

Have you ever walked into a room and had a feeling, maybe it is excitement or a sense of calm? The energy fields of color are what you notice first when you enter a space. This is why using color psychology in my Well Home Design for Life Plans is critical to maximize the type of mind and body response you want to achieve. Most people are familiar with warm and cool color tones. However, your response to color is very individualized based on the color symbolism of your cultural background. For instance, for most people blue is a calming color often seen in bedrooms. But for others blue can be depressing. For many, walking into a red room increases your heart rate and provides a sense of energy and stimulation. For others, red ignites fear and agitation. Yellows and oranges can trigger hunger pains which is why McDonald's uses a lot of yellow and red while casual dining restaurants use orange hues.

Grube notes we experience color through all five of our senses.[70] She explains color has a smell such as seeing a lemon and having it message the brain about a fresh scent. Colors have sounds as well as you read about pink noise as a sleep aid, but also hot pink is a loud color, whereas lavender

---

[70] A condition known as synesthesia (also spelled synaesthesia) is often seen in those on the autism spectrum. It is defined as a 'mixing of the senses.' For example, someone would see colors when they hear sounds, link specific letters to colors or report that musical notes evoke different tastes. This is different from multisensory experiences to enhance wellness.

is a soft color. You also taste with your eyes sensing yellow and green foods will be sour or tart and oranges and pinks will be sweet. And when it comes to touch, you seek colors that can literally change your perception of the temperature in the room making you feel 10 degrees warmer or cooler. Following are the positive and negative interpretations of color and various studies conducted on color psychology and health. It is a guide on how to think about color in your home environment.

Figure 21: The eye sees 1 million colors creating its own Pantone color system.

Color Psychology

WHITE

In Western culture white means clean, pure, freedom while in Asian culture white means death. The color white also represents innocence and youth – think of brides or first communions. Doctors wear white coats to imply sterility but some patients (including myself) feel triggered by "white coat syndrome," also known as white coat hypertension. This syndrome accelerates the stress response and leads to higher blood pressure readings often based on anxiety when interacting with health care professionals. When used in home design, white can be a perfect blank canvas on which to reflect colorful images, or hang photos that are comfort sources but older eyes require a lot of contrast with mostly white walls.

BLACK

Black is seen as a powerful color, which may explain why black is the most popular choice for luxury vehicles. But it is also used for graduation robes of educational achievement and symbolizing the authority of priests, pastors, judges and law enforcement officers. People often describe the color as sexy, powerful, mysterious, and even ominous. in Western cultures, black is also the color most associated with death and grief. Before more modern medicine in the mid-19th century identified germs and microbes, Hippocrates identified the four humors: blood, phlegm, yellow bile and black bile. This last humor was associated with melancholy, depression and cancer - all were believed to emanate from black bile secretions. These types of diseases were seen as living in darkness. As with many conditions created by neurological disturbances, visual stimuli of certain colors and contrast sensitivity are important to understand in the care of these loved ones. For instance, Alzheimer's patients avoid stepping onto any black carpets, rugs or other areas as they perceive this as a hole they will fall into.

RED

Red is mostly associated with energy and action. It can actually increase heart rates which is why it is used for urgent or important messages such as stop signs, red lights and warning labels. Red is also associated with the color of life and love. But for others, red can create fear, agitation and represents sin (think of Halloween devil costumes or the red room in the erotic romance novel, *Fifty Shades of Grey*). One study looked at brain scans of neurologically impaired patients after seeing the color red. In both Parkinson's patients and those with traumatic brain injuries (TBI), the color red created negative and distressing reactions. Yet, another study of Alzheimer's patients showed increased eating and drinking – 25% for food and 84% for liquid – when the food was served on dishware with red versus baseline white, the color of most people's dishes.

Pink, a variation on red, is considered feminine but up until World War II, pink was associated with both little girls and little boys. Pink is seen as a color of innocence, romance, and happy, joyful thoughts. Researchers found a deep rosy shade known as "drunk-tank pink," also called Baker-Miller pink, used in prisons, jails and psychiatric wards calmed patients and inmates although recent critics debate that the effect was only temporary.

Color Psychology

ORANGE

The color orange is part of the warm family of colors along with reds and yellows. It is the color mostly associated with the sun and with fire, both of which bring us warmth. In Avicenna's time, it was used for healing lungs and to increase energy levels through application of coral and orange jade. Orange foods and environmental design are found to stimulate the appetite. Placing orange flowers, fruits or other décor or art, especially in a dining area or kitchen, will stimulate regular healthy eating. Orange color therapy has even been found to stimulate the thyroid to boost metabolism. Orange is also a color associated with a sense of mastery as well as being cheerful, friendly and confident. And it is the color most associated with gratitude, thoughtfulness and being considerate. Because orange colors are dominant when we go from fall (leaves, pumpkins, etc.) to winter, it is seen as a color associated with transitions and adaptability. It is a color most often used to help a person recover from disappointments, a wounded heart, or a blow to one's pride.

YELLOW

For the last 30 years, Leatrice Eiseman, color specialist and executive director of the Pantone Color Institute has conducted research on color psychology. During a TV interview she remarked, "The first words that consistently come to mind when people see the color yellow are 'sunshine,' 'warmth,' 'cheer,' 'happiness' and sometimes even 'playfulness.'" She also shared that most children choose the yellow crayon in a box first because it is "fun." This stems from its association with a crucial player in our solar system – the sun. Yellow also plays a role in boosting dopamine in the brain. According to *Psychology Today*, seeing flowers, particularly bright yellow, triggers reward signals in your brain. This is tied to our ancient brains when food was more abundant in the spring when flowers were blooming. Seeing yellow flowers meant food sources would be easier to find and this signaled less stress, more pleasure and increased happiness.

The use of yellow was also employed to treat World War I soldiers suffering from shell shock in 1917 London. While psychology was still a relatively new field mostly rejected by the medical establishment, at the McCaul Convalescent Hospital psychologist Howard Kemp-Prosser believed in a new theory that the right colors could help those suffering from a variety of mental ailments. Kemp-Prosser painted the psychiatric ward with blue ceilings to simulate the daytime sky but the most predominant color was yellow – walls, medicine cabinets, even food trays – to simulate sunshine. The theory became popularized by the British press as the "colour cure." While science debated whether the colour cure had any validity, other hospitals and care centers, including Red Cross units in Australia and other countries, adopted the color scheme to aid emotionally distressed veterans. Even the *British Journal of Nursing* acknowledged "colour medicine" was beneficial in transporting the afflicted soldiers from the brown dust and red carnage of the Battle of the Somme and other horrendous scenes of war to the hopeful, bright living environment of springtime.

Color Psychology

BLUE

Blue is the color of seas and skies and is also associated with motivation and sparking creative behavior. It signifies trust, strength, stability, harmony and loyalty which is why so many major brand companies use the color in their logos (Facebook/Meta, AT&T, Pfizer, American Express and Walmart to name a few). One-half of people worldwide – despite gender, age and culture differences – chose blue as their favorite color two to four times more than any other color. This is interesting since blue is the rarest color in nature where you seldom see blue animals, blue plants or blue food. But blue can also signify death and depression. If a person's lips and pallor are blue the body is experiencing hypothermia as the person freezes to death. This is also true for spoiled food as blue tinge on meat products typically means decay. One research study had weight loss participants replace their refrigerator light bulbs with blue bulbs or wear blue-tinted glasses to discourage snacking and overeating. And blue moods are tied to depression. Picasso's Blue Period happened when he sank into a major depression after the death of a fellow artist.

Blue can also be a deterrent to crime with one city using blue lights in high crime areas such as railway stations seeing crime drop 9% and suicides ceased. Some airports have blue lighting in international terminals to help "wake" passengers up from jet lag. While blue lights serve a positive function when it comes to illegal activity, blue light emissions from smartphones, TV, computers and tablets, especially in the bedroom at night, will disrupt circadian rhythms of 24/7 light and dark cycles that promote restful sleep. Turning off all digital devices with these blue lights before bed is recommended to improve your sleep health.

PURPLE

Purple is often connected to royalty, power, privilege, luxury, wisdom, magic and spirituality. Purple is also seen as a color that connotes a creative and unique personality. Just think Prince and his famous "Purple Rain" song and movie which the artist said was inspired by envisioning red blood mixed with blue sky to signify the end of the world. He believed being with the one you love, allows faith and god to guide you through the purple rain. On the other hand, purple is also associated with courage and valor. The highest honor for bravery in U.S. military service is the Purple Heart, an award created by George Washington to give soldiers in the Revolutionary War. It was also the color chosen by the women's suffrage movement in the early 1900s representing freedom and dignity and was chosen by the Alzheimer's Association to show calm yet passionate advocacy for those with dementia.

Because purple lights include a red hue, they are recommended over blue lights for getting restorative sleep because they do not disrupt circadian rhythms (although most experts advise amber orangey-red nightlights are best). However, purple lights have also been found to decrease sex drive. And, older eyes have a hard time distinguishing pastel purples such as lavender unless contrasted with darker colors.

Color Psychology

GREEN

Green is a powerful color and falls into the cool color tones along with blues (versus warm tones of red, orange, yellows) when it comes to color psychology. From an emotional standpoint, green makes most people feel refreshed and relaxed. It is also cited as the color we most associate with nature and the green movement for eco-friendly practices. Since ancient times, green has been associated with fertility and a thriving life. Green has been shown to create calm, reduce respiration and muscle tension as well as lower the pulse and blood pressure which is why surgeons often wear teal (green/blue) scrubs to help calm patients.

Scientists in one study found more people were likely to recall positive words written in green, leading researchers to theorize that green carries more positive emotional connotations. And, green is commonly used to convey financial success even serving as the color of paper money. However, green can also be associated with envy ("green-eyed monster") and not feeling well ("he looks green at the gills").

Hues of green are considered the most optimistic color especially for older adults. According to a study published in *Psychology and Aging*, green color tones sparked more positive effects in memory and recall. As we age, vision starts to change because at age 60 the pupils need three times the light needed when at age 20. Since the eye translates light into colors and the human retina identifies colors between 400 and 700 nanometers, the color green – located at about 550 nanometers – is the easiest color for the retina to perceive. Because it is on the cool end of the color spectrum, your eyes do not have to adjust to see green because it uses a shorter wavelength. This makes hues of green the best color choice for attracting older eyes. And perhaps because we "see" better when looking at green, having green plants and living walls in a work environment has been shown to boost innovation and creative-thinking.

The Healing Art of Chromatherapy

More than 2000 years ago Egyptians, Indians and the Chinese used healing arts based on chromatherapy, also known as color therapy, phototherapy or light therapy. The ancients mixed primary colors of yellow, red and blue in the form of minerals, stones, salves, crystals and dyes to bring the body back into balance and treat diseases making chromatherapy an essential healing art.

It was Abu 'Ali al-Husayn Ibn Sina, better known as Avicenna (AD 980), a Persian physician, who advanced the healing art of colors. He created the first color chart on how temperature could be used as a treatment showing red moved the blood, blue or white cooled it and yellow reduced muscular pain and inflammation. He also discovered a person with a nosebleed should avoid looking at anything of a brilliant red color and should avoid red light that stimulates the sanguineous humor, whereas blue (water, ice) would soothe it and reduce blood flow.

His discoveries were influenced by the ancient Egyptians who had color-healing rooms as part of their temples. Each room emitted rays or waves of colors associated with those healing properties where patients were color diagnosed and treated with the prescribed color. The ancient Greek city of Heliopolis also became famous for its healing temples and its practice of heliotherapy - therapeutic sunlight treatment.

Centuries later, a 19th century Scandinavian researcher, Niels Ryberg Finson, was suffering from a rare metabolic disease, Niemann–Pick disease, and used heliotherapy (phototherapy) sunlight sessions to alleviate the painful symptoms of his genetic disorder. His successful experiments helped him overcome his reduced appetite, abdominal extension, slurred speech and unsteady gait. Eventually he used phototherapy to cure skin tuberculosis, resulting in his Nobel Prize in Physiology in 1903. His pioneering work in phototherapy has led to modern day radiation therapies.

Many of our current biomedical practices are based on principles of chromatherapy. Surgeons use a carbon dioxide laser that emits an infrared beam to make incisions; the argon laser used by ophthalmologists to treat eye conditions – glaucoma, diabetic retinopathy and some retinal holes and tears – uses a radiating green beam to stem bleeding tissues and ultra-violet light is used to treat acne and psoriasis. When it comes to light therapy, purple LED is a combination of red and blue wavelengths with dual benefits of both skin clearing (blue light) and anti-aging (red light). Purple is also beneficial for cellular oxygenation and regeneration to promote enhanced skin fitness and vitality similar to how purple foods contain anthocyanins, the type of antioxidants that prevent and repair cellular damage. After aggressive and invasive treatments such as Botox, fillers or lasers, ultraviolet light therapy is recommended to reduce inflammation and visible acne marks and encourage wound healing.

The modern godfather of chromatherapy is Edwin Babbitt, a 19th century American "psychophysician" who prescribed red for paralysis, physical exhaustion and chronic rheumatism; yellow as a laxative or nausea-inducing agent for bronchial difficulties; blue for inflammation, sciatica, meningitis, nerves, headaches, irritability and sunstroke. Much of Babbit's experimenting led to today's understanding of circadian rhythms – the light and dark cycles of sleep science – as well as the visual processing and ultraviolet radiation effects of your 24/7 light and dark cycles. Science is now turning to chromotherapy as a therapeutic treatment that uses the visible color spectrum of electromagnetic radiation to cure diseases including advancements in red light therapy and virtual light therapy for those with seasonal affective disorder (SAD) and Alzheimer's patients who experience sundowning, that some researchers believe is based on circadian rhythm disorder. The power of color in your emotions and environments is no longer seen as pop psychology. Color psychology and chromatherapy are essential tools in your wellness plan.

chapter 28

Digital Detox Dynamic Duo: Hygge and Niksen

Fans of Marie Kondo, the popular decluttering queen, were startled when she told the *Washington Post* in 2023 that she was feeling burnout after having her third child, saying she has "kind of given up" and admitted, "My home is messy… but I realize what is important to me is enjoying spending time with my children at home." Bravo Kondo!

Somehow, we find ourselves in this place where if we are not busy or productive or decluttering every single second, we feel we are failing. But if Queen Kondo, the t-shirt-rolling, category and color curator of spices, sweaters and shoes, can take a break, then it is time for you to do the same. Part of staying busy in the modern world means being tethered to your digital device. A Nielsen Report found Americans spend on average 11 hours a day – that is almost half of your entire day – gorging on media whether we are watching, listening or reading. No wonder we are getting less sleep and have no time for self-care, we are too busy scrolling and streaming. How do we unplug from this noise pollution?

Welcome to the era of *hygge* and *niksen* or as I call them the dynamic duo of digital detox from Denmark and the Dutch. About a decade ago, the world discovered the Danish art of *hygge*. When I wrote about this practice of "warm coziness" in my first book, *A Cast of Caregivers*, hygge was still relatively unknown outside of Denmark. But over the last 10 years, this practice has spawned several books, clubs and more evidence-based science on its effectiveness as a way for caregivers to practice self-care. For those unfamiliar with hygge, it is the art of unplugging from technology and the warp speed at which we live our lives. It is about finding warmth (a fireplace, cozy socks, a warm pet, cup of coffee or cocoa), curling up with a good book or knitting or even playing an old-fashioned board game such as Monopoly or Clue with family and friends. Candlelight replaces artificial lights and snuggling is encouraged. It is all about taking time to pause for soul relief.

Not to be outdone by Denmark's hygge, the Dutch offer us *niksen*, known as *niks* to insiders. This is similar to hygge but when we say *digital detox*, we really mean step away from the technology and even from social company. Niksen is the purposeful art of doing nothing similar to what Claire Weekes prescribed for anxiety of "masterly inactivity." It is not meditation that requires focus and effort, it is more like the elastic thinking you read about in Emotional Wellness. Letting your mind wander and just staring out a window or onto a wide vista to observe your surroundings without engaging or focusing too hard on what is happening around you. Instead of being *mindful* it is being *mindless*.

While this sounds simple – and yes, the health benefits have been tracked by science – it is a lot harder than you think. Try spending a few minutes not doing *anything*. No conversation, no reading, no playing with the dog nor doomscrolling, literally *nothing*. Researchers in the Netherlands observed how some people were originally uncomfortable with this "nothingness" assignment. The art of just "being" is hard. But suddenly you see, hear, smell things you had not noticed. A ladybug crawling along a windowsill, leaves fluttering in the breeze, the clouds rolling by, the smell of flowers – niksen creates a very aware multisensory experience because you slowed everything down to be present.

Advocates for niksen say you do not have to just stare into space. You can lie down and listen to music but do not allow your mind to ruminate on tasks you should be doing or things that upset you. Instead think happy, positive thoughts. You can also do a mindless activity like dishwashing. With automatic dishwashers, few of us get our hands in the suds anymore. But as I wrote in Blue Wellness, having your hands in warm, soapy water as you do a few dishes can be soothing and allows your mind to wander while you get a tactile benefit of the water. One Florida State University study done on dishwashing and mindfulness found participants reported a decrease in nervousness by 27% and an increase in mental inspiration by 25%. *Business Insider* reported both Bill Gates and Jeff Bezos use it to spark their creative thinking.

Other quiet, analog practices found to help with de-stressing include journaling. A recent Pinterest survey showed from 2021 – 2022 there were more online searches for "journal writing prompts therapy" (up 220%), "writing therapy" (up 1,840%), and "art journal therapy" (up by 3,755%). Music therapy and art activities are also on the rise.

As mentioned earlier, the younger Gen Z (also known as iGen) population is enthusiastically embracing the art of unplugging. A New York City-based group calling themselves The Luddite Club[71], is comprised of teenagers tired of tech tyranny whose mission is to promote "self-liberation

---

[71] This is a nod to the 19th century Luddite movement in England where textile workers rebelled against the onslaught of the Industrial Revolution and its latest machinery technology that were replacing their livelihoods.

from social media and technology." Most of the club members use '90s style flip phones and the club encourages members to abolish doomscrolling to help overcome social media burnout and to escape surveillance by digital tech lords. These tech freedom fighters are finding better mental health by meeting weekly in New York City parks to practice analog social activity: reading books to each other, sketching each other on drawing pads and conversing in an environmentally beautiful tech-free safe zone.

Marie Kondo's mantra was to only keep things that spark joy in your life. By using your hands to create joyful or comforting analog activities that replaces typing "likes," "shares" or emojis on your smartphone is how to do digital detoxing that would make Kondo and our Danish and Dutch friends proud.

Financial Wellness

Jeanne Calment (1875-1997)

Your eyes are not playing tricks – the birth and death dates for Jeanne Calment are correct. Calment was a French woman whose story has become gerontology folklore and not just because she is the longest living human on record surviving 122 years.

Known for her wicked wit, Calment said she smoked two cigarettes a day until she was 119 and only then kicked the habit because she could not see well enough to light up. She learned how to fence at age 85 and rode a bicycle until age 100. But it is the real estate deal Calment brokered when she was 90 years of age that has gerontologists sharing this oral history about how living longer can surprise us.

Calment had outlived her husband, her daughter and even her grandson by her ninth decade and with no heirs remaining, she wanted to ensure her last few years of life would be lived in the comfort of the Arles, France home where she had spent most of her life. Engaging a notary republic, André-François Raffray, who at age 47 was half Calment's age at the time, Calment signed a life estate contract with Raffray, similar to what we call a reverse mortgage. The agreement made Raffray the owner of her property at the time of Calment's death in exchange for her right of occupancy through the end of her life (which Raffray assumed would be mere months). In exchange for taking ownership of the apartment upon her death, Raffray agreed to pay Calment 2500 francs a month until she passed away. This was the deal of a lifetime. Or so he thought.

As you already know, Calment lived another 32 years out-surviving Raffray by two years. In fact, at the time of Raffray's death, he had paid $180,000 to Calment, more than double the home's value. His family continued making those payments another two years until Calment passed away.

During an interview shortly before her death, Calment was asked about her good fortune in her real estate deal. With a twinkle in her eye, Calment said she had once written Raffray a note stating, "Forgive me for still being alive, but my parents didn't raise second-rate goods."

chapter 29

Healthspan and Wealthspan Financial Planning

Jeanne Calment embodied what Roman poet Virgil (70-19 BC) philosophized, "The greatest wealth is health." It is hard to separate health and wealth as they are intertwined in American life. If you have a higher socioeconomic status (better paying job, higher education level), you typically have better health, because you can afford healthier food and more preventive health care such as a gym membership or home gym, weight loss programs, nutritional supplements, etc. Conversely, if you struggle financially, your health can be jeopardized by not having health insurance or the ability to pay for expensive procedures, medications and therapies not to mention living in *food deserts* where the most nutritious meal is McDonald's or the local gas station goodies. Financial insecurity and devastation such as losing a job or suffering huge losses in the stock market, can have deleterious effects on your mental health. Thus, the goal is to have your wealthspan equal your healthspan.

We know financial wellness plays a role in happiness and emotional health which is why we call it the Joyconomy. It may not be the most important ingredient but not having a certain level of financial security pushes other areas of wellness out of balance. Money does not buy happiness but it can alleviate stress and worry about money woes. One of the reasons I chose to use Financial Wellness as one of my seven elements of wellness is because it is not just about your income or occupation. Certainly how much money you make is going to affect your emotional, social and other elements of wellness, but Financial Wellness is also about your relationship with money and how your relationships affect your day-to-day finances. Financial Wellness is about planning for your dreams as well as planning for long-term care and caregiving costs of older loved ones. These financial factors might be a blip on your current list of life needs but will cost you later in life. And when it comes to big ticket items in life, affording health care and long-term care, buying and maintaining a home and finding opportunities to escape on vacations are three of the biggest cash outlays you will make in life and they all need planning ahead.

In many ways you should be looking at Financial Wellness planning the same way you practice preventive health care. Every year you have an annual wellness visit with your doctor[72] yet, at what age do most of us seek help from a financial planner? Unless you are making a ton of money as a hedge fund manager, you may feel you do not have enough money for anyone to manage.

While most financial advisors are looking for clients who have $1-5 million+ in assets to oversee, it does not mean sitting down with a financial expert in your 20s is out of the question. After all, it takes a long runway to have the time to meet financial goals such as paying off student loan debt, estimating costs of starting a family or purchasing a home, etc. The reason to start earlier rather than later is saving for retirement, home purchasing

---

[72] Unless you are managing a chronic illness that may mean you see a team of specialists more frequently.

and long-term care for yourself or older family members are often ignored to only focus on shorter term goals.

But even if you are in mid-life, it is never too late to start a sound financial plan. In a Prudential survey, two-thirds of women (66%) say planning for their own long-term care costs is a very important retirement goal, but only 9% are very confident they will be able to save enough to cover the costs when the time comes.

How much money do you need to be happy? A 2023 study took an updated look at this previously researched question and found there is a threshold where 30% of people are the happiest with earnings around $100,000 topping out at $500,000, after which there is no positive effect on life satisfaction levels for higher wage earners. About 15% of the participants with reported incomes above $100,000 said the income had no bearing on their happiness levels. This sounds reasonable until you throw an unforeseen event such as caregiving for a loved one into the financial picture.

What is fascinating is just how bad we are at forecasting what will really make us happy. As mentioned in Emotional Wellness, psychology researchers Dan Gilbert and Timothy Wilson took a look at how well people do at planning a happy future. The results were captured in their concept called *affective forecasting*. Similar to the poor accuracy rates of TV's weather forecasters, Gilbert and Wilson found individuals are woefully inaccurate in predicting what will create a sustainable level of satisfaction and happiness in life. They found most expectations were unrealistic, anticipatory imagination of future events are flawed, and past experience created an "impact bias" influencer model when it comes to peering into your personalized crystal ball of the future. All of this makes your ability to plan for a happy future unsuccessful. Part of this is based on looking only at immediate, material achievements like the red Ferrari or

Sprinkles cupcake examples that may bring pleasure but do not always offer meaning. If we were really good at predicting our future happiness, we would not have garages and attics filled with useless junk, we would not have divorce lawyers, and we would not have tattoo removal services.

> Humans are bad at forecasting what really makes us happy.

Why are we so bad at predicting our future happiness? Gilbert points to your ease of remembering (the past) versus your difficulty in imagining (the future). It is easier to look back over the last 10 years and identify what made you happy as opposed to looking 10 years into the future and trying to imagine what will bring happiness. You also cannot forecast for only sunny days. There will be storm clouds and other life events to upset your financial wellness. To ensure your happiness is not derailed for these unforeseen events, you have to plan for them as much as you can and caregiving is one of those events no one plans for but almost everyone encounters in life.

Much of what you hear today is about "living in the present." Being mindful and present-oriented is more about your relationships and how to participate fully and thoughtfully with people who matter in your life. It does not apply to long-term happiness in terms of financial planning. For that you have to become a future forecaster and adopt the Gen C Continuum mindset I posed in the beginning – it is not a matter of if you will become a caregiver and have out-of-pocket costs of care, it is simply a matter of when.

The Costs of Care

When we look at the statistics of living longer it all seems hopeful until you realize many of the 20-30 bonus years you will get may not all be lived in good health. Studies show most people start to feel some of the impacts of aging – what we scientifically call "wear and tear" – around age 50. If your life expectancy is about 82 years old that means 30+ years of managing aches, pains, arthritis, declining eyesight and hearing, etc. Some of the issues can be resolved with the latest innovations in hearing aids, hip, knee and shoulder replacement surgeries and more but according to the U.S. Administration on Community Living, 7 out of 10 people age 65+ will need some type of long-term care or caregiving help in their remaining lifetime.

This care in your later years is delivered one of three ways: 1) a family member who takes on the tasks and responsibilities to keep a loved one in their home; 2) a professional caregiver or home health aide who comes into the home; or 3) becoming a resident in a senior living or memory care community. All three have significant costs involved – costs that more than half of older adults erroneously believe the government will cover. Medicare, that adults age 65+ receive from the government based on lifetime employment credits, covers only hospital and physician visits (and only 80% of those costs unless you opt for a Medicare Advantage, Medigap or Medicare supplement plan). This means the cost of long-term care is the sole responsibility of the older adult and their family. Medicaid, a program provided by the federal government but administered and overseen by local state governments,[73] is the means tested social safety net program delivered to individuals who meet

---

[73] This means services and costs vary state by state.

certain lower income thresholds, qualifying pregnant women and children and individuals receiving Supplemental Security Income (SSI).

The conundrum for family caregivers is knowing how your financial future may be rocked by caregiving costs today. A 2022 report by Martha Deevy, associate director at the Stanford Center on Longevity found a majority of Americans age 50-74 have a median retirement savings of $128,000. Even when coupled with expected social security income and potential future earnings in a freelance, gig worker or part-time role, it will not cover the needed savings of at least $1.18 million to support a 30-year retirement, according to an *AARP Magazine* article.[74]

In the "2023 Cost of Care Survey," a minimum of $162,000 - $317,000 is needed for the national average of a typical three-year stay in assisted living or skilled nursing facility. While only 11% of older Americans have long term care insurance plans that may provide benefits to cover those costs, these plans can still have limitations on how long benefits will last (typically three years) which means if your loved one outlives the benefit period, the costs will be all out-of-pocket. In a 2022 survey, 59% of older adults expect a spouse or adult child to pay for or provide the care they need. Many older adults only move to a long-term care facility after months or years of home-based care provided by the family caregiver (sweat equity and cost of time) or a home care professional fee for service (on average $60,000 a year plus any necessary home modifications for safety and accessibility at home such as bathroom grab bars, better lighting, prevention of falls such as removing rugs, carpets and avoiding stairs that you will read about in the Peter Pan Phenomenon below.)

---

[74] This calculation is based upon average returns of 6% and inflation at 2.5% or for higher wealth individual investments and savings that are 10 to 12 times current income levels.

Caregivers of those with Alzheimer's and related dementias will experience the most expensive care with the average family spending a minimum of $360,000 for 2-3 years for a loved one to be cared for in a memory care community. During the pandemic, many of my Well Home Design for Life plans for private clients were for family caregivers of a loved one with dementia since many families were either making the decision to keep loved ones at home longer or to move a loved one from a memory care community back home so they could be with them.

While my plans follow universal design and wellness biophilic design principles, I also incorporate what I call the five Cs of age and dementia-friendly design: Curves, Contrast, Color, Clutter-free and Comfort Sources.[75] When it comes to designing homes to make it easier for an adult with Alzheimer's to stay in their home longer, there are additional considerations because Alzheimer's adults interpret their living environments differently from other older adults. With memory loss, confusion, agitation, balance issues, anxiety and disorientation, specific modifications include safety measures such as an iGuard Stove to turn off a stove left on that can result in a deathly home fire, special shower and bath needs for temperature and balance controls from Moen and color sensitivity such as removing black rugs that Alzheimer's adults see as a black hole they may fall into. Home modification costs for dementia-friendly design can range from $10,000 - $80,000+ depending on individual needs and the stage of the disease.

Cindy Hounsell, president and founder of WISER (Women's Institute for Secure Retirement), a nonprofit advocacy group in Washington, D.C. that helps guide women to a better financial future, came on my podcast

---

[75] I wrote about dementia-friendly design for *USA Today* – you can find that on my Snug Home section of my Caregiving Club web site.

to launch a free caregiver financial hub from WISER with comprehensive checklists and information on care costs.

"There is a gap in what people understand about costs of long-term care but also what is actually available to them as benefits from Social Security and Medicare," said Hounsell. "For instance, you can start drawing on your Social Security savings in your 60s, for Medicare you can receive those benefits starting at 65 but there is a premium you have to pay to access the Medicare benefit that most people are not aware of."

Hounsell explains this Medicare premium can be taken out of your Social Security benefit so if you thought you would get $1,000 a month from Social Security and now you are only getting $835 because the Medicare premium – based on income deducted – is $165 from the total – this deduction can be a big difference in financial planning for an older adult on a fixed income.

And while you hope your older loved one has made sound savings plans for retirement and long-term care costs consider national studies showing 78% of caregivers are financial contributors covering some or most of the costs of personal care. Pew Research reported 83% of parents in their 50s and 60s are financially caring for children under age 18 while also paying for older parents - known as the Sandwich Generation.

To cover these costs family caregivers spend on average 20% of their annual income – this is *after* costs that are covered by the loved one's Medicare benefits, Social Security, supplemental health plans, long term care insurance and personal savings. Most older parents do not want to be a financial burden to their adult children yet in aggregate family caregivers spend $190 billion out-of-pocket annually on medications, home care, home modifications, rent or mortgage, groceries, transportation, pet care and more to ensure the proper care of their older loved ones.

And caregivers are also stealing from their own retirement. A 2017 AARP report found 21% of those over age 50 had tapped their savings to cope with a life event such as divorce, caregiving or a medical emergency for themselves or a loved one in the past five years thus saving $270,000 less for retirement.

Although men have been stepping into the primary role of caregiver, mostly for spouses or older parents, a government report, "Families Caring for An Aging America," showed women will spend on average 10% of their adult life as a caregiver to an older loved one. One reason according to the Center for Retirement Research at Boston College shows older parents receive almost double the care hours from adult daughters (31%) compared to adult sons (16%). Pew Research reported prior to the pandemic, more than 39% of women said they had reduced their work hours to care for a child or older family member, compared to 24% of men. And more women (27%) said they had quit their job to care for a child or family member, compared to 10% of men.

A dark side of caregiving is the need to protect older loved ones from elder abuse, especially financial exploitation and fraud. According to the FBI's Internet Crime Complaint Center (IC3), more than 92,371 older adults were victims of fraud losing almost $1 billion in aggregate in 2020. While the average loss is $500 per incident, in late 2022, the FBI Cyber Crimes Unit caught up with two grandparent scam criminals who fleeced more than 70 older victims for $2 million, some of the individuals losing $30,000 or more. There are various types of identity theft, insurance scams, medical claims scams and natural disaster fraudsters, but the grandparent scams are where the perpetrators pose as a grandchild in an emergency needing money quickly (such as "Grandma, my hockey team bus had an accident and I need money to fly home"). In the past, these criminals used young women to pose as the grandchild with a youthful voice, but today's scammers are using artificial intelligence (AI) to "voice clone" the actual grandchild's voice from social media making it even tougher to know what is real and what is fraud.

On my podcast, I talked with Liz Loewy, a former prosecutor of elder abuse cases in the Manhattan District Attorney's Office and now co-founder and chief operating officer of Eversafe, an online fraud protection and financial monitoring service for older adults.

"You have to look at more than just identify theft and a credit report, scammers go to bank accounts, retirement accounts, investment accounts, home title and real estate information found online to scam older adults," said Loewy. "As well, a dormant credit card found in a drawer somewhere that is taken by someone who has access to the home won't show up on a credit report but monitoring services can catch the anomaly quickly and shut it down. Each individual has personal financial habits, even unpaid bills are an alert and we bring that to the senior's or their trusted advocate's, such as a family caregiver's, attention."

For dementia caregivers the risks of fraud is higher with 50% of those with Alzheimer's suffering from elder abuse, many of these cases are financial abuse. The warning sign is if your older loved one is scammed out of their life savings you could wind up helping out financially so protecting family members from fraud helps you as well.

All of these additional financial stressors are taking their toll on family caregivers and their health. Several studies show the physical and mental health implications of unforeseen caregiving and financial costs.[76] The National Alliance for Caregiving's "Caregiving in the U.S. 2020" report

---

[76] As former chairman of NAC and key family caregiving strategist at UnitedHealthcare, I was involved in the first national studies on caregiver health and costs of care. The first health risk study in 2004 showed 17% reported their health as "fair or poor" with 53% of those reporting their health worsened affecting their ability to care and 91% reported depression over their loved one's condition and their lack of self-care time. More recent studies show caregiver health remains at risk.

found the number of family caregivers who report their health as "fair" or "poor" was 21% - an increase of 4% since 2017. A Pew Research Center study found 4 in 10 U.S. adults (41%) have experienced high levels of psychological distress at least once with up to 80% of family caregivers reporting negative emotional health. The financial aspect of caregiving is one most people do not plan for and therefore become blindsided by later in life. Planning ahead can save you money and mental health distress.

From Peter Pan Housing to Forever Homes

One of the biggest financial costs you will have throughout your life is where you live. Homeownership is the goal of most people but it takes a lot of savings and what about maintaining it for a lifetime? According to the Harvard Joint Center for Housing Studies, while the U.S. economy shrank 3.5% in 2020, people still invested in home improvements that were up 3% to create a $420 billion industry. Most of these were DIY renovations that came from staring at the walls in our homes for two years during the pandemic.

You may love your home but what are you doing to ensure it can be your forever home? The 2021 American Community Survey conducted by the U.S. Census Bureau, estimated almost half of owner-occupied homes were built before 1980, with around 35% built before 1970 making the average home today about 40-50 years old. And while almost 9 in 10 Americans want to stay in their homes as long as possible, as they grow older the home renovations planned mostly miss the mark on the modifications needed to allow them to live there forever.

According to AARP, only 1% of the 100 million U.S. homes feature any universal design defined as the building and construction principles that make environments and spaces ageless, accessible and adaptable. Yet by 2037, households with someone over age 80 will double to more than 14 million. On one end of the homeownership spectrum we have 47% of 75-year-old women living alone, also known as solo agers; while on the other end the number of three-generation households with at least one person age 65 or older almost doubled in 10 years with 1.7 million multigen homes in 2006 to 3.2 million in 2016.

In his "New Tools for Better Home Modifications," Jon Pynoos, a professor at USC focused on environmental gerontology and especially aging in place home modifications,[77] coined the term Peter Pan housing, "A significant number of frail older people and people with disabilities live in homes that do not fit their needs. These houses and apartments can be described as 'Peter Pan Housing' designed for people who never age." The missing link to solve this dilemma is universal design.

Typically, people make some small accommodations for health or aging challenges such as grab bars in showers and bath or handrails for steps and stairs. But many believe these types of changes scream, "I'm old and frail!" and diminish the design aesthetic of their home. However, brands such as Lowe's Livable Home division, Pottery Barn's Accessible Home line of furnishings and décor, Sherwin Williams's Senior Living and Living Well paint collections, Moen's biometric and Kohler's chromatherapy bath accessories and fixtures are showing manufacturers and interior designers are joining the growing legion of builders who plan for accessibility and age. In addition, kitchen and bath appliance giant, Kohler, is adding more wellness into its product lines. Innovations include its Konnect Smart Bath

---

[77] Pynoos was one of my USC graduate school professors and inspired my love for ageless home design. Aging in place is a term used in long-term care to identify those who want to stay living in their homes as long as possible.

line using chromatherapy with voice or motion-controlled lights integrated into bathroom mirrors, tubs and toilets that automatically turn blue light in the morning (to wake you up) and amber/orange at night (to maintain your circadian rhythms for sleep). In 2023, Kohler debuted Sprig, its botanical water infusion line for shower and bath with six aromatherapy infusion pods with scents that create energy, calm and sleep.

The Homes Renewed coalition is helping older adults and family caregivers find these products more easily through its Purple Tag symbol. Products that meet the universal design criteria receive this designation, similar to how the Environmental Protection Agency (EPA) issues Energy Star certifications for energy efficient appliances.

A study done by Notre Dame University School of Architecture showed 50% of 75-year-olds were making home modifications to make life easier and more accessible and 60% of 55-70-year-olds made upgrades and renovations to make their home more age-friendly after being a caregiver for an older parent. Most homeowners who decide to incorporate universal design changes to their home contract with a professional who understands Americans with Disabilities Act (ADA) compliance. This type of investment in a forever home is well worthwhile. Consider that universal design upgrades reduced the hours of care needed by a family caregiver in that home by 42% per week.

These changes for making your home or your loved one's home a forever home include: Lever handles instead of door knobs to avoid twisting and turning the wrist; adjustable beds to aid in sleep and address snoring issues that impact cardiovascular health; non-slip rugs or bath mats and walk-in tubs or no step entry showers to prevent falls at home – 80% of which happen in the bathroom; distinct contrast between counters and floors or walls as well as good lighting around task areas such as the kitchen or reading spaces since older eyes at age 60 need 2-3 times the illumination of a 20-year-old; and avoiding furniture with sharp, hard edges and replacing with curved tables, counters, chairs and couches.

And Millennials are embracing some of the universal design/biophilic design principles not for aging but for wellness. Design elements such as walk-in bathtubs are easier for bathing children and also offer hydrotherapy jets and chromatherapy for weekend warriors with tired muscle aches. Pull-down and pull-out shelving makes bending and reaching easier for any age, and smart home technology and sensor design is no longer seen as just beneficial for older adults but for everyone.

Using universal design with multisensory biophilic design is the trend of the future for homeowners of all ages.

chapter 31

The Escape Plan: How to Take a Wellcation

The third essential element of your Financial Wellness plan is ensuring you have periodic escapes from the stressors of everyday life. A report from the Center for Economic Policy and Research called the U.S. the "no vacation nation" and a recent survey found 90% of Americans have taken only half of their allowed paid vacation time with 1 in 5 saying they have taken five days or less leaving five vacation days unused. While it is important to get a few minutes a day or during the week to escape – such as with daydreaming or doing a few minutes of digital detox – you also need the ability to get away physically for longer periods. This is your Wellcation plan, a significant contributor to the Joyconomy.

According to a Global Wellness Institute (GWI) 2022 study, for every $800 spent on your wellness needs, happiness levels rise by 7% and life expectancy goes up by 1.26 years. The ability to get away from the stressors of daily life and explore taps into your ancient brain and genetic predisposition for wanderlust. One study found not taking a vacation increased your risk for a heart attack by 30% and even a long weekend getaway of three days can reduce stress levels.

The challenge for most is reconciling the need to get away with the cost as financial pressures and economic concerns continue to pump the breaks on spending money on longer stay or international travel. For those who are putting plans and budgets together the travel trends seem to fall into three categories: returning to your roots, self-care (including sleep tourism), and educational travel.

As noted in Social Wellness, one way to address mental health and emotional burnout is to embrace your ancestry. Heritage tours have been on the rise for years but given how much time we spent with families over the last few years at home, we now have a desire to learn more about our roots. These trips go beyond typical tourism such as having a genealogist do some of your ancestry research ahead of time to then plot your visits to the hometowns of your forebearers. These are often the types of vacations where adult children and parents or "skip-gen travelers" – grandparents and grandchildren vacationing together – explore family histories both in domestic and international travel.

Many of these destinations support the ageless-ness of intergenerational travelers, similar to the magic behind Walt Disney's vision in creating his theme parks that made them "the happiest places on Earth" for all ages. But now instead of "It's a Small World" ride, these trips actually take you to the country of your family's origins and connect you to your cultural roots.

Even Airbnb has gotten into the picture with an accessible travel filter to find universally design homes. Travelers interested in staying in an age-friendly designed home can vacation at places like The Werner House, an Infinite Living Collaboration in Columbus, Ohio, that includes adjustable beds and sleep science bedrooms, walk-in hydrotherapy tubs, adjustable kitchen counters, hot and cold plunge pools and a seated sauna, cognitive and balance workout equipment created by NASA and the latest smart home technology. The Freebird Club, started in Ireland but now global, offers travelers age 50+ a stay with homeowners who are also 50+. This is both a social lodging concept where hosts can serve as local guides.

When it comes to self-care travel, the hospitality industry is catering to a new kind of traveler: the wellness explorer. In the past, you might indulge in a massage or spa treatments or soothe in a sauna while at a resort to do something else such as play golf or tennis or indulge during a business trip. The new trend in travel is to take the vacation specifically to find the latest spa, sauna, hot springs and wellness practices but also the social and self-care soothing you need.

This wellness travel evolution from the yoga retreats and medical spas of the past are focusing on both self-care and social wellness. There are travel packages to Greece through Healing Holidays to help you explore your grief through immersive experiences such as dance therapy. There are also travel packages called "radical sabbaticals" for Jane Austen and "Downtown Abby" fans in the English countryside and TV influenced trips such as a fashionista's dream vacation inspired by "Emily in Paris" or dude ranch getaways to Montana and Wyoming to tap into your inner Dutton based on the success of "Yellowstone." These destinations mix personal wellness with group discussions among like-minded entertainment fans that achieve Social and Emotional Wellness.

Another key aspect of self-care travel is the sleep tourism trend. Everything from AI-designed mattresses for adapting your optimal sleep environment to sleep concierges who can find you weighted blankets, sound vibrational pillows, lavender scents for the room or even a hypnotherapist, are now a natural part of resort spas and offered at some Hilton, Hyatt and Marriott hotel locations. And biophilic-designed hospitality properties are not the only thing going green. Kimpton Hotels recently announced its "Plant Pals" program where you can ask the concierge to send you one of a selection of locally sourced plants that not only provide air care oxygenation for your room but creates a nature environment to promote calm and brain health during your stay.

When it comes to educational travel, the sky's the limit. One of the biggest travel trends in 2023 is indigenous trips to Australia's Outback and Great Barrier Reef to learn Aboriginal rituals or take an actual walkabout tour (also known as Dreamtime) led by indigenous guides. The same type of knowledge vacation is happening in North American tribal lands where vacationers learn more about Native American tribal wellness practices on reservation land sleeping out under the stars. Not to be outdone, Europe offers Celtic retreats where resorts located in Ireland, Scotland and Wales forest areas offer *wyda*, a type of yoga infused with ancient pagan and druid influences practiced at sunrise and sunset. And Caribbean getaways are curating emotionally themed wellness retreats such as: Love, Strength, Dream, Acceptance.

While caregivers feel they have to give up travel while caring for an older loved one, as I wrote about in *A Cast of Caregivers*, there are respitality services where your loved one can visit an assisted living for a short stay (one day to a couple of weeks) or home care can help watch over a loved one at home. This is also the time to tap into the sibling or friend who wants to help by having them contribute to the care cost or fill in on temporary caregiver duty while you get a much-needed break.

After suffering through a couple of years of almost non-existent travel during the pandemic, everyone was ready to fly away. However, in 2022 and 2023, airline passengers experienced one of the worst outrages in customer service imaginable with frequently delayed and cancelled flights creating a backlash from thousands of stranded frequent flyers.

Some travelers pivoted from this airline trauma to taking a road trip. This vintage travel trend includes using old-fashioned printed maps to seek off-the-beaten path surprises channeling Jack Kerouac or Huell Howser. AARP reported 61% of American travelers age 50+ will take road trips in 2023, mostly to save on costs of international travel and the stress of airline travel. The Automobile Club of America (AAA) reported they printed 123% more maps in 2022 than the year before, and it is not just boomers using analog navigation. AAA noted one-half of its membership is comprised of Millennial and Gen Z age travelers.

While gasoline prices are still sky-high as of this writing (and electric car infrastructure is still catching up to far afield destinations), road trips are something you can enjoy with family and friends because it creates a bubble of intimacy. As opposed to plane or train travel where you can go to sleep for several hours, road trips energize most people by firing up your ancient brain to seek and explore. You have intimate conversations and there is more bonding than in other types of travel.

I love the spontaneity of a road trip where you are surprised by unplanned delights and meeting new people. For caregivers there is a psychological calmness to not planning since everything in your normal life has to be overplanned. One thing I learned caring for my father -- and many of my friends and colleagues have echoed this same experience – is how much we enjoyed a good joy ride mostly back to my hometown to cruise around reminiscing and taking in the old sights. It might only be an hour but exploring my dad's neighorhood or discovering new places filled our afternoons in his last days (oxygen tank and all) and gave us both beautiful memories. The same was true for my stepfather who loved the sea, a legacy of his days in the Navy. Even after his painful infusion treatments for cancer, we would find peace and solace taking a little Duffy boat around Balboa Island where he was still the captain of our family ship. The sea air, the skies melting into the water, the wind in your hair is healing travel indeed.

The No Excuses Wellcation: Virtual Travel

> "One must travel to learn."
> -- Mark Twain, *Innocents Abroad*

I know I am lucky to have had these outings with my loved ones right up to the very end of their lives. But for some caregivers, that is not possible. A bedridden or non-ambulatory loved one makes road trips and Duffy rides unmanageable. Traveling with a loved one in late stages of cancer or Alzheimer's can also be challenging. But there is a way to still take a trip with your loved one from the comfort of home.

Virtual tourism really took off during the pandemic but shows no signs of stopping especially for older adults who either cannot or choose not to endure strenuous travel. The advantage of virtual travel for older adults is there is no need to pack a bag and have the stress of getting to a favorite destination. You also do not need to worry about having the energy for a multi-day trip, you can go where you want in one hour. You can sit in the comfort of your home or your senior living community and enjoy the experience almost like being there in person. It also addresses the need to help older adults overcome feelings of social isolation and to be engaged in an adventure instead of just an activity such as bingo or arts and crafts. As opposed to passive TV watching of a documentary on Ireland, you can explore the Emerald Isle with a live guide.

There are two options when it comes to virtual travel: either using a virtual reality (VR) headset for a full immersive experience, or joining a travel group where you participate online such as Zoom and join your travel guide and fellow travelers as the local on-site guide takes the group in real time to the pyramids in Egypt, an African safari and other worldwide destinations.

Companies such as Rendever, MyndVR, Viarama and VR Genie from Equality Labs, all use the latest VR headsets to allow older adults to swim with the dolphins, climb to the top of the Christ the Redeemer statue in Rio de Janeiro, fly to the moon, skydive and even walk down the streets of their hometown. These travel excursions became a hit in assisted living and memory care where groups of residents can travel virtually together to different destinations and share their memories with each other. There is also the opportunity to help wounded and disabled veterans join a Veteran's Day Parade as if they are really there and in one nursing home, MyndVR filmed a swing band and singer in 1940s attire playing Frank Sinatra tunes giving residents the feeling they were sitting right in the front row of an "old blue eyes" concert. One woman who was a refugee from Cuba, traveled back in time to her hometown outside of Havana for the first time in 60 years.

The downsides of VR travel are it is not a live experience, you are watching either something previously filmed even though you may feel like you are live in the environment. Which means once you have experienced a destination, there is no spontaneity or different experience to be had as you would with real world trips even to the same city. Also, for many older adults, especially those with dementia, vision problems or neurodegenerative health issues, the VR headsets can be heavy and the 360-degree aspect can make anyone who is not a videogaming teenager nauseated and dizzy.

This brings us to a new breed of virtual travel where headsets are not needed and the experience, while maybe less immersive, is actually live and interactive. Two companies are leading this new virtual tourism category yet with different approaches.

Discover Live caters to travelers of all ages and offers bespoke travel services. Travelers customize their trip or event based on where and when they want to travel, how many screens (travelers can be located in different places) they will need and have the ability to ask for special travel guide experiences. The travel guides are live on-site and use smartphones and GoPro video headsets to take travelers into the Louvre Museum in Paris or on a gondola ride in Venice. You can also explore Madrid at night or other customized requests you would not get with a typical tour. This is also a great option for event planning such as destination weddings, family reunions, girlfriend trips or heritage trips with grandchildren where not everyone can attend in person.

Another company, Wowzitude, was created specifically for older travelers in mind. Founded by a travel agent with 30 years of experience who wanted to help her mother, who was a world-class travel lover but could no longer make the trips later in her life, Wowzitude actually has planned trips, similar to travel packages, where next Tuesday it is Paris and Thursday it is Singapore. Virtual travelers are sent interesting local information ahead of their trip such as a recipe for an Italian meal for dining while touring Florence or a list of the best whiskeys or wines if in Scotland or Napa Valley or great music and movies connected to your trip to Rome, such as the classic "Roman Holiday" with Audrey Hepburn or the recent "House of Gucci" movie with Lady Gaga. What is different from Discover Live is during a Wowzitude trip you meet fellow travelers from around the globe. As you enjoy the live tour guide commentary, you can ask questions of your guide and chat with other travelers just like on a typical tour. This is great for solo agers who want the stimulation of travel and the social connections of meeting new people.

When it comes to escaping, you have many options for getting away to refill your tank or take a trip – even virtually – with a loved one. Do not think of wellcations as a luxury or indulgence, it is another important part of your financial wellness plan.

Spiritual Wellness

The Story of the Red Cardinal

Throughout many centuries and many cultures, birds have been symbols that hold hidden meanings. The spirituality of birds comes from their lightness of being, their freedom of flight, their ability to rise above adversity and find strength during challenging times. Birds also thrive in nature reminding you to not be weighed down by stress but to seek the solace of the outdoors. They live in warm, comforting nests and flock together for safety and socialization. In fact, a flock of birds is said to bring good luck and for caregivers is a sign of having friends who help you soar above your daily struggles.

When it comes to red birds, this colorful bird of life – the red cardinal – is a spiritual symbol found in many cultures. In Native American lore, red birds represent loving relationships and devotion. Specifically, the Choctaw tribe saw cardinals as symbols of enduring love since cardinals, unlike most other birds, are monogamous and remain with their mate long after eggs are hatched. In Asian folklore, red birds represent transformation. In Latin cardinal means *hinge* or *pivot* – exactly what caregivers have done with their lives – pivoted into new responsibilities. The cardinal also represents a devoted guardian and the blood ties of eternal family bonds.

Folklore tells us a visit from a red cardinal represents a sign from a loved one who has passed. The origins of this story may have come from ancient times when birds often symbolized heavenly visitors, messengers to the gods, or even the gods themselves in feathered form. This belief has been part of ancient Egyptian, Celtic, Maori, Irish, and Hindu spiritualism, as well as the lore and legends of many Native American tribes, including the Lakota, Odawa, Sioux and Algonquin. The bright red plumage distinguishable even during stark winter months, reminds you of the living spirit of your loved one whose soul is still with you. Our red feathered friends also remind family caregivers to slow things down, observe the wonders of nature, pause for reflection, practice self-care. And even after your caregiving journey has ended, cardinals remind you that you are never alone because your loved one watches over you.

Gratitude and the God Code

A recent Pew Research survey on religious affiliation showed one-third of Americans describe themselves as atheist, agnostic or "nothing in particular." However, 90% of those surveyed considered themselves "spiritual" (SBNR means spiritual but not religious). While a majority of the country still identifies with a religion (mostly Christian), the percentage has fallen over the last decade from 75% in 2011 to 63% in the 2021 poll. A separate 2022 Gallup Poll mirrored this same drop showing a belief in God had fallen to its lowest level in 78 years.

How do religion and spirituality differ? In most religions there are rules and rituals such as going to church, synagogue or mosque on certain days, fasting at certain times of the year or preparing food in a specific way. There are also rituals such as communion for Catholics, bar mitzvahs in Judaism or Muslims praying five times a day facing Mecca. Other people feel they have spirituality in their life, believe in a higher power than themselves but practice an eclectic mix of mystical or unorthodox philosophies and theologies.

In *Learned Optimism,* the godfather of positive psychology, Martin Seligman, writes, "When our grandparents failed, they had comfortable spiritual furniture to rest in. They had, for the most part, their relationship to God, their relationship to a nation they loved, their relationship to a community and a large extended family. Faith in God, community, nation and the large extended family have all eroded over the last 40 years and the spiritual furniture that we used to sit in have become threadbare."

When you live a life where there is no higher power than yourself, you not only put tremendous and unrealistic pressure on your emotional health, you emphasize your sense of isolation and "aloneness." This is not what your ancient brain is seeking. Many millennia ago, being cast out of your tribe meant despair and death.

In this increasingly secular world, we are replacing a higher power with high-tech. This is making you less happy and more isolated. It fuels emotional despair, anxiety and depression because you are constantly connected to negative messaging, bullying and insipid lifestyles of the Narcissist Nation while you have lost your connection to God and spirituality. You can also experience internal guilt when you violate or ignore your deepest values and your spirituality. Arthur Brooks, a Harvard professor who writes and speaks on happiness, said 30% of how religious you are is based on genetics and your upbringing, the rest is faith. By turning your back on your spirituality, you abandon your faith in the future.

There is also a flip side of the benefits of spirituality and religion that should be noted. Certain religious groups may be too judgmental and make you feel guilty or rigid doctrines may make you more anxious or depressed. Also, some religions reject traditional medicine and replace it with faith-healing that may put your health and well-being at risk. And rejecting those outside of your faith may make you less tolerant and lead to more social isolation.

As you have read throughout this book, the goal for your Spiritual Wellness is balance. In the Me Time Monday program I help you address feelings of spiritual bankruptcy in the same way the program helps you change your time poverty to time affluence. When you focus on gratitude and embrace a higher power, you experience soulfulness that brings joy.

In the Social Wellness chapters I began by sharing the quality of your relationships is the key element that sustains you. In the context of your relationships, there are two that often seem to get overlooked: the relationship you have with yourself – self-awareness, self-reflection, self-confidence, self-love – is easier to achieve if you also have a relationship with a higher power. If you have a relationship with yourself buoyed by a relationship with your faith, you are never alone.

I am not here to promote one religion over others. But having no religion in your life is a sure recipe for hopelessness. For myself, I find God in nature. As mentioned in Environmental Wellness, Edwin Babbitt, a 19th century American physician, spiritualist and psychologist, had a simple but sophisticated definition of God's existence: nature.

Babbitt highlights the "sacred teachings of a leaf" showing the balance and harmony God has infused in everything he has created. All leaves have a center vein holding the two sides of the leaf together. It is this "center" that shows you nothing can exist without a solid foundation and that delicate balance is essential in life. The collaboration of the two sides of the leaf working together to bend and grow shows your need for the social aspect of a life in balance – one side is self, the other is social. The veins along each side of the leaf represent freedom, diversity, individuality and self-reliance and do not impede one another thereby representing justice.

As the leaf grows it shows progression and while there is strength there is also delicacy and vulnerability in its existence mirroring the resiliency *and* fragility of your world. The leaf mostly follows a shape with curved lines not block or grid lines giving you a "comforting curve" design that resonates with your ancient brain. Finally, the leaf draws its sustenance from the earth, sunlight and rain (water) as you do. Babbitt called his leaf theory "truth is beauty" teachings. We often forget we are like the leaf – part of nature and held to the same balance and harmony standards to achieve a good life.

While I find spirituality in nature, science-meets-spiritualty author, Gregg Braden, believes God is inherently inside all of us. His research claims there is a special genetic code God had imprinted on all humankind's DNA something he explored in *The God Code,* his 2005 book that captured the attention of theologians, scientists and others. Rather than definitively answer how we were created, Braden's biggest mission was to show how despite our cultural, racial, religious and other differences, we are all the same created by one maker.

Regardless of your religious beliefs, you can embrace a key principle of spirituality: gratitude. Scientists believe gratitude involved evolutionary adaptation that allowed humans to survive and thrive by creating communal, social circles of reciprocal altruism. It is your social glue where you reward yourself by "paying it forward."

While gratitude is a tenet of many religions it also plays a powerful role in supporting your physical and mental health. Some health benefits of gratitude include: amplifying the good in your life that you see in yourself and others; rescuing you from toxic feelings by offsetting chronic negativity you may feel; and connecting you with others by strengthening and solidifying your relationships with friends, family, neighbors and co-workers. In one study just 15 minutes of writing in a gratitude journal created better and longer sleep. In an 11-week study, people who kept a weekly gratitude journal exercised 40 minutes more per week than the control group. And researchers found grateful people experience fewer aches and pains and report feeling healthier than people who do not practice gratitude.

One study conducted by USC researchers led by psychologist Glenn Fox, sought to understand how gratitude affects brain health. The results were insightful highlighting gratitude is not just about the dopamine release or reward center of brain activity but it also involves morality, social rewards and bonding as the brain scans showed these corresponding areas of the brain light up.

The other finding from research is gratitude continues to grow over time. An important study found expressing gratefulness through written thank you letters (even if never sent) had a cumulative effect growing after four weeks and increasing again after 12 weeks. The key is to focus on *people* not *things* you are grateful for and to add as many details or explanation for why you feel this gratitude for this person. Just like the rings inside of a tree trunk as it ages, gratitude can grow to make you healthier and live longer.

Here is a little game I created and shared in the Me Time Monday workshops. I often find myself griping (in my head) about things – a car that cut me off, a salesperson who sees you need help but remains on his/her smartphone texting away, someone who leaves a shopping cart in a parking space, etc. At one point I felt I was becoming very negative about everything and it was not making me feel good. I decided to allow myself to gripe about these little transgressions just to purge the toxic feeling from my system but then I *immediately* have to come up with something I am grateful about. I call it the Gripes & Gratitude Game.

Most experts agree gratefulness is very personal. While some people can simply think about their gratitude to experience health benefits, it is not just the thought, but the act of gratitude that achieves balance in life.

Before I Die . . .

"The truth is, once you learn how to die, you learn how to live."
— Mitch Albom, *Tuesdays with Morrie*

In the aftermath of Hurricane Katrina that devastated the coastlines and inland areas of Mississippi, Louisiana and especially the city of New Orleans, the residents faced unbelievable losses in businesses, homes and loved ones. Five years later, while still coping with the hurricane's destruction, Candy Chang, an installation artist who was living in NOLA at the time, lost a dear friend. Her grief was profound and unrelenting. While she struggled with her depression and ruminated on all the things her friend had wanted to still do in life, she also thought of her city and wondered if others were still struggling too. In her TED Talk, she says, "I am in love with New Orleans. My soul is always soothed by the giant live oak trees shading lovers, drunks and dreamers for hundreds of years. And I trust a city that always makes way for music."

Chang decided to take an abandoned home in her neighborhood and erect a huge blackboard across its outer walls. At the top she had spray painted "Before I Die..." in large letters and underneath numerous lines where passersby could take the colorful chalk she left out and fill in the blanks. She said she did it to help the city heal from its trauma and its hurting. She felt the moment was right for everyone to think about what and who really matters before they are gone. Within one day the entire blackboard was filled in with wishes.

The overwhelming response reflected the thoughts of New Orleans citizens of all ages and backgrounds. Word spread of this healing art project and literally consumed the world. To date, hundreds of blackboard walls have been installed in 78 countries, 5,000 cities and in more than 36 languages.

When I heard Chang talk at a Motion Picture & Television Fund Women's Conference, she shared why this simple idea had taken hold globally. Chang said it is easy to get caught up in your day-to-day life and forget what matters to you. She also felt the wishes were about universal themes on life: Love, Well-Being, Helping Others, Travel/Exploring, Family. The walls were public spaces that became healing spaces. For many it was a place to grieve and find hope, to "console, celebrate and be alone together."

Here are some examples of the messages left on the walls over time: "Abandon all insecurities," "I want to be someone's cavalry," "Be completely myself" (New Orleans). Other cities around the globe expressed similar thoughts: "Come to terms with who I am" (Washington), "Slow down for a moment and maybe even stop" (Portsmouth, New Hampshire), "Find serenity" (Vicenza, Italy), "Stop being afraid" (Jerusalem), "Lose my fear of death" (Trujillo, Peru), "Find what I'm looking for" (San Francisco).

As I listened to Chang's story, I was struck by one comment she made, "Two of the most valuable things we have are time and our relationships with others." This was right before I lost my father to cancer. I had taken a leave of absence from work to help care for him and also to have time to write my first book. It was financially challenging but the gifts of our conversations and the quality time we spent together, after a life of not having much relationship with him at all, would never be able to be replaced by a paycheck. I observed the closer he came to dying, the more spiritual he became. My Dad did not fear death and he did not have a bucket list because he lived his bucket list throughout his life. But he was in a rush to make up for lost time with a daughter he hardly knew.

A few years later I lost my stepdad, who really was the father who raised me. I had been very close to my stepdad, he was an entrepreneur who taught me to be fearless, to love jazz, to love fishing and to love road trips. His curiosity knew no bounds and he gave that gift to me. Similar to my father, my stepdad had done so much in life – U.S. Navy veteran, successful entrepreneur, father and husband – and he had no fear he was leaving a life with things undone. I know he would have liked to stick around a little longer just to be with my Mom, but he knew she was a survivor and she would be OK.

The loss of these two men in my life – one the glamourous, globe-trotting, risk-taking Formula One race car driver; the other a reliable, engaged, kind, encouraging and patriotic paternal guide who taught me resiliency and gratitude – made me think what does it mean to have a "good death?"

The Institute of Medicine defines a good death, or successful dying, as "free from avoidable distress and suffering for patient, family, and caregivers, in general accord with the patient's and family's wishes, and reasonably consistent with clinical, cultural, and ethical standards." However, critics from all scientific disciplines jumped on this stating no one can define a good death. Instead, they hypothesize a successful death is the natural transition from successful aging – or as gerontologists frame it, *optimal aging*. By practicing a good life now, we train ourselves for a good death and beyond.

When we think of spirituality, it has two parts: the spirituality rooted in your daily life and the spirituality that prepares you for death. The Latin root for spirituality is *spiritus* that means soul, ghost, courage, breath. When I wrote my first book, I shared the wisdom of Elisabeth Kübler-Ross who is the well-known psychiatrist who identified the five stages of grief: Denial,

Anger, Bargaining, Depression and Acceptance. Her co-author, David Kessler, expanded on the five stages of grief in his 2019 book where he wrote the sixth stage of grief is *Meaning*. It is not enough to simply accept tragic and traumatic events or loss in your life. To become whole again you must find meaning from your suffering and your struggles. Spirituality helps with finding meaning in your life.

Maybe the question is not "what is a good death?" maybe it is "what is a good life?" This is what gratitude is all about. It is your personal value system that creates a meaningful life. You will not need a bucket list because you are living those dreams every day and you will not fear death because you realize there is a higher power. I am forever grateful I learned these lessons from my father and stepfather.

Finding the Rainbow Bridge

> "Until one has loved an animal, a part of
> one's soul remains unawakened."
> -- Anatole France

There is a spiritual aspect of animals that helps heal your soul. Most pet owners know the loss of your trusted, non-judgmental companion can be as devastating as the loss of a loved one. I find it hard as a Christian that the faithful believe animals do not have souls and therefore, will not be reunited with us in heaven. One look into the eyes of dogs I have loved tells me God would not do that to us. After all, when you spell God backwards doesn't it spell Dog?

I am not the only saddened Christian when it comes to pets and heaven. Scottish artist and animal lover, Edna Clyne-Rekhy, obviously felt the same way more than 60 years ago when she poured her grief over the loss of her beloved dog, Major, into "The "Rainbow Bridge" poem. The poem reads you will be reunited with your pet after crossing the rainbow bridge together once in heaven. This chain letter to Clyne-Rekhy's close friends became a 1994 "Dear Abby" column. Since then, the poem has been bringing comfort and solace to those who know the intense loss of a pet.

One U.K. survey found almost half of respondents (45%) believe their pets end up in the same place they do when they die. Numerous Biblical authors agree. One author, Brian Burgess writes, "Animals are innocent and are not in need of salvation and that it was never our Heavenly Father's desire that we or his animals would suffer death. The pets that we had to say goodbye to are alive in heaven right now in their spiritual bodies and we will see them again."

This spiritual connection is not just left to the dogs. In 2005, a stray kitten wandered into a nursing home in Providence, Rhode Island. The cat was named Oscar and he quickly became a beloved pet in the facility known for finding those in their last hours of life and sitting near them to comfort them. Rather than being seen as a bad omen, residents, staff and family thought of Oscar as an angel who had come to help their loved one pass away peacefully. Oscar's legend grew with the book, *Making the Rounds with Oscar*, chronicling how this cat brought comfort and companionship for those taking their final journey. Sadly, in 2022, Oscar passed away himself at age 17. Staff and visitors gathered to commemorate the cat who in his lifetime brought solace to hundreds of humans.

Soul Food: Musical Menus, Sonic Seasoning and A Dash of SOC

The world-renowned classical pianist, Arthur Rubinstein, lived until age 95 and for 80 of those years he performed in front of live audiences. Regarded as the greatest Chopin interpreter of his time, Rubenstein admitted in his autobiography his ability to practice 8-10 hours a day became more difficult as he aged. His eyesight, nimble fingers and stamina were all starting to revolt requiring him to create a new way to continue his mastery of the classical repertoire he loved.

He applied a gerontology approach developed in the '90s by Paul and Margaret Baltes known as the Selective Optimization with Compensation (SOC) theory or *behavioral plasticity*.

SELECTIVE – This is about one of our seven A's of Caregiving: Adaptation. It means you continue to do things you love with some compromise. By reducing the number of classical masterpieces he played in concert, it allowed Rubinstein to also reduce his practice time and maximize his cognitive reserve. Piano playing, unlike bike riding, is an activity that requires continued practice to stimulate memory as part of neuronal activity.

OPTIMIZATION – By focusing his practice sessions on fewer pieces, Rubinstein maximized not just his memory capacity but his expertise for each piece. This is a classic example of less quantity but higher quality.

COMPENSATION – In some of the pieces, there were faster movements where Rubenstein's fingers needed to move rapidly and effortlessly across the keys of the piano. Given his age-related issues of arthritis and decline in dexterity, Rubinstein employed a classic compensation solution. He simply slowed the pace of his playing at the beginning of the piece. Thus, when the moment came for the faster pace, he could easily speed up his play without the audience being the wiser to the slower pace in the beginning.

Another music legend, jazz icon Dave Brubeck, used SOC not because of advancing age but because of a debilitating accident as a young man. In 1951, he dove into the surf in Hawaii and damaged several neck vertebrae and his spinal cord suffering residual nerve damage in his fingers. As a 32-year-old jazz pianist, hunching over the keys exacerbated the pain in his back and fingers. Like Rubenstein, Brubeck was not as dexterous playing speedy single note runs. Instead, Brubeck had a special upright piano designed so he could maintain his long hours of practice in his home studio by playing standing up. Because of the injury to nerves in his hands, he also adapted his style to create the complex blocky chords that became Brubeck's signature on his classic pieces, "Time Out" and "Blue Rondo à la Turk."[78]

What these music legends teach us is using a method of problem-solving such as SOC is a great example of how aging or disability does not mean abandoning one's passions but rather adapting to maintain the joy in life. This same method can be applied to life in general, such as adapting home environments to achieve optimal healthspan and wellspan

---

[78] "Time Out" became the first jazz album to go platinum and sell a million copies (and by the way, Brubeck was my stepfather's favorite jazz artist, a love he passed on to me).

via accessible Well Home For Life Design or adapting your frenetic work schedule to take on caregiving.

When it comes to caregiving, the application of SOC by these musical legends can also be the prescription for caregivers as a way to maintain life balance. One friend of mine became a family caregiver for both of her older parents, one of whom had Alzheimer's, while also juggling full-time work. While she employed a home care worker to look after her parents while she was at work, on at least two occasions, she returned home to find her parents had fired the home care worker because they "didn't like strangers in their home." My friend was at her wit's end on how to solve this dilemma.

I told her about the SOC theory and could it be applied to her problem? We discussed it and came up with a brilliant solution. She adapted her work from home schedule with her employer to have a blended virtual and in-office hours (known as flex time). Thus, she already had her "selectivity" in place when she would be home with her parents and when she would not.

She also hired a personal assistant to do all the little chores she either did not have time for or would take her away from being with her parents. Instead of paying a home care worker to replace herself as a caregiver, she hired an assistant to replace herself as the person who got an oil change for her car, picked up the dry cleaning, went to the post office or Fed Ex, etc. This "optimized" her time where it had the most value – with her parents – instead of doing other menial tasks.

Finally, she "compensated" by tapping into delivery services for her parent's medication needs and apps like Instacart to help with grocery shopping. And, since her parents loved pets, she hired pet therapy services along with a professional caregiver to bring in dogs, cats, rabbits, for those times she would have to be at the office. Instead of her parents feeling there was a stranger in their home, they felt useful petting and playing with the animals. With just a little SOC she solved her caregiving challenges.

Musical Menus and Sonic Seasoning

In the lexicon of self-care and wellness we talk about spirituality in terms of what feeds your soul, and for many people it is music. I have written about how I love all jazz[79], my Mom loves Elvis, one of my best friends loves The Who and Candy Chang loves the blues music that breathes life into New Orleans. We know how medicine can help purify the body, but it is music that purifies the soul. It is humankind's universal language as well as the body's natural pain reliever and mood booster.

Music can be a history tour such as remembering what tune you loved while in high school, or the song played at your wedding or some other milestone life event that releases serotonin and dopamine in the brain. Music can also create endorphins that divert your attention away from pain and help boost your endurance, especially if working out. Research published in *Scientific American* also found music can enhance your metabolic efficiency that is your body's ability to preserve glycogen and burn fat as fuel.

When it comes to music and meals, most restaurants have used ambient sounds to enhance your dining experience for years. But today's researchers are taking this to a whole new level. One study found prolonged periods of stress increased cortisol levels that in turn reduced the intensity for taste of both sweet and sour foods. Altered taste perception can lead to

---

[79] My list is long but includes: Dave Brubeck, Django Reinhardt, Ella Fitzgerald, Coltrane, Bird, Toots Thielemans, Chuck Mingus, Wes Montgomery, Regina Carter...

appetite loss and even increased depression as your brain reacts to the loss of pleasurable tastes closely tied to smell.

After age 40, about 19% of adults show the sense of taste declines with about 3 in 10 suffering from tastelessness in food by age 80. In fact, 15 million people have problems with smell and 7.5 million have problems with taste. The loss of sensitivity with taste and smell increases as we age but can also be associated with certain congenital disorders or viruses such as COVID-19. This loss of smell is known as anosmia affecting 3% of people over age 40 in the U.S. We often talk about taste and smell together because your olfactory nerves control smell and are responsible for 80% of gustation (what you taste) and both of these senses together are responsible for your flavor experience consisting of five main tastes: sweet, sour, salty, bitter and savory (also known as umami). One of the reasons smell is one of your most powerful senses is the message from the moment of sniffing travels directly to your brain's hippocampus (memory) and amygdala (emotions) regions.

An expert in the world of taste, smell, flavor and multisensory experiences in a music-infused environment is world-renowned gastrophysicist, Charles Spence, a professor of experimental psychology and head of the Crossmodal Research Laboratory at the University of Oxford. Our lives are full of spiritual rituals and Spence's research is in examining the rituals of eating and music and how to optimize the dining experience for health. His research is focused on gastrophysics, an emerging field of science that blends chemistry and physics and applies them to the fundamentals of gastronomy and cooking into what he calls "multisensory dining."

I have interviewed Spence for my podcast, articles and this book, and every time I learn fascinating ways our five senses are at the center of wellness and health. Spence has consulted for global brands such as Starbucks in the

U.K. where he helped to launch a new coffee product with a disco ambient soundscape and found customers who originally tasted bitterness in the recipe, now reported the coffee tasted 10% sweeter after listening to Donna Summer. For British Airways, Spence developed a "Sound Bite" menu for long haul flights pairing meals with certain music. Most frequent flyers report food loses 30% of its taste appeal on planes. In Spence's study passengers using the music selections reported 38% enhanced flavor in their meals.

Working with music producers, composers, chefs and nutritionists, Spence creates sonic seasoning (soundscapes such as "sounds of the sea" for seafood) and musical menus (instrumental or vocal songs) that enhance food and the dining experience in the brain. For instance, when it comes to the taste of coffee, Spence said he "can't turn water into wine yet" but he can take black coffee (and foods) that can be a bit tart and if he wants it to be sweeter, he uses music with tinkling high piano notes, windchimes or singers with high pitch such as Mariah Carey and Taylor Swift that signals the brain into sweetening the palate. On the opposite end of the taste spectrum, if he uses low pitch bass music – think of the baritones of Frank Sinatra or Johnny Cash – it makes the coffee taste more bitter and foods taste more savory. Several other studies show soft music (think classical or smooth jazz) prompts you to make healthier eating choices whereas loud, aggressive music (think heavy metal or hip hop) trigger unhealthy eating habits.

By maximizing sensory acuity, you can apply Spence's research findings to health and wellness. For instance, for those with Type 2 diabetes who need to reduce sugar in their diet, eating to a soundtrack of Celine Dion or Brian Wilson of the Beach Boys, can help make the food taste sweeter. For those with high blood pressure who need to reduce salt, put on Barry

White, Johnny Hartman, Nina Simone, Cher or Karen Carpenter to help increase the savory taste of the meal.

Spence's latest research in hospitals, long-term care and memory care communities focuses on the high level of noise in these facilities that disrupt pleasurable dining but also how to address the lack of patient and resident tastebuds. "As we age our senses decline but in the case of hearing or eyesight we have solutions such as hearing aids or eyeglasses to maintain the optimal level of these senses," Spence explained. "When taste and smell go, we don't have any solutions for that."

This became personal for Spence when he realized his mother was losing too much weight after moving into a memory care community. He found the only thing she would eat was ice cream that was not going to meet her nutritional needs. His first thought was the ice cream might just be nostalgia from her younger years but he realized it was mostly about the temperature of the cold dessert, the cool sensation coating her mouth was all she had to hold onto to bring her pleasure while eating.

"Because of the high level of daily medications older adults take, they need, for instance, up to 12 times more salt in their soup to get the same flavor they had before the medications diluted their tastebuds," Spence told me. "This in turn is bad for hypertension which is where the sonic seasoning strategies may help address this issue."

Collaborating with the facility's chef, music experts and the dementia care staff, Spence created a multisensory experience to encourage his mother's appetite. First, he took her favorite food, tomato soup, and with his gastronomic team created a "Cream of Tomato" ice cream with less fat and more protein. While the ice cream looked pink and therefore may trigger the brain to think sweet, Spence made a label for the bowl with the old tomato soup label and served the culinary invention using a floral chintz tablecloth and napkins similar to the ones his mother remembered from home. He also played her favorite World War II-era songs by British singer Vera Lynn.

By creating an entire multi-sensory environment – similar to reminiscence therapy where it is immersive and interactive – it triggered in his mother's brain pleasing nostalgic memories of her younger years. Spence said the experiment helped his mother blossom and find more life satisfaction in her later days. While Cream of Tomato soup ice cream may sound odd to Western diners, Spence says other countries, specifically Japan, have been creating savory ice creams for years. And, along with the taste and texture, using soundscapes including sounds of the sea to enhance the taste of seafood-based meals has proven successful in various research studies.

"There is no reason sonic seasoning should be limited to high-end dining experiences," advised Spence. "By engaging multisensory dining in any environment – hospital, memory care or at home – we bring both nutrition and pleasure back to one of our most basic activities: the joy of eating."

Motivation Through Music and Mozart

Throughout most of this book I have related our modern wellness practices and needs to our ancient lives millions of years ago when our brains began their phenomenal development. Music is no exception. What is different today is we consider music as entertainment, a sensory experience that makes you happy, sad, energetic or calm. But our ancient connection to music was more about infusing meaning into our communal, tribal lives through rituals – something that taps into our deepest feelings of spirituality.

Ancient cultures such as Aboriginal peoples in Australia followed *songlines* in the Outback as their spiritual version of our GPS.[80] Ancient pipes or flutes evolved into bagpipes that we mostly associate with Celtic history in Scotland but originated in the Middle East. The bagpipes were used to identify different clans as each had their own òra ("song" in Gaelic), and later it was used by flutes and drums in military strategy to muster soldiers and signal certain movements to troops. Even in today's modern world, each country has its own national anthem to bind us together as a people and culture and is a source of pride during ceremonies such as the Olympics medal presentations.

As we evolved, music remained a constant in our lives used to celebrate (weddings, birthdays, holidays) and to commemorate lifestage events (graduations, funerals). Most religions have music as part of the worship services, and although some fundamentalist Muslims do not believe in music as part of their *salah*, or prayer ritual, they do include music as accompaniment to various folk tales.

In the Emotional Wellness section, I mentioned entrainment, known as beat-matching. Researchers found this synchronization with our environment begins in utero as the heart rates of fetuses match the beating heart of their mother. Music picks up on this synchronicity where we see heart rates match the beat of the music. This makes music an important tool in your wellness routine.

Studies have shown most people listen to music in the afternoons and evenings between 4-8pm. However, it is morning where you should "tune in" to help set the tone for the rest of your day. Energetic, fast beat music can get your heart rate up but you want to use a playlist of songs familiar to you and tunes that do not have complicated lyrics but rather repeat an easy

---

[80] Songlines, are also known as dreaming tracks, and use ceremonial songs to help guide the traveler's way in the Outback.

chorus. Why? Your brain is used to concentrating on words so if the words are familiar, they promote energy. A new song or one that has complicated lyrics makes your brain concentrate on the song rather than energizing your wake-up neurons that promote alertness and vigor.

Putting people in the right mood to be productive and active is not new. An example is the famous department store CEO John Wanamaker, who installed an organ in his department store in 1909 to energize his employees in the morning. Similarly, a radio program called "Music While You Work" was developed in the early 1940s to play music for factory workers to maintain positivity during war time.

Classical music with slow tempos has been shown to help promote better sleep and to optimize reading or schoolwork. One study found women with insomnia went to sleep more quickly after listening to their favorite classical music continuously for 10 nights. One reason why classical music works as a sleep aid is most pieces have 60-80 beats per minute (BPM) that corresponds with the body's resting heart rate.

Although somewhat controversial among scientists who debate the validity in the study results, Gordon Shaw, a University of California at Irvine (UCI) physicist was the researcher who famously identified "The Mozart Effect." Shaw conducted studies among his college students as well as three-year-olds using Mozart's Sonata for Two Pianos in D major. He found in the college student group there was a temporary increase in the study participant's IQs while among the pre-schoolers, there was a 30% increase in spatial testing even after six months when compared to young peers not listening to music. The toddlers also had better concentration, higher math scores, better verbal skills and more self-control.

While Shaw never felt Mozart-listening alone would make you smarter, he felt it was a warm-up for the brain's parietal and frontal regions that house intelligence. If you compare this to a physical workout, listening to Mozart is your stretching routine before you get into real complex thinking exercises. Over the years, Shaw continued his studies using MRI brain scans to show those who listened to Mozart as opposed to Beethoven consistently scored higher on tests, however he was never able to identify why.[81]

Mozart may make you smarter but when it comes to health, we know the *music as medicine* movement is real, especially for those with dementia. A leader in this space is SingFit, based on musical health technology. SingFit engages the participants in music-making – singing, swinging arms, tapping toes, swaying side to side – using your loved one's favorite tunes, most from days gone by known as "the oldies." Created by the sister-brother team of Rachel Francine, a technology industry veteran, and Andy Tubman, a certified music therapist, they based their medical music health solution on an idea from their inventor, opera-singing father.

One SingFit study that included 250 assisted living community residents joining group sing-a-longs one to seven times a week showed a 43% increase in mood, with many participants going from "sad" or "melancholy" to "content" and even "overjoyed." Tubman advises singing in a group or having a family caregiver join their older loved one using a consistent routine of three to four sessions a week for 40 minutes per session to increase oxytocin for these individuals and create deep neurological work and brain plasticity. Francine who was a caregiver for her mother with dementia, said, "SingFit is scalable medicine not just for those with

---

[81] I like Mozart but I am devoted to Beethoven and will sacrifice the IQ points to listen to Beethoven String Quartet No. 14, Op 131, Moonlight Sonata, Emperor and Ode to Joy.

dementia but for many chronic conditions, including hypertension, autism, Parkinson's and those with brain injuries."

Research has shown music memory is kept in the auditory cortex region of the brain and is one of the last memories to atrophy in Alzheimer's patients. This makes music therapy essential in keeping those with dementia engaged. For anyone who has seen the documentary, "Alive Inside," where catatonic dementia residents in memory care come alive tapping their toes and singing along with a favorite tune of their past, the power of music in your brain is almost biblical. The renowned neurologist and psychologist, Oliver Sacks, detailed how "music occupies more areas of your brain than language does – humans are a musical species." For family caregivers who struggle to communicate with dementia loved ones, the music-brain connection is a powerful key to unlock lost memories.

But you want to choose your playlist wisely. Studies have found while classical or pop tunes can calm aggressive behavior, prolonged listening to heavy metal music can increase the risk of aggression, anger, antisocial behavior, substance abuse, suicidal ideation, anxiety and depression. Another study found aggressive lyrics, including some rap and hip hop songs, increase feelings of hostility.

Another part of our Spiritual Wellness is to cope with episodes of grief and hopelessness. While seemingly counter-intuitive, research has found sad music can actually lift your spirits. Aristotle observed tragedies performed in theaters with dramatic music allowed the audience to binge then purge on negative emotions, a benefit he called *catharsis*. In one study about a third of the participants had a positive mood boost after listening to music many may find sad but these participants had embedded memories of certain music as a pleasurable or memorable experience. Some feel the blues has a melancholy vibe, country music ballads can make you cry, and sadcore – a sub-genre of alternative rock – has bleak lyrics and downbeat tempos. Examples include: Billie Holiday's "Strange Fruit," "Hurt" by Johnny Cash and most hauntingly Lana Del Rey's "God Knows I Tried."[82] Researchers of a 2014 study on mood and music genres found "certain psychological rewards, such as regulating or purging negative emotions, retrieving memories of important past events, and inducing feelings of connectedness and comfort" are the positive aspects of turning to melancholic music moments.

In my Me Time Monday workshop, I have participants create a personalized playlist including energetic "make you want to dance" tunes, calming songs, etc. We also watch one of my favorite YouTube videos – Old Hollywood clips with Fred Astaire, Gene Kelly, Rita Hayworth, Gwen Verdon and more set to modern music such as "Uptown Funk" and "Dancin' on the Ceiling." There is something celebratory about music and movement that taps into our tribal and spiritual origins. Think about the last time you danced or at least tapped your feet and swayed with the music. If it has been more than a week – time to add a little Me Time Monday music break into your wellness plan.

---

[82] The songs that always tear me up (but I love hearing them) are Harry Chapin's "Cat's in the Cradle," Joni Mitchell's "River" and Peggy Lee's "Is That All There Is?"

chapter 34

Dragonflies and Post Traumatic Growth

Approximately 300 million years ago, long before dinosaurs roamed the Earth, one of the first organisms to inhabit the planet were dragonflies. In China, people associate the dragonfly with prosperity, harmony and good luck while among Native Americans, dragonflies are a sign of happiness, speed and purity. In the Hopi and Pueblo tribes, the dragonfly was considered a medicine animal, associated with healing and transformation and killing a dragonfly was considered taboo among the Pueblo people. In Japan, dragonflies are a national emblem and are seen as symbols of happiness, strength and courage with ancient Japanese samurai using dragonflies on their *mon*, known as a heraldic crest, to symbolize victory.

While the myths and symbolism of dragonflies varies (many Western cultures still feel dragonflies are signs of mischief) most agree dragonflies are mysterious insects that offer poetic insights when it comes to caregiving and wellness.

First, dragonflies have perfect agility with the ability to not only fly backwards but have each wing work independently giving them unparalleled aerodynamics to fly sideways, straight up or down or just hover in one spot like a helicopter. NASA, among other global space programs, study the aeronautics of dragonflies to innovate modern drones, satellites and spacecraft. This adaptability and flexibility is a message for caregivers to be open to change and to also pause for moments of reflection and not feel you have to be in constant motion.

Second, dragonflies can see more than most living things. Their heads are 90% eyes and they have almost 360-degree vision, with just one blind spot directly behind them. The ability to be *present* and to be realistic about what you see is key for caregivers. And understanding you may have a blind spot when it comes to your loved ones lets you be realistic about striking the balance in caring for your loved one as much as caring for yourself.

Third, because dragonflies are cold-blooded, they have difficulty regulating body temperature whereas warm-blooded humans have no such trouble. To address this, dragonflies will assume the obelisk posture similar to a handstand-like position in yoga. This helps them prevent overheating on sunny days. The abdomen is raised until its tip points at the sun, minimizing the surface area exposed to solar radiation. For caregivers, the reminder is to take time to raise your face to the sun or practice a little yoga. While the dragonfly is regulating body temperature, you are regulating overwhelming emotions.

Fourth and last, dragonflies are seen as magical, beautiful creatures mostly because of the iridescent hue on their body and gossamer wings. It is why dragonflies, more than any other insect, are found in ancient carvings, pottery, illustrations and other works of art. Dragonflies spend most of their life underwater until their metamorphosis into the brilliant flying creatures we see. Some believe it is this lengthy incubation in salt water that gives dragonflies their beautiful *iridescence*, a word derived in part from the Greek word, *iridos,* meaning rainbow. In this context, the dragonfly becomes the perfect symbol for the Me Time Monday program. It is about light and water – two things that draw you into nature and wellness. It is also a reminder to caregivers to live life colorfully and to embrace caregiving as a dragonfly embodies change, transformation, adaptability, self-care to emerge from feeling underwater in your caregiving role to having a growth mindset to find silver linings in your experience.

How Growth Mindset and Gerotranscendence Lead to Post Traumatic Growth

"... my old age sits light upon me... and not only is not burdensome, but is even happy."
— Cicero (106-43 BC)

Around the same time neuroscientists were learning about brain plasticity and how to create new brain cells, Carol Dweck, a psychology professor at Stanford University, was investigating human motivation. She found that mindset faced a similar dilemma as brain cells where scientists originally thought you only get so many neurons at birth and that is it. Dwek's research looked at the talents and opportunities you are born with and wondered is that all you get or can you grow these areas for more success in life? What she uncovered is people with a *growth mindset* believe their talents and opportunities for success in life can be developed. On the flip side are people who have a *fixed mindset* believing the talents they are born with remain unchangeable.

As opposed to personality or emotions, people with growth mindset simply worry less about looking smart and focus their energy instead on learning. AARP reported more than one-half of older Americans embrace lifelong learning and upskilling programs. Growth mindset does not let failure or age define you it simply becomes a pivot point for further learning. A breakthrough or achievement you seek can be just around the corner and with hard work you will achieve your goal.

Using a similar hypothesis to lifelong learning, Lars Tornstam, a Swedish sociologist and author, began studying what he called *gerotranscendence* in the

'80s. While Dweck's work has been mostly with younger generations and also business management groups for workplace development, Tornstam has focused his research on older adults and this gero-optimistic trend.

Gerotranscendence is when older adults have a decreased interest in superfluous social interaction and seek more moments of solitude rather than constant, yet meaningless, social activity. They also worry less and ignore nagging problems instead focusing on positive experiences. Social isolation and loneliness are issues gerontologists find concerning, but Tornstam advises occasional quiet and seclusion are not always a bad thing.

It also taps into another psychologist's work, Erik Ericksen's eight stages of psychosocial development. This theory includes the seventh stage of lifelong development where people in their mid-40s to 60s either embrace *generativity* (a desire to give back and to share wisdom found through life with younger generations often felt to be the most fruitful stage of nurturing and creation); or *stagnation* (failure to contribute, to be engaged or to be passionate about anything in life). Erickson labels the seventh stage as "Care" in our lifelong development, when we spend the most time caring for children or older parents.

If you gather all these hypotheses on motivation and development from Dweck to Tornstam to Erickson, there are those who continue to thrive through life and those who do not. What creates this difference?

The difference for these two disparate groups is the ability to tap into your spirituality for hopefulness, resiliency and happiness. For others who struggle there is *post-traumatic growth* (PTG). When you are faced with overwhelming stress and emotional distress, you survive by tapping into your reservoirs of resiliency. Think of first responders – from warfighters preserving your freedom to the heroes at ground zero after 9/11 to the health care workers during the pandemic to law enforcement officers and firefighters who start every day not knowing if they will come home. The wear and tear on mental health of this daily assault and build-up of stress of highly traumatizing events have many suffering from post-traumatic stress disorder (PTSD). Every day citizens can also experience PTSD from a trauma such as a car accident, a neighborhood shooting or a physical assault. The symptoms of PTSD can include flashbacks, panic attacks (accelerated heartbeat, breathing and sweating), severe anxiety and disturbing thoughts.

Whether you suffer from PTSD or lack of resiliency, the five areas of PTG identified in the '90s by University of North Carolina researchers, Richard Tedeschi and Lawrence Calhoun, help: spiritual changes, personal strength, relationships, appreciation of life and new possibilities. Moving past the trauma and a sense of vulnerability to a place of strength is what PTG is all about. Through PTG you accept that you only have so much control over the devastating events in life. Sometimes that requires letting go gracefully of the trauma and finding meaning in what you experienced.

There are some people who expressed feeling PTSD during the pandemic who would fall into the category of chronic trauma rather than the acute trauma experienced by first responders. The lack of spirituality in the U.S. is a factor in more people feeling anxious and fearful or traumatized by events that should not typically trigger those intense emotions. During PTG you learn to put context around challenging events. One example is a social media meme that went viral during the pandemic, "The Greatest Generation was asked to go to war and save the world, you are being asked to sit on the couch, eat pizza and binge watch Netflix. Trust me, you can do this." This is not to pass judgment on anyone's feelings of trauma but as noted in Emotional Wellness, we live in our own bubbles where context for life is everything.

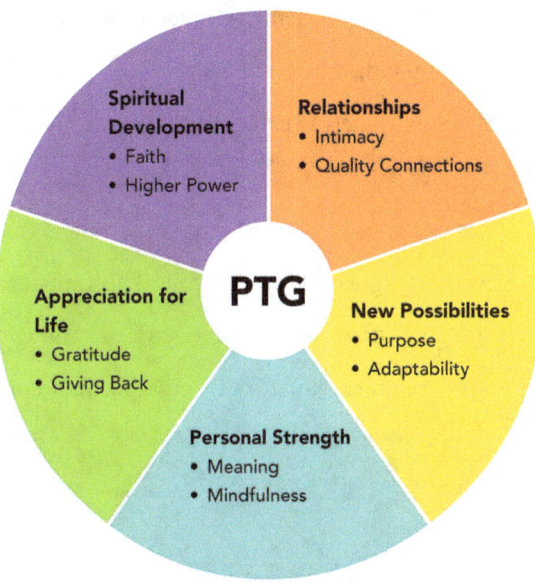

Figure 22: 5 Areas of Post Traumatic Growth (PTG)
adapted from Tedeschi, Calhoun (1996)

While the pandemic may have triggered PTSD for some, consider living through the Great Depression in 1929 or the Holocaust in Nazi Germany. Perspective and the ability to step outside your bubble and have empathy for other's struggles helps you achieve post-traumatic growth. By engaging in conversations with others who have experienced trauma, or by volunteering to help those impacted by traumatic events, you can overcome your problems through empathy and increase your appreciation for life.

PTG helps build resiliency which is at an all-time low, especially among younger generations. A survey conducted in 2020 during the height of the pandemic showed 60% of adults and children lacked the resiliency to cope with crisis events. This group could potentially be using a fixed mindset. However, a more recent study published in the *Journal of Psychiatry* in 2022 revealed 88% of respondents felt they gained knowledge, coping skills and increased resiliency post-pandemic – much more in alignment with a growth mindset. In Finland, which has ranked No. 1 in global happiness surveys since 2017, there is a 500-year-old cultural tradition known as *sisu* that loosely translated means "determination and fortitude." This ability to tap into inner locus of control and find strength and grit is what the five elements of PTG are designed to do for you. The transformation from enduring a psychological struggle and adversity that allows you to grow spiritually is not about being resilient but re-establishing core beliefs that allow for resiliency in the future.

Caregiver Walkabout: Finding Awe and Awesomeness

In my first book, I was inspired by research on indigenous people in Australia's Outback and how a special ritual resembled the journey caregivers take. It is worth repeating here as I write about finding awe and your personal awesomeness:

Caregiver Walkabout

There is a cultural tradition among Australian Aborigines that very closely resembles the journey caregivers take. It is called a *walkabout* and is a rite of passage for adolescent boys to become men. These young boys have no choice on whether they want to do this or not – it is a long-held tradition these people believe connects them to the land they love. They are sent out alone into the Outback, sometimes spending months in solitude. Many of the boys follow ancient *songlines* or *dreaming tracks* where they learn to find food and shelter – the same types of food and rock formations their ancestors found before them. During this quest, they develop deep self-awareness and when they return to their families they have a greater sense of who they are, their importance to their family and their heritage.

In many ways, caregivers are on a walkabout. You may feel you had no choice to become a caregiver. You may spend months or years feeling all alone in your journey. But along the way, you learn about food, shelter (and legal paperwork and insurance rules) in the care of your aging or ill loved one. When you return from your caregiving journey, hopefully you will feel a sense of connectedness to your past and your future. In this journey called life, you understand your purpose, your role. And while you may have felt alone in the *Caregiving Outback*, friends, experts and others were helping to guide you. They were in the stars and the whispers of the wind at night. When you open your eyes and realize you are or will be a caregiver, you will know you are not alone. Welcome to the cast of caregivers.

– Sherri Snelling, *A Cast of Caregivers*

While science tells you social heath and maintaining quality relationships is the key to health, happiness and longevity, there is something to be said about the solace of solitude. Pythagoras, Ralph Waldo Emerson and as you have just read, Lars Tornstam, believed mornings spent in solitude are when nature speaks to your imagination in ways that cannot be heard when you are in other's company. And, while Thoreau takes the prize as someone who truly understood solitude spent in nature and Socratic self-reflection ("Know thyself"), many gerontologists believe to be able to create social fitness and social convoys of quality relationships, you must first have a quality relationship with yourself and that begins with having moments just to yourself. Some fear seeking solitude can lead to loneliness. But as I wrote in Social Wellness, being alone does not mean you are lonely. Loneliness is defined by the *quality* of your relationships not the *quantity* of time you spend with others.

Other cultures have something similar to the young Aboriginal boys in the Outback. Many Native American tribes have vision quests[83] where one fasts for four days alone at a sacred site in nature with the purpose of obtaining advice, seeing into the future and seeking protection. Blacks during the antebellum era followed a similar connection to the nighttime sky but for different reasons. While Aboriginal boys are seeking manhood, and Native Americans are seeking answers, Blacks were seeking freedom. The oral storytelling used by escaping slaves along the Underground Railroad journey often included *signal songs* that provided shibboleths for directions to freedom in the North. Harriet Tubman used "follow the drinking gourd" to mean the Big Dipper as a signal to find this constellation in the night sky that identified the North Star, Polaris. This observational astronomy was passed down through generations of former slaves to their descendants still needing to read the night sky during the dark days of the Jim Crow era.

Ancestral storytelling is another way to find your sense of "awesomeness" or help your child achieve the same while simultaneously giving your older loved one a starring role in an important family activity. A Boston College study found depression decreased in both grandparents and grandchildren who spent quality time together. Another U.K. study among 1,500 school-age children found stronger emotional health among those children who had close, interactive relationships with grandparents. Additional research has shown family stories or intergenerational narratives, as shared among

---

[83] Vision quest is an umbrella term. Individual tribes use different names.

grandparents and grandchildren, help build relevancy for the older adults and resiliency and a sense of self among younger generations. Family stories are shown to be a great tool in creating empathy in both generations.

Part of finding your awesomeness is realizing where you came from and I do not mean the geography but your ancestry. There is a sense of empowerment in learning the history of your family. As discussed in the Caregiver Wellness Journey chapter, there is a Native American philosophy called the Seventh Generation Principle. While this ancient tribal philosophy has ethical, moral, scientific and realistic value, there is a variation on this future-thinking that focuses on self and your role in seven generation planning. This perspective considers the oldest relative or family friend who touched or knew you as an infant. It could have been a grandparent or today even a great-great-grandparent. Then you visualize the oldest relative or family friend who touched or knew your oldest relative, again maybe a grandparent or great-grandparent.

When you take a moment to consider this throughline in your lineage, you can appreciate the continuity of care it took to have all these generations lead to you. Many people experience this realization when they research their family history and genealogy. Insights into your history is the inheritance you can use to build upon your internal strengths. There is a sense of continuity and recognition in knowing about the generations that came before you that is comforting and empowering. Native American cultures have maintained oral family histories through many generations that is a life enriching gift.

Besides finding your awesomeness, spirituality also allows you to experience awe - a sense of wonder that is often something experienced solo. Awe is a unique blend of curiosity and uncertainty. While this would seem to create anxiety, instead it fills your soul with spirituality. Finding moments of awe are the peak experiences Abraham Maslow wrote about in his motivational theory of self-transcendence. These experiences are often described as removing the barriers to go beyond your boundaries and find moments of pure joy.

The awe factor of watching the Northern Lights or a shooting star or just staring at the galaxy with the hundreds of stars you can see at night reminds you of how small you are and how your daily struggles are part of a larger story being written across the universe and across time. Learning about your ancestry gives you perspective on life's challenges and fears. Contemplating your role in the universe does the same thing. A 2021 study found experiencing moments of awe on a daily basis, reduced stress levels and increased self-reported feelings of life satisfaction. Other research stated feeling awe can lower inflammatory cytokines, that are created in response to the body's invaders – they mobilize immune cells to fight the pathogens such as viruses or flus.

Awe is an anti-inflammatory.

While studies show 75% of our sense of awe comes from nature, the sensation of having your breath taken away or staring in wonderment can be a nature scene such as a sunset, a snowy mountaintop or a blooming field of flowers, but it can also be watching a loved one sleep soundly, contemplating a beautiful work or art or architecture, witnessing a child's birth or holding the hand of a loved one as they take their last breath. Some psychologists call this *sunset mode*, a term that defines a mindset allowing you to take all of life's emotions in but realize the moment will not last. It is similar to watching a sunset that invites you to take in the awe of the moment as the sun sinks into the horizon. This philosophy is also found in

Buddhism where impermanence is the cornerstone of Buddhist teachings and practice: All that exists is impermanent; nothing lasts. In our world of scientific certainties, we are surprisingly OK with experiencing the mystery of awe. This is because when you encounter awe you also experience faith and faith replaces fear in your soul.

One of the strengths of solitude and experiencing awe is you become healthfully self-aware. You are not distracted by other's attitudes or intruding beliefs, you are able to have the space to believe in wonder and miracles and redefine your values in life. As Vincent Van Gogh said, "I know nothing with any certainty but the sight of the stars makes me dream."

By now you have discovered that finding well-being is a multi-faceted effort. It is not just about your physical body nor your emotions, intellect, financial wellness nor even your social connections. However, if your life is soul-less there is a hole that needs to be filled. For Abraham Maslow, self-transcendence captured some of the aspects of achieving spirituality. For others, Csikszentmihalyi's flow theory is rising above self to an almost spiritual awakening of the conscious mind. Famed psychologist William James offered that spirituality achieves a type of divine non-sectarian and non-institutional level of living that corresponds with Buddhism or Emerson's existentialism of self-improvement, self-reliance and communing with nature. But in the end, spirituality, just like your wellness plan, is not defined by experts it is defined by you.

One awe-inspiring moment I will never forget was working on the Opening Ceremonies for the 1984 Los Angeles Summer Olympics. As a young intern, my role was mostly to take notes, check performers in for rehearsals and grab coffee for everyone. Even though I sat through numerous rehearsals, there was one performance I knew would have everyone transfixed and it was based on music and entrainment – the magic of synchronicity. It was the awe-inspiring moment when 84 pianists sitting at baby grand pianos in the peristyles of the L.A. Coliseum rolled in playing George Gershwin's "Rhapsody in Blue." It is moments like this that make me grateful for the opportunities I have had in life.

There are many things that feed our souls such as music, art, star gazing and while these seem like external elements, they can transform our emotions and take us out of the chaos of a crazy world and into a place where there is calm, comfort and wonder. As Martin Luther King, Jr. said, "Faith is taking the first step even when you don't see the full staircase."

Conclusion:
Me Time Monday for a Wonderful Life

In the classic holiday film, "It's a Wonderful Life," the Jimmy Stewart character, George Bailey, is the epitome of stress and burnout towards the end of the movie. He is a caregiver to everyone but himself and a classic case of a mental health breakdown. He even contemplates suicide until Clarence the almost-angel reminds him of what is important in life. It is his social connections – the lives he touched and made better. In the end, his gratitude for those relationships saves George Bailey.

If you apply the lesson of George Bailey to your life, and as you have read throughout this book, self-care is not always a solo sport. You are the foundation but you need friends, family and a spiritual relationship to really achieve well-being. I started the book saying your longest caregiving relationship is with yourself. But it is also the passengers and travelers you choose to take the journey with who make all the difference.

The other great lesson of this movie is that life is imperfect and sometimes that is wonderful. We do not want George to cave into Potter's cunning offer because we know he will be more miserable even if his financial woes are eliminated. Instead, what George needed is what we are seeing in wellness today: a little cold water therapy (diving into the frigid river to save Clarence), doing good deeds for others (which actually does make George a rich man and is his salvation), feeling Zuzu's petals in his pocket (connecting him to nature and life-affirming biophilia). George learned that having a purposeful, meaningful life is the mission. He learned that living a simple life can be a happier life. He showed us that character, not cash, counts. He becomes grateful for the support of friendships and having a confidante who has your back (his wife, Mary). Clarence helps him see that life's sacrifices can also be life's rewards and that no one is a failure who has friends.

As I have highlighted throughout this book, self-care and wellness are not about changing you, they are about realizing what you already have and simply recharging it. If you adopt George Bailey's lessons on life it will be a joyful journey and a wonderful life.

Your Me Time Monday Survey

You have read about nature and neuroscience, learned about the seven elements of life that keep you in balance, understand how to find your flow using microflows and how to use Mondays and other routines and tips along your wellness journey.

Now it is time to map out your wellness plan – the Me Time Monday plan just for you. By treating the seven elements of your life as gardens that need tending to survive, it will help you achieve the balance you need for a joyful ride through life.

Following is my Me Time Monday Survey for you to start crystallizing where you are on your wellness journey. By answering these questions you will start to see where you might want to add more activity to achieve that balance. It also helps your brain to visualize the answers. This is how you begin to map your wellness needs. There is no score – this is not a competency test. Remember wellness is about being self-aware and pursuing progress not perfection in your wellness goals. Only you can assess and decide where you want to focus and where you need more wellness practices in your life.

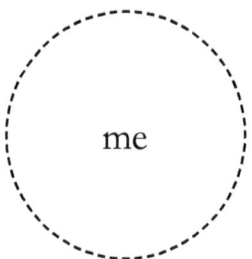

- Write down up to 7 things that you feel are valuable in your life (your ikigai) – the activities, experiences that support your self-care wellness plan (leave important relationships for the Social Wellness questions below)
  1.
  2.
  3.
  4.
  5.
  6.
  7.

- Between your biological well-being, your psychological well-being and your social well-being – rank these 3 in priority order of your current well-being status
  #1 –
  #2 –
  #3 -

- Based on the 7 colors in the Wellness graphic – which color best describes you or which color is your favorite? Why?

- What is your flow? How often do you practice it?

- Do you feel like your life has passion, purpose and meaning?

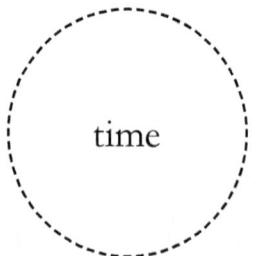

- Of the things you wrote down under "me" as your ikigai, how much time per day or per week do you spend on these valuable self-care activities?

- Write down a list of the things you do automatically every day – the habits or routines you have (take a shower, brush your teeth, comb your hair, drive to work/school, make breakfast/lunch/dinner, etc.)

- Do you already practice habit-stacking with healthy behaviors layered on top of routine behaviors (go ahead list them)? If not, which daily routine do you feel you have time to add 2-7 minutes to during the day?

- Do you feel you could dedicate 7 minutes a day to at least one element of your wellness?

- How much time do you spend on Me Time?
  _____ daily
  _____ weekly

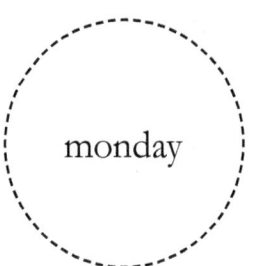

- Of the 7 elements of Me Time Monday (Physical, Emotional, Social, Intellectual, Environmental, Financial Spiritual) rank them in the order that you feel you are succeeding at or where you are spending most of your time

Physical	Emotional	Social
Intellectual	Environmental	Financial
	Spiritual	

- Are Mondays a day you look forward to as a fresh start or do you get the Sunday scaries the night before?

  I look forward to Mondays _____

  I dread Mondays _____

- How do you reward yourself for performing a self-care practice or other good deed, even if performed for someone else?

- Are you successful at setting a New Year's Resolution and sticking to it or do you abandon your goals at some point during the year?

- Do you write down what you want to accomplish or need to tackle on Friday or Sunday afternoon/evening and then let go of the anticipatory stress of Mondays?

- Check your calendar on Mondays – do you have Me Time scheduled each day for at least 7 minutes with a self-care activity?

Physical

- Do you cross-train your body? (walking, stretching, weight lifting)?

- How many hours of sleep do you get per night?

  | _____ | _____ | _____ |
  | Less than 5 hours | 5-6.5 hours | 7-9 hours+ |

- How many minutes/hours do you check your smartphone/tablet or watch TV/stream a show, or read a book before you going to bed? _____ minutes nightly (on average)

- How many ounces of water do you drink daily?

  | _____ | _____ | _____ |
  | 64 oz or less | 91-125 oz. | ½ your body weight in oz. |

- How many colors (foods) of the rainbow do you eat daily?
  1   2   3   4   5   6   7

- Do you eat your meals during sunlight hours?

- Do most of your meals take at least 30 minutes?

- Of the 21 meals (or more if you do little meals throughout the day) you eat each week, how many are spent eating alone?

- Do you play music in the morning before you start your day?

Emotional

- On a scale of 1 to 5 (5 being "best") where would you rank your happiness level on most days?

- If you were to pick something you already do or want to learn that becomes your "flow" what would it be?

- Do you consider yourself more Optimistic or Pessimistic? Why?

- Pick 7 things that bring you joy – find time to practice at least one of these things every week

- On a scale of 1 to 5 (5 being "highest") how would you rank your resiliency and ability to face life's challenges?

- How many minutes a day do you spend on social media?

- What is your Emotional Vibrational Score after using social media for more than 15 minutes?
  _____ (Peace, Joy, Love, Enlightenment)
  _____ (Neutral, Courage, Pride, Acceptance)
  _____ (Anger, Fear, Grief, Gult, Apathy, Shame)

Social

o   Fill in your Social Convoy Model graph below:

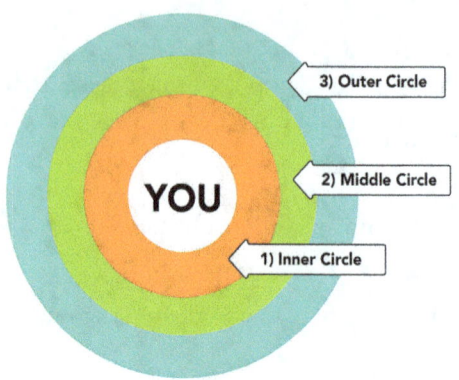

o   If there was an emergency (personal or disaster-related event) who is the one person you can call at 3am for help?

o   How long do you typically go without talking to someone (phone or face to face; not texting or on social media)?

o   How many times a week do you "play" (play with your kids or grandkids, play games with spouse, friends or pet)?

o   How many times a day do you laugh (on average)?

o   How many hugs do you get/give per day (on average)?

o   Do you feel you belong to a "tribe?"

Intellectual

- How many times a day/week do you practice brain exercises or focus on multisensory (5 senses) activity?

- Is there something new you have learned in the last year or started a new hobby such as playing pickle ball, cooking a new recipe, learning a new language or how to play a musical instrument? Did you learn it alone or with others?

- How many fiction novels have you read in the past year?

- Have you had a comprehensive eye exam in the last 12 months?

- How many minutes did you spend daydreaming over the last 7 days?

- Do you feel your job increases your well-being or decreases it?

- Do you have a "best friend" at work?

- Do you feel supported by work supervisors and colleagues about your caregiver responsibilities?

- Does your workplace have:
    _____Biophilic designed space?
    _____Faith-friendly culture?
    _____Caregiver support and education?

Environmental

- Does your home make you feel:
    - Happy and joyful? _____ Peaceful and safe? _____

- Can you gaze upon items that fill your heart with memories and joy?

- Are you proud to have people in your home?

- Do you have a sanctuary space (I call it "the snug")?

- Do you have biophilic elements in your home? Walk into each room in your home and see if you can identify some part of nature (greenery, wood, water, wind/air, fire) in the sensory design (sight, sound, smell, touch, taste)?

- How many green houseplants do you have?

- How many minutes do you spend weekly in nature (walks, hikes)?

- How many times a week do you gaze upon a body of water (river, lake, ocean, pool)?

- How many minutes daily do you do a digital detox (hygge, niksen)?

- When was the last time you hand-washed the dishes?

Financial

- How much money do you estimate you spend monthly/annually on your personal wellness or self-care activities or products?

- Is your home ready for you to live there forever or would you have to make adaptations to make it safe and accessible at age 80-90?

- Have you had the conversation with older loved ones about costs of caregiving, including assisted living, memory care, home care or home modifications? Do you know if you would need to contribute to help with costs of care? Do you have a long-term care plan?

- Since the pandemic, have you taken a wellcation (stayed at a resort, taken a road trip or engaged in virtual travel)?

- If you travel for business, do you take some time to spend on your wellness needs (massage or facial, soak in the tub, play golf, etc.)?

- How many months has it been since your last vacation?

- How many days were you on that vacation?

Spiritual

- Do you believe in a higher power than yourself?

- How many minutes a day do you spend in prayer or meditation?

- Do you practice daily gratitude?

- How often do you practice yoga, tai chi or other breathing-based, meditative activity?

- Do you listen to music when you eat? If so, what genre of music?

- Do you have a growth mindset or fixed mindset?

- Have you pruned your toxic or meaningless relationships?

- Do you know your family history/ancestry and the family stories?

- When was the last time you felt awe? What was it about?

- What is awesome about you?

- Fill in this statement:
  Before I die _____

Me Time Monday – Mapping Wellness

To give you examples of how to use the Me Time Monday (MTM) graphic as a guide to understanding your wellness needs, here is an example from my workshop.

Your Home Environment

Step 1: Create the plan. What do you want to specifically change or add based on the answers to your questions above?

Step 2: Take microflow baby steps. What is something you can do every week for 7-10 minutes to make these changes?

Step 3: Reward your successes or reset your schedule each week.

One Last Thing... Thank You

Thank you for taking this Me Time Monday wellness road trip with me. For everyone who is or has been a caregiver, I say "thank you" for all the gifts you gave and continue to give your loved ones. For those not yet caregivers, I hope these chapters helped you see how to not swerve off the wellness road when you take on those added responsibilities. And, if you are the friend, partner or employer of a caregiver, take note on how you can support the wellness plan for life's amazing caregivers.

When you think about your lifespan, most people see it as an arc where you begin by shooting up but then as healthspan declines and lifespan increases, you start a downward descent like a shooting star.

Instead, life is like shooting for the moon. You begin grounded to earth but eventually aspire to reach higher and find new frontiers. The human elements of hope and happiness drive you ever upwards. Once in orbit you become like the moon – a natural satellite that continues to stay aloft. Just as Magellan navigated the seas, Lindbergh navigated the skies and Armstrong navigated space, you are an explorer of what makes you joyful. Enjoy the ride.

P.S. If you want to continue to learn more and tap into my Me Time Monday Wellness Hacks – 52 Tips for Self-Care, check out the web site at: CaregivingClub.com and follow Me Time Monday on social media (I know it is re-engaging you in social media but only with positive messages about the balance between technology and nature in your life!).

acknowledgements

There are many people I need to thank connected to this book (and my life) but I start with my inner circle especially my Mom who not only gave me encouragement and listened to my agonizing over every detail and every word but she also read through various drafts making great notes and provided her excellent design guidance. I also have to thank my two besties, Molly Ballantine and Vicki Guttridge, who have been part of my social convoy inner circle since college and who also read through chapters to give me my target reader's perspective. A trusted mentor, colleague, friend and fellow author on longevity, Mary Furlong, has been a fan of Me Time Monday over the last decade and was a champion for this book from the beginning. And my brother, Tom, kept me from looking like a sports moron by ensuring I used correct terminology for the Tom Brady story.

I am grateful for the many experts and fascinating people I have had the privilege of interviewing through the years for my articles, podcasts and specifically those featured in this book: Marta Benson, Susan Black, Ken Deering, Dr. Annie Fenn, Rachel Francine, Kathryn Grube, Cindy Hounsell, Bonnie Kaplan, Lawrence Kosick, Liz Loewy, Henry Mahncke, Dani Klein Modisett, Tricia Norton, Steve Nygren, Rick Renner, Mark Schulz, Charles Spence, Art Toga, Andy Tubman, Sue Wadden and Jay Wei.

I also appreciate what I have learned from my excellent editors at PBS Next Avenue through the years including Julie Pfitzinger and Rich Eisenberg – you have helped make me a better writer. A special thank you to my agents at APB Speakers Bureau including Charles Spofford. And a big thank you to my team at Luckenbooth Press especially Una Fraser. Special thanks to my book jacket and internal book graphics designer, Joanna Ata of Liatto Design.

Other friends and colleagues who have provided much-appreciated support while I balanced my professional life while writing this book and have offered me many opportunities and sage advice in my career include: Brooks Kenny, Michelle Hudspeth, Merritt Meade Loughran, Laurie Mahoney, Mary Sutton, Kathy Aicher, Melina Montoya, Alex Witt, James Grant, Elliot Jacobson, Michael Carroll, Saudia Gajadhar, Nicole Hennessy, Cherry Dumaual, Peggy Neu, Ron Hernandez, Drew Holzapfel, Janet Beers, Alex Sherman, Lauren Peszt, Bill Coppel, Dr. Jessica Zitter, Jeannie Pierce, Alex Montgomery, Martin Ng, Louis Tenenbaum, Sherwin Sheik, Carrie Shaw, Beth Sanders, Dr. Leslie Saxon, Dr. Rohit Varma, Dr. Inderbir Gill, Dr. Mark Humayun, Dr. Berislav Zlokovic, Dr. Helena Chui, Dr. Steven Giannotta, Dr. Rosemary Laird, Myrna Blyth, Susan Donley, Toula Wooten, Debbie and Rocky Cifone, Dr. Pamela Saunders, MJ Contino. Also, a shoutout to my professors and friends at the USC Leonard Davis School of Gerontology including: Donna Benton, Maria Henke, Orli Berman, Jon Pynoos, Paul Nash and Andrei Irimia, my professors at MIT Sloan School of Management certification course on Shaping Jobs of the Future: Thomas Kochan, Elisabeth Reynolds and Barbara Dyer.

And finally, to the two loves in my life I cannot do without: Brent Parkhouse who always makes me laugh, who is generous and kind and wise and always "has my six" (he's also a great dog dad); and to Penny, my beloved furry companion, who during the writing of this book never left my side, licked my face, warmed my feet, encouraged me to take play breaks and nudged me with her nose to remind me when it was time to go to bed. You make my life joyful.

illustrations

Note: All images used with permission by copyright holders below.

Caregiver Wellness Journey

Section Image - Wellness Forest ©ImageKing/Dreamstime

Figure 1 - 6 generation family ©SWNS

Figure 2 - 7 generation family ©Michael O'Brien: www.obrienphotography.com

Figure 3 - Gen C continuum
Yoga icon: ©Veronika Ershakova / Dreamstime; Man with dog, son with older mom, couples:©Leremy/Dreamstime; Parents with baby, little boy: ©Microvone / Dreamstime; Older couple with hands: Takt818 / Dreamstime; Graphic with content: ©Caregiving Club, Inc.

Figure 4 - Wellness Timeline
©Dreamstime artists: Cavemen = ©Korkwellum; Ayurveda = ©Webtechops Llc; TCM = ©Denys Drozd; Hippocrates = ©Stas11; Roman Baths, Hannah Wooley, Dr. John Travis, National Wellness Institute - ©Kanate; Avicenna = ©Aleksandr Lysenko; Hydrotherapy = ©DreamstockIcons; Homeopathy = ©Raja Rc; Central Park = ©Aleksandr Mansurov; Edwin Babbitt = ©Serkorkin; Dr Monkey Gland = ©Elena Kozyreva; Dr Halbert Dunn - ©VectorMine; Capital Bldg, Workplace = ©Sergey Lavrentev;
Birren/USC, Flexner Report = ©Tuktukdesign; Jack LaLanne = ©Ihorzigor; Brain = ©Pavlo; Goop = ©Malachianastasia; Apple = ©Skarin92

Me Time Monday

Section Image - MTM Clock/Colors
Clock: ©Photobeps / Dreamstime; Beach: ©Anatoly Tiplyashin / Dreamstime; Beach Lettering: ©Sultan Malçok / Dreamstime; Color Wheel: ©Caregiving Club, Inc.

Figure 5 - BPS Balance graphic
Yoga post icon: ©Veronika Ershakova / Dreamstime; ©Caregiving Club, Inc.

Figure 6 - Old Brain, New Brain
Brain Image: ©Mkkans/Dreamstime; Graphic with content: © Caregiving Club, Inc.

Figure 7 - In utero facial expressions
©FETAP (Fetal Taste Preferences) Study, Fetal and Neonatal ResearchLab, N Reissland Durham University: Laughter-face reaction scan image.jpg – A 4D scan image of the same

fetus showing a laughter-face reaction afterbeing exposed to the carrot flavour. Cry-face reaction scan image.jpg– A 4D scan image of the same fetus showing a cry-face reaction after beingexposed to the kale flavour.

Figure 8 - Telomeres   ©Caregiving Club, Inc. (Adapted from E Blackburn, 2005).

Figure 9 - Blue/Black, White/Gold Dress   ©Roman Designs

Figure 10 - Maslow's Pyramid   ©Caregiving Club, Inc. (Adapted from A. Maslow, 1943)

Physical Wellness
Section Image - Hannah Wooley
©Wellcome Images, a website operated by Wellcome Trust, a global charitable foundation based in the U.K.
Figure 11 - Sleep Cycles   ©Vaeenma / Dreamstime
Compilation - Rainbow Diet
Carrot, Broccoli, Grapes icons: ©Skarin92 / Dreamstime; Tomato, Avocado icons: ©Amornism / Dreamstime; Graphic with content: ©Caregiving Club, Inc.
Compilation - Sunshine Diet
Sunshine icon: ©Skarin92 / Dreamstime; Graphic with content: ©Caregiving Club, Inc.

Emotional Wellness
Section Image - Sully Miracle on the Hudson
©Brendan McDermid/Reuters; Sully inset: ©Bladerunner 88 / Dreamstime
Figure 12 - Flow & Ballerina Ferri
Ferri image: ©Leslie Spatt / ArenaPAL; Flow graph: ©Caregiving Club, Inc. (Adapted from M. Csikszentmihalyi, 1990)
Figure 13 - Happiness U-Curve
Adapted from: Stone, A. A., Schwartz, J. E., Broderick, J. E., & Deaton, A. (2010). A snapshot of the age distribution of psychological well-being in the United States. *Proceedings of the National Academy of sciences, 107*(22), 9985-9990

Figure 14 - 6 emotions   ©CurrentCrescent/Dreamstime.com; (Adapted from P. Eckman, 2003)

Figure 15 - Vibrational Frequency   ©Spideyspike32/Dreamstime

Figure 16 - 4 Hormones   ©CurrantCrescent / Dreamstime

Figure 17 - OCEAN Personality Chart   ©Caregiving Club, Inc. (adapted from Costa &McCrae, 1980)

Social Wellness
Section Image - Skeletons   ©Dagmar Hollmann / Wikimedia Commons https://commons.wikimedia.org/wiki/File:Mantua2.jpg
Figure 18 - Social Convoy
©*Convoy Model and Aging Families* Figure 2. The Hierarchical Mapping Technique (Adapted from T. Antonucci, 1986)

Intellectual Wellness

Section Image - Tom Brady ©Sports Images / Dreamstime

Figure 19 - 5 Senses in Brain ©Nikolay Plotnikov, Serkorkin/ Dreamstime Graphic with content: ©Caregiving Club, Inc.

Environmental Wellness

Section Image - Central Park ©Melpomenem/Dreamstime

Figure 20 - Harper's Bazaar/Six Senses

Harper's Bazaar ©Yates Collection of Saratogiana, Skidmore College; Six Senses Wellness Club – ©Six Senses

Figure 21 – Rainbow Eye ©Philip Steury / Dreamstime

Colors - ROYGBIV Colors ©Caregiving Club, Inc.

Financial Wellness

Section Image - Jeanne Calment ©Wikicommons

Spiritual Wellness

Section Image - Red Cardinal ©Gerald Marella / Dreamstime

Figure 22 - PTG Graph ©Caregiving Club, Inc. (Adapted from: Tedeschi, R. G., & Calhoun, L. G., 1996)

Me Time Monday for a Wonderful Life

Section Image - Life is Wonderful Beach ©Anyaberkut / Dreamstime

MTM - Home Environment Map ©Caregiving Club, Inc.

notes

Caregiver Wellness Journey

Chapter 2 - Caregiving Redefined

BBC News (June 16, 2021). Woman overjoyed at birth of great-great-great-grandchild in Edinburgh.

Czeisler, M. É., Drane, A., Winnay, S.S., Capodilupo, E.R., Czeisler, C.A., Rajaratnam, S.M.W., Howard, M.E. (2021). Mental health, substance use, and suicidal ideation among unpaid caregivers of adults in the United States during the COVID-19 pandemic: Relationships to age, race/ethnicity, employment, and caregiver intensity. *Journal of Affective Disorders, Volume 295*, Pages 1259-1268, ISSN 0165-0327

Embracing Carers (2020). *The global carer well-being index: who cares for the carers? Perspectives on COVID-19 pressures and lack of support.* EMD Serono, Rockland, MD.

Finch, C. E., & Pike, M. C. (1996). Maximum life span predictions from the Gompertz mortality model. *The Journals of Gerontology Series A: Biological Sciences and Medical Sciences, 51*(3), B183-B194.

Fuller, J. B., & Raman, M. (2019). The caring company. *Harvard Business School, 17.*

Shen, L. (October 14, 2021). Today's youth have a 50% chance of living to age 104. What does that mean for the economy? *Fortune.* New York, New York.

Stepler, R. (April 21, 2016). *World's centenarian population projected to grow eightfold by 2050.* United Nations charts in Pew Research report.

Vitaliano, P. P., Zhang, J., & Scanlan, J. M. (2003). Is caregiving hazardous to one's physical health? A meta-analysis. *Psychological bulletin, 129*(6), 946.

Vespa, J., Medina, L., Armstrong, D.M. (2020). *Demographic turning points for the United States: population projections for 2020 to 2060.* Current Population Reports, P25-1144, U.S. Census Bureau. Washington, D.C.

Chapter 3 - Wellness Hijacked

Blei, D. (January 4, 2017). The false promises of wellness culture. *JSTOR Daily.*

Garcia-Rada, X., Steffel, M., Williams, E., Norton, M. (September 28, 2021). The paradox of marketing to caregivers. *Harvard Business Review.*

Hamilton, D. (1986). *The monkey gland affair.* Chatto & Windus.

Mahdawi, Arwa, (January 18, 2020). Gwyneth Paltrow has capitalized on vaginal shame and celebration. *The Guardian.*

Me Time Monday

U.S. Surgeon General's Office (May, 2023) *Our Epidemic of Loneliness and Isolation: The U.S. Surgeon General's Advisory on the Healing Effects of Social Connection and Community.* Washington, DC.

Chapter 5 - Nature/Neuroscience

Accius, J., & Suh, J. Y. (2019). *The longevity economy outlook: How people ages 50 and older are fueling economic growth, stimulating jobs, and creating opportunities for all.* AARP Thought Leadership.

Al'Absi, M., Nakajima, M., Hooker, S., Wittmers, L., & Cragin, T. (2012). Exposure to acute stress is associated with attenuated sweet taste. *Psychophysiology, 49*(1), 96–103.

Al-Shamahi, E., Chambers, R., Dodd, I. & Jayanti, H. (2018) *Neanderthals: Meet Your Ancestors* [documentary film]. United Kingdom. BBC.

Arain, M., Haque, M., Johal, L., Mathur, P., Nel, W., Rais, A., Sandhu, R., & Sharma, S. (2013). Maturation of the adolescent brain. *Neuropsychiatric disease and treatment, 9*, 449–461. https://doi.org/10.2147/NDT.S39770

Emerson, R. W. (1940). *Nature (1836)*. K. W. Cameron (Ed.). Scholars' facsimiles & reprints.

Falk, J. H., & Balling, J. D. (2010). Evolutionary influence on human landscape preference. *Environment and behavior, 42*(4), 479-493.

Goyal, M. S., Blazey, T. M., Su, Y., Couture, L. E., Durbin, T. J., Bateman, R. J., ... & Vlassenko, A. G. (2019). Persistent metabolic youth in the aging female brain. *Proceedings of the National Academy of Sciences, 116*(8), 3251-3255.

Harvey, B. M., Klein, B. P., Petridou, N., & Dumoulin, S. O. (2013). Topographic representation of numerosity in the human Parietal cortex. *Science, 341*(6150), 1123-1126.

Jaffe. E. (March 20, 2014). The fascinating neuroscience of color. *Fast Company*.

Ratcheva, V., Leopold, T. A., & Zahidi, S. (2020, February). Jobs of tomorrow: mapping opportunity in the new economy. *In World Economic Forum, Geneva, Switzerland.*

Raghanti, M. A., Edler, M. K., Stephenson, A. R., Munger, E. L., Jacobs, B., Hof, P. R., ... & Lovejoy, C. O. (2018). A neurochemical hypothesis for the origin of hominids. *Proceedings of the National Academy of Sciences, 115*(6), E1108-E1116.

Raichle, M. E. (2006). The brain's dark energy. *Science, 314*(5803), 1249-1250.

Ustun, B., Reissland, N., Covey, J., Schaal, B., & Blissett, J. (2022). Flavor sensing in utero and emerging discriminative behaviors in the human fetus. *Psychological Science, 33*(10), 1651-1663.

Vitaliano, P. P., Zhang, J., & Scanlan, J. M. (2003). Is caregiving hazardous to one's physical health? A meta-analysis. *Psychological bulletin, 129*(6), 946.

Wilson, E. O. (1984). Biophilia. In *Biophilia*. Harvard University Press.

Chapter 6 - Wellness in the Womb

Roseboom, T. J., Painter, R. C., van Abeelen, A. F., Veenendaal, M. V., & de Rooij, S. R. (2011). Hungry in the womb: What are the consequences? Lessons from the Dutch famine. *Maturitas, 70*(2), 141-145.

Watson, K. T., Simard, J. F., Henderson, V. W., Nutkiewicz, L., Lamers, F., Nasca, C., ... & Penninx, B. W. (2021). Incident major depressive disorder predicted by three measures of insulin resistance: a Dutch cohort study. *American Journal of Psychiatry, 178*(10), 914-920.

Chapter 7 - Stress Effect

Adelman, R. D., Tmanova, L. L., Delgado, D., Dion, S., & Lachs, M. S. (2014). Caregiver burden: A clinical review. *JAMA, 311*(10), 1052-1060.

Blackburn, E. H. (2005). Telomeres and telomerase: Their mechanisms of action and the effects of altering their functions. *FEBS letters, 579*(4), 859-862.

Cannon, W. B. (1932). *The wisdom of the body.* W.W. Norton & Company, New York.

Echouffo-Tcheugui, J. B., Conner, S. C., Himali, J. J., Maillard, P., DeCarli, C. S., Beiser, A. S., ... & Seshadri, S. (2018). Circulating cortisol and cognitive and structural brain measures: The Framingham Heart Study. *Neurology, 91*(21), e1961-e1970.

Guidi, J., Lucente, M., Sonino, N., & Fava, G. A. (2021). Allostatic load and its impact on health: A systematic review. *Psychotherapy and psychosomatics, 90*(1), 11–27.

Nagoski, E., & Nagoski, A. (2020). *Burnout: the secret to unlocking the stress cycle.* Ballantine Books.

Sapolsky, R. M. (2004). *Why zebras don't get ulcers: The acclaimed guide to stress, stress-related diseases, and coping.* Holt paperbacks.

Swensen, S., Strongwater, S., & Mohta, N. S. (2018). Leadership survey: immunization against burnout. *NEJM Catalyst, 4*(2).

Taylor, S. E., Klein, L. C., Lewis, B. P., Gruenewald, T. L., Gurung, R. A., & Updegraff, J. A. (2000). Biobehavioral responses to stress in females: tend-and-befriend, not fight-or-flight. *Psychological review, 107*(3), 411.

Wong, A. (June 9, 2022). "Pandemic babies are behind after years of stress, isolation affected brain development." USA Today.

7 Elements of Wellness
Chapter 8 – MeTime Monday Program

Anderson, J.C. (May 15, 2012). Maya Angelou opens women's health And wellness center, calls disparities "embarrassing." *HuffPost.*

Ayers, J.W., Althouse, B.M., Johnson, M.J., Cohen, J.E. (2014). What's the Healthiest Day? Circaseptan (weekly) Rhythms in Healthy Considerations. *American Journal of Preventive Medicine, 47,* 73-76.

Brooks, A. (July 2, 2014). *A formula for happiness.* Aspen Ideas Conference. The Aspen Institute.

Clifton, J. (2022). *Blind Spot: The Global Rise of Unhappiness and How Leaders Missed it.* Gallup Press.

Cole, J. (July, 2020). *The coronavirus disruption project: How we are living and coping during the pandemic.* The Center for the Digital Future at USC Annenberg.

Dai, H., Milkman, K.L., & Riis, J. (2013). The fresh start effect: Temporal landmarks motivate aspirational behavior. *Management Science, 60,* 1-20.

Duncan, R.D. (September 6, 2022). What 'happiness' really means to your Life, work and wellbeing. *Forbes.*

Dunn, H. L. (1961). *High level wellness: A collection of twenty-nine short talks on different aspects of the theme 'high level wellness for man and society.'* Charles B. Slack.

Fry, J., & Neff, R. (2010). Healthy monday: Two literature reviews. *Johns Hopkins School of Public Health: Baltimore, MD, USA.*

Gervais, Z. (January 28, 2020). The average American abandons their New Year's resolution by this date. *New York Post.*

Gilbert, D. (2009). *Stumbling on happiness.* Vintage Canada.

Heitmann, B. (September 28, 2018). Your guide to winning @work: decoding the Sunday scaries. LinkedIn official blog. LinkedIn and Harris Poll.

Hwang, H. L., Tu, C. T., & Chan, H. S. (2019). Self-transcendence, caring and their associations with well-being. *Journal of advanced nursing, 75*(7), 1473–1483. https://doi.org/10.1111/jan.13937

Miller, G. A. (1956). The magical number seven, plus or minus two: Some limits on our capacity for processing information. *Psychological review, 63*(2), 81.

Jonauskaite, D., Abu-Akel, A., Dael, N., Oberfeld, D., Abdel-Khalek, A. M., Al-Rasheed, A. S., ... & Mohr, C. (2020). Universal patterns in color-emotion associations are further shaped by linguistic and geographic proximity. *Psychological Science, 31*(10), 1245-1260.

Jabr, F. (March 20, 2013). Let's get physical: The psychology of effective workout music, *Scientific American.*

Koltko-Rivera, M. E. (2006). Rediscovering the later version of Maslow's hierarchy of needs: Self- transcendence and opportunities for theory, research, and unification. *Review of general psychology, 10*(4), 302-317.

Lally, P., & Gardner, B. (2013). Promoting habit formation. *Health psychology review, 7*(sup1), S137- S158.

Mann, T. (1927). *The magic mountain.* Alfred A. Knopf.

Maslow, A. H. (1943). A theory of human motivation. *Psychological review,* 50(4), 370.

Maslow, A. H. (1967). A theory of metamotivation: The biological rooting of the value-life. *Journal of humanistic psychology, 7*(2), 93-127.

Miller, G. A. (1956). The magical number seven, plus or minus two: Some limits on our capacity for processing information. *Psychological review, 63*(2), 81.

Morris, D. (1994). *The naked ape: A zoologist's study of the human animal.* Random House.

Norcross, J. C., & Vangarelli, D. J. (1988). The resolution solution: longitudinal examination of New Year's change attempts. *Journal of Substance Abuse, 1*(2), 127–134.

Orsama, A., Mattila, E., Ermes, M., van Gils, M., Wansink, B., & Korhonen, I. (2014). Weight rhythms: Weight increases during weekends and decreases during weekdays. *Obesity Facts, 7,* 36-47.

Peralta, A. (February, 2023). *Wellness+senses: Multisensory integration.* Global Wellness Trends Report 2023. Global Wellness Institute, Miami, FL.

Puig, M. V., Rose, J., Schmidt, R., & Freund, N. (2014). Dopamine modulation of learning and memory in the prefrontal cortex: insights from studies in primates, rodents, and birds. *Frontiers in neural circuits, 8,* 93.

Reed, P. G., & Haugan, G. (2021). Self-Transcendence: A Salutogenic Process for Well-Being. In *Health Promotion in Health Care–Vital Theories and Research* (pp. 103-115). Springer, Cham.

Researchgate, (November, 2020). *Staying at home: How well did Americans maintain their health behaviors?* Researchgate for Healthy Monday Campaigns.

Saunders, B. T., Richard, J. M., Margolis, E. B., & Janak, P. H. (2018). Dopamine neurons create Pavlovian conditioned stimuli with circuit-defined motivational properties. *Nature neuroscience, 21*(8), 1072–1083. https://doi.org/10.1038/s41593-018-0191-4

Schmitz, T. W., De Rosa, E., & Anderson, A. K. (2009). Opposing influences of affective state valence on visual cortical encoding. *Journal of Neuroscience, 29*(22), 7199-7207.

Snelling, S. (2013). *A cast of caregivers: celebrity stories to help you prepare to care.* 461-466. Balboa Press.

Stephenson, N. (1992). *Snow crash.* Bantam Books.

Stone, A. A., Schneider, S., & Harter, J. K. (2012). Day-of-week mood patterns in the United States:

On the existence of 'Blue Monday','Thank God it's Friday'and weekend effects. *The Journal of Positive Psychology, 7*(4), 306-314.

Toffler, A. (1970). *Future shock*. Bantam.

Toups, K., et. al., (July, 2022). Precision medicine approach to Alzheimer's disease: successful pilot project. *Journal of Alzheimer's Disease 1*(2022-1-11).

Unpublished data gathered from New York-based gyms and the Johns Hopkins recreation center (2013).

Wallisch, P. (April 12, 2017). Two years later, we finally know why people saw "the dress" differently. *Slate*.

Witzel, C., Racey, C., & O'Regan, J. K. (2017). The most reasonable explanation of "the dress": Implicit assumptions about illumination. *Journal of Vision, 17*(2), 1-1.

World Health Organization (WHO), (March 2, 2022). [Press release] "COVID-19 pandemic triggers 25% increase in prevalence of anxiety and depression worldwide."

Yin, H. H., & Knowlton, B. J. (2006). The role of the basal ganglia in habit formation. *Nature Reviews Neuroscience, 7*(6), 464-476.

Zhu, C. W., Scarmeas, N., Ornstein, K., Albert, M., Brandt, J., Blacker, D., ... & Stern, Y. (2015). Health-care use and cost in dementia caregivers: Longitudinal results from the Predictors Caregiver Study. *Alzheimer's & Dementia, 11*(4), 444-454.

Physical

Campbell, O. (March 1, 2021). Part of being a domestic goddess in 17th century Europe was making medicines. *Smithsonian Magazine*.

Chapter 9 - Sleep

Blume, C., Garbazza, C., & Spitschan, M. (2019). Effects of light on human circadian rhythms, sleep and mood. *Somnologie : Schlafforschung und Schlafmedizin = Somnology : sleep research and sleep medicine, 23*(3), 147–156. https://doi.org/10.1007/s11818-019-00215-x

Centers for Disease Control and Prevention. (2022). Sleep health.

Chang, A. M., Aeschbach, D., Duffy, J. F., & Czeisler, C. A. (2015). Evening use of light-emitting eReaders negatively affects sleep, circadian timing, and next-morning alertness. *Proceedings of the National Academy of Sciences, 112*(4), 1232-1237.

Christensen, M. A., Bettencourt, L., Kaye, L., Moturu, S. T., Nguyen, K. T., Olgin, J. E., ... & Marcus,

G. M. (2016). Direct measurements of smartphone screen-time: relationships with demographics and sleep. *PloS one, 11*(11), e0165331.

Hale, L., Troxel, W., & Buysse, D. J. (2020). Sleep Health: An Opportunity for Public Health to Address Health Equity. *Annual review of public health, 41*, 81–99. https://doi.org/10.1146/annurev-publhealth-040119-094412

Office of National Statistics, (August, 2020). *Internet access: households and individuals*. 2020 Dataset Edition. United Kingdom.

Ong, J. L., Lo, J. C., Chee, N. I., Santostasi, G., Paller, K. A., Zee, P. C., & Chee, M. W. (2016). Effects of phase-locked acoustic stimulation during a nap on EEG spectra and declarative memory consolidation. *Sleep Medicine, 20*, 88-97.

Pagel, J. F. (2010). Drugs, dreams, and nightmares. *Sleep Medicine Clinics, 5*(2), 277-287.

Papalambros, N. A., Santostasi, G., Malkani, R. G., Braun, R., Weintraub, S., Paller, K. A., & Zee, P. C. (2017). Acoustic enhancement of sleep slow oscillations and concomitant memory improvement in older adults. *Frontiers in human neuroscience*, 109.

Precedence Research (July, 2022). Report on the Global Sleep Aids Market.

Robillard, R., Dion, K., Pennestri, M. H., Solomonova, E., Lee, E., Saad, M., ... & Kendzerska, T. (2021). Profiles of sleep changes during the COVID-19 pandemic: Demographic, behavioural and psychological factors. *Journal of sleep research, 30*(1), e13231.

Sharma, R. A., Varga, A. W., Bubu, O. M., Pirraglia, E., Kam, K., Parekh, A., ... & Osorio, R. S. (2018). Obstructive sleep apnea severity affects amyloid burden in cognitively normal elderly. A longitudinal study. *American journal of respiratory and critical care medicine, 197*(7), 933-943.

Skeldon, A. C., Phillips, A. J., & Dijk, D. J. (2017). The effects of self-selected light-dark cycles and social constraints on human sleep and circadian timing: a modeling approach. *Scientific reports, 7*(1), 1-14.

Uchino, B. N., Cribbet, M., de Grey, R. G. K., Cronan, S., Trettevik, R., & Smith, T. W. (2017). Dispositional optimism and sleep quality: A test of mediating pathways. *Journal of Behavioral Medicine, 40*(2), 360-365.

Walker, M. (2017). *Why we sleep: Unlocking the power of sleep and dreams.* Simon and Schuster.

Williamson, A. M., & Feyer, A. M. (2000). Moderate sleep deprivation produces impairments in cognitive and motor performance equivalent to legally prescribed levels of alcohol intoxication. *Occupational and environmental medicine, 57*(10), 649-655.

Zitting, K. M., Vujovic, N., Yuan, R. K., Isherwood, C. M., Medina, J. E., Wang, W., ... & Duffy, J. F. (2018). Human resting energy expenditure varies with circadian phase. *Current Biology, 28*(22), 3685-3690.

Chapter 10 - Diet and Nutrition

Agarwal, P., Leurgans, S. E., Agrawal, S., Aggarwal, N., James, B. D., Dhana, K., ... & Schneider, J.

A. (2023). Association of Mediterranean-DASH Intervention for Neurodegenerative Delay and Mediterranean Diets With Alzheimer Disease Pathology. *Neurology.*

Aubrey, A. (December 31, 2011) "The average American ate (literally) a ton this year." National Public Radio.

Bosch, J. A., Nieuwdorp, M., Zwinderman, A. H., Deschasaux, M., Radjabzadeh, D., Kraaij, R., ... & Lok, A. (2022). The gut microbiota and depressive symptoms across ethnic groups. *Nature Communications, 13*(1), 1-14.

Boles, D. Z., DeSousa, M., Turnwald, B. P., Horii, R. I., Duarte, T., Zahrt, O. H., ... & Crum, A. J. (2021). Can exercising and eating healthy be fun and indulgent instead of boring and depriving? Targeting mindsets about the process of engaging in healthy behaviors. *Frontiers in psychology, 4262.*

Colten H.R., Altevogt, B.M., (2006). *Sleep disorders and sleep deprivation: An unmet public health problem.* Institute of Medicine (U.S.), Committee on Sleep Medicine and Research, Washington, DC.: National Academies Press 2, Sleep Physiology. Available from: https://www.ncbi.nlm.nih.gov/books/NBK19956/

Du, H., Li, L., Bennett, D., Guo, Y., Turnbull, I., Yang, L., ... & China Kadoorie Biobank study. (2017). Fresh fruit consumption in relation to incident diabetes and diabetic vascular complications: a 7-y prospective study of 0.5 million Chinese adults. *PLoS medicine, 14*(4), e1002279.

Durack, J., & Lynch, S. V. (2019). The gut microbiome: relationships with disease and opportunities for therapy. *Journal of Experimental Medicine, 216*(1), 20-40.

Fairfield, H. (April 3, 2010). Factory food. *New York Times.*

Fenn, Annie (October 2022). *The brain health kitchen cookbook*. Workman Publishing, Inc., New York, NY.

Fernandez M. L. (2006). Dietary cholesterol provided by eggs and plasma lipoproteins in healthy populations. *Current opinion in clinical nutrition and metabolic care, 9*(1), 8–12. https://doi.org/10.1097/01.mco.0000171152.51034.bf

Ferrières J. (2004). The French paradox: lessons for other countries. *Heart (British Cardiac Society), 90*(1), 107–111. https://doi.org/10.1136/heart.90.1.107

Gholami, N., Hosseini Sabzvari, B., Razzaghi, A., & Salah, S. (2017). Effect of stress, anxiety and depression on unstimulated salivary flow rate and xerostomia. *Journal of dental research, dental clinics, dental prospects, 11*(4), 247–252. https://doi.org/10.15171/joddd.2017.043

Guiliano, M. (December 26, 2007). *French women don't get fat: The secret of eating for pleasure*

Han, B. H., Brennan, J. J., Orozco, M. A., Moore, A. A., & Castillo, E. M. (2023). Trends in emergency department visits associated with cannabis use among older adults in California, 2005–2019. *Journal of the American Geriatrics Society.first.* Vintage. New York, NY.

Kaplan, B., Rucklidge, J. (April 20, 2021). *The better brain: Overcome anxiety, combat depression, and reduce ADHD and stress with nutrition*. Harvest. Boston, Mass.

Kaplan, B. J., Rucklidge, J. J., Romijn, A., & McLeod, K. (2015). The emerging field of nutritional mental health: Inflammation, the microbiome, oxidative stress, and mitochondrial function. *Clinical Psychological Science, 3*(6), 964-980.

Li, P., Gao, L., Yu, L., Zheng, X., Ulsa, M. C., Yang, H. W., ... & Leng, Y. (2023). Daytime napping and Alzheimer's dementia: A potential bidirectional relationship. *Alzheimer's & Dementia, 19*(1), 158-168.

Machado, V., Botelho, J., Escalda, C., Hussain, S. B., Luthra, S., Mascarenhas, P., ... & D'Aiuto, F. (2021). Serum C-reactive protein and periodontitis: a systematic review and meta-analysis. *Frontiers in immunology*, 3054.

Mahdi G. S. (2006). The Atkin's diet controversy. *Annals of Saudi medicine, 26*(3), 244–245. https://doi.org/10.5144/0256-4947.2006.244

Martineau, A. R., Jolliffe, D. A., Hooper, R. L., Greenberg, L., Aloia, J. F., Bergman, P., ... & Camargo, C. A. (2017). Vitamin D supplementation to prevent acute respiratory tract infections: systematic review and meta-analysis of individual participant data. *BMJ, 356*.

Radjabzadeh, D., Bosch, J. A., Uitterlinden, A. G., Zwinderman, A. H., Ikram, M. A., van Meurs, J. B., ... & Amin, N. (2022). Gut microbiome-wide association study of depressive symptoms. *Nature Communications, 13*(1), 1-10.

Schlosser, E. (January 31, 2002). *Americans are obsessed with fast food: The dark side of the all-American meal*. CBS News.

Scott, C., & Johnstone, A. M. (2012). Stress and eating behaviour: implications for obesity. *Obesity facts, 5*(2), 277–287. https://doi.org/10.1159/000338340

Snelling, S. (Host). (March 3, 2022). *Brain food, books & creating cozy reading nooks*, Season 2, Episode 4 - interview with Bonnie Kaplan, "Caregiving Club On Air," [podcast]. Caregiving Club and Resonate Recordings.

Snelling, S. (Host). (March 20, 2023). *National Nutrition Month with Brain Health Kitchen author, Happiness Day & Reading Nooks for Niksen Breaks*, Season 3, Episode 23 - interview with Dr. Annie Fenn, "Caregiving Club On Air," [podcast]. Caregiving Club and Resonate Recordings.

Sukkar, S. G., & Muscaritoli, M. (2021). A clinical perspective of low carbohydrate ketogenic diets: A narrative review. *Frontiers in Nutrition, 8.*

Wheeler, S. (July 1, 2018). 42% of Americans are vitamin D deficient. Are you among them? Cleveland Clinic News online

Zhang, B., Wang, H. E., Bai, Y. M., Tsai, S. J., Su, T. P., Chen, T. J., Wang, Y. P., & Chen, M. H. (2022). Bidirectional association between inflammatory bowel disease and depression among patients and their unaffected siblings. *Journal of gastroenterology and hepatology, 37*(7), 1307–1315. https://doi.org/10.1111/jgh.15855

Chapter 11 - Nature's Cleanse

Dmitrieva, N. I., Gagarin, A., Liu, D., Wu, C. O., & Boehm, M. (2023). Middle-age high normal serum sodium as a risk factor for accelerated biological aging, chronic diseases, and premature mortality. *EBioMedicine*, 104404.

Chapter 12 - Matthew Effect

Baker, L. D., Frank, L. L., Foster-Schubert, K., Green, P. S., Wilkinson, C. W., McTiernan, A., ... & Craft, S. (2010). Aerobic exercise improves cognition for older adults with glucose intolerance, a risk factor for Alzheimer's disease. *Journal of Alzheimer's Disease, 22*(2), 569-579.

Bask, M., & Bask, M. (2015). Cumulative (dis) advantage and the Matthew effect in life-course analysis. *PloS one, 10*(11), e0142447.

Boere, K., Lloyd, K., Binsted, G., & Krigolson, O. E. (2023). Exercising is good for the brain but exercising outside is potentially better. *Scientific Reports, 13*(1), 1140.

Broadhouse, K. M., Suo, C., Singh, M. A. F., Gates, N., Wen, W., Sachdev, P., ... & Valenzuela, M. J. (2017). What happens to the hippocampus 12-months after training? Longitudinal linear mixed effects model analysis of mild cognitive impairment in the smart trial. *Alzheimers Dement J Alzheimers Assoc, 13*(7), P260.

Carson, R. (2009). *Silent spring.* 1962.

Collyer, T. A., Murray, A. M., Woods, R. L., Storey, E., Chong, T. T. J., Ryan, J., ... & Callisaya, M. L. (2022). Association of Dual Decline in Cognition and Gait Speed With Risk of Dementia in Older Adults. *JAMA Network Open, 5*(5), e2214647-e2214647.

Dannefer, D. (1987, March). Aging as intracohort differentiation: Accentuation, the Matthew effect, and the life course. In *Sociological forum* (Vol. 2, No. 2, pp. 211-236). Kluwer Academic Publishers.

Ferraro, K. F., Shippee, T. P., & Schafer, M. H. (2009). Cumulative inequality theory for research on aging and the life course. In V. L. Bengston, D. Gans, N. M. Pulney, & M. Silverstein (Eds.), *Handbook of theories of aging* (pp. 413–433). Springer Publishing Company.

Joseph K. S. (1989). The Matthew effect in health development. *BMJ* (Clinical research ed.), 298(6686), 1497–1498. https://doi.org/10.1136/bmj.298.6686.1497

Kandola, A., Hendrikse, J., Lucassen, P. J., & Yücel, M. (2016). Aerobic exercise as a tool to improve hippocampal plasticity and function in humans: practical implications for mental health treatment. *Frontiers in Human Neuroscience, 10*, 373.

Kerr, J., Sallis, J. F., Saelens, B. E., Cain, K. L., Conway, T. L., Frank, L. D., & King, A. C. (2012). Outdoor physical activity and self rated health in older adults living in two regions of the U.S. *The international journal of behavioral nutrition and physical activity, 9*, 89. https://doi.org/10.1186/1479-5868-9-89

Luther, C. (2011). Jack LaLanne dies at 96; spiritual father of U.S. fitness movement. *Los Angeles Times.*

Müller, J. P. (1912). *My system: 15 minutes' work a day for health's sake.* Ewart, Seymour.

Pinterest (2023). *Pinterest predicts primal movement.* Pinterest global search data analysis period Sep. 2020 to Sep. 2022; Sparkler and Pinterest qualitative community analysis in BR, JP, UK and the US, Sep 2022.

Saint-Maurice, P. F., Graubard, B. I., Troiano, R. P., Berrigan, D., Galuska, D. A., Fulton, J. E., & Matthews, C. E. (2022). Estimated number of deaths prevented through increased physical activity among US adults. *JAMA internal medicine, 182*(3), 349-352.

Yarborough, S., Fitzpatrick, A., & Schwartz, S. M. (2022). Evaluation of cognitive function in the Dog Aging Project: associations with baseline canine characteristics. *Scientific reports, 12*(1), 1-11.

Yoshida, R., Sato, S., Kasahara, K., Murakami, Y., Murakoshi, F., Aizawa, K., ... & Nakamura, M. (2022). Greater effects by performing a small number of eccentric contractions daily than a larger number of them once a week. *Scandinavian Journal of Medicine & Science in Sports.*

Emotional

Couric, K. (February 8, 2009). "60 Minutes: Saving flight 1549." CBS News, New York

Sullenberger, C., Zaslow, J. (2009). *Highest duty: My search for what really matters.* William Morrow & Company.

Chapter 13 - Flow

Csikszentmihalyi, M. (1990). Flow: *The psychology of optimal experience.* Harper & Row.

Hunt, M. G., Marx, R., Lipson, C., & Young, J. (2018). No more FOMO: Limiting social media decreases loneliness and depression. *Journal of Social and Clinical Psychology, 37*(10), 751-768.

Chapter 14 - Happiness

Bartels, M., Ragnhild, B.N., Armitage, J., van de Weijer, M., Vries, L., Haworth, C. (March 18, 2022). *Exploring the biological basis for happiness.* Chapter 5, World Happiness Report 2022. Sustainable Development Solutions Network and Gallup World Poll data.

Blanchflower, D. G. (2021). Is happiness U-shaped everywhere? Age and subjective well-being in 145 countries. *Journal of Population Economics, 34*(2), 575-624.

Brooks, A. (July 2, 2014). "The formula for happiness." Presentation at Aspen Ideas Festival, Aspen Institute, Washington, D.C.

The Economist, (December 16, 2010). *The U-bend of life: Why, beyond middle age, people get happier as they get older.*

Gallup, (2022). Gallup *Global Emotions Report.* Gallup, Washington, D.C.

Lyubomirsky, S. (2011). Psychology: holding on to happiness. *Nature, 471*(7338), 302-303.

Lyubomirsky, S., Sheldon, K. M., & Schkade, D. (2005). Pursuing happiness: The architecture of sustainable change. *Review of general psychology, 9*(2), 111-131.

Proto, E., Oswald, A., (2020). *National happiness and genetic distance: A cautious exploration 2015-2020.* Colchester, Essex: UK Data Service. 10.5255/UKDA-SN-854125

Seligman, M. E. (2012). *Flourish: A visionary new understanding of happiness and well-being.* Simon and Schuster.

Snelling, S. (February 13, 2018). 5 ways to find happiness as a family caregiver. *PBS Next Avenue.*

Stone, A. A., Schwartz, J. E., Broderick, J. E., & Deaton, A. (2010). A snapshot of the age distribution of psychological well-being in the United States. *Proceedings of the National Academy of sciences, 107*(22), 9985-9990

Chapter 15 - Vibrations

Cowen, A. S., & Keltner, D. (2017). Self-report captures 27 distinct categories of emotion bridged by continuous gradients. *Proceedings of the National Academy of Sciences, 114*(38), E7900-E7909

Eckman, P. (2003). *Emotions revealed: Understanding faces and feelings.* Orion Publishing Company.

Ivanov, P. C., Ma, Q. D., & Bartsch, R. P. (2009). Maternal–fetal heartbeat phase synchronization. *Proceedings of the National Academy of Sciences, 106*(33), 13641-13642.

Keyes, C. L., Dhingra, S. S., & Simoes, E. J. (2010). Change in level of positive mental health as a predictor of future risk of mental illness. *American journal of public health, 100*(12), 2366-2371.

Kirkpatrick, T. (May 10, 2022). *Mental health app installs decline more than 30% since January 2021.* Apptopia.com

Liu, T. (2018). The scientific hypothesis of an "energy system" in the human body. *Journal of Traditional Chinese Medical Sciences, 5*(1), 29-34.

Muehsam, D., & Ventura, C. (2014). Life rhythm as a symphony of oscillatory patterns: electromagnetic energy and sound vibration modulates gene expression for biological signaling and healing. Global advances in health and medicine, 3(2), 40–55. https://doi.org/10.7453/gahmj.2014.008

Pederson, T. (July 19, 2014). Melancholy Danes? Not so much, and genetics may show why. *PsychCentral.*

Pikovsky, A., Rosenblum, M., & Kurths, J. (2002). Synchronization: a universal concept in nonlinear science. *American Journal of Physics 70,* 655 https://doi.org/10.1119/1.1475332

Sin, N. L., & Lyubomirsky, S. (2009). Enhancing well-being and alleviating depressive symptoms with positive psychology interventions: A practice-friendly meta-analysis. *Journal of clinical psychology, 65*(5), 467-487.

Wilson, M., & Cook, P. F. (2016). Rhythmic entrainment: Why humans want to, fireflies can't help it, pet birds try, and sea lions have to be bribed. *Psychonomic bulletin & review, 23*(6), 1647–1659. https://doi.org/10.3758/s13423-016-1013-x

Wilson, T. D., & Gilbert, D. T. (2005). Affective forecasting: Knowing what to want. *Current directions in psychological science, 14*(3), 131-134.

Chapter 17 – Pajama Class, Positivity, Personality

Boehm, J. K., Chen, Y., Koga, H., Mathur, M. B., Vie, L. L., & Kubzansky, L. D. (2018). Is optimism associated with healthier cardiovascular-related behavior? Meta-analyses of 3 health behaviors. *Circulation research, 122*(8), 1119-1134.

Cauley, J. A., Smagula, S. F., Hovey, K. M., Wactawski-Wende, J., Andrews, C. A., Crandall, C. J., ... & Tindle, H. A. (2017). Optimism, cynical hostility, falls, and fractures: the Women's Health Initiative Observational Study (WHI-OS). *Journal of bone and mineral research, 32*(2), 221-229.

Costa, P. T., & McCrae, R. R. (1980). Influence of extraversion and neuroticism on subjective well- being: Happy and unhappy people. *Journal of Personality and Social Psychology, 38*, 668–678.

Costa, V. D., Tran, V. L., Turchi, J., & Averbeck, B. B. (2014). Dopamine modulates novelty seeking behavior during decision making. *Behavioral neuroscience, 128*(5), 556.

Felt, J. M., Russell, M. A., Ruiz, J. M., Johnson, J. A., Uchino, B. N., Allison, M., ... & Smyth, J. (2020). A multimethod approach examining the relative contributions of optimism and pessimism to cardiovascular disease risk markers. *Journal of behavioral medicine, 43*(5), 839-849.

James, W. (1890). *The principles of psychology*. Henry Holt and Company.

Koga, H. K., Trudel-Fitzgerald, C., Lee, L. O., James, P., Kroenke, C., Garcia, L., ... & Kubzansky, L. D. Optimism, lifestyle, and longevity in a racially diverse cohort of women. *Journal of the American Geriatrics Society*.

Langer, E. J. (2009). *Counterclockwise: Mindful health and the power of possibility*. Ballantine Books.

Lee, L. O., James, P., Zevon, E. S., Kim, E. S., Trudel-Fitzgerald, C., Spiro III, A., ... & Kubzansky, L. D. (2019). Optimism is associated with exceptional longevity in 2 epidemiologic cohorts of men and women. *Proceedings of the National Academy of Sciences, 116*(37), 18357-18362.

McCrae, R. R., & Costa, P. T. (1987). Validation of the five-factor model of personality across instruments and observers. *Journal of personality and social psychology, 52*(1), 81.

McCrae, R. R., Costa, P. T., de Lima, M. P., Simões, A., Ostendorf, F., Angleitner, A., ... & Piedmont, R. L. (1999). Age differences in personality across the adult life span: parallels in five cultures. *Developmental psychology, 35*(2), 466.

Rahm, T., Heise, E., & Schuldt, M. (2017). Measuring the frequency of emotions validation of the Scale of Positive and Negative Experience (SPANE) in Germany. *PloS one, 12*(2), e0171288. https://doi.org/10.1371/journal.pone.0171288

Roizen, M., Linneman, P., Ratner, A. (2022). *The great age reboot: cracking the longevity code for a younger tomorrow*. National Geographic.

Tindle, H. A., Chang, Y. F., Kuller, L. H., Manson, J. E., Robinson, J. G., Rosal, M. C., Siegle, G. J., & Matthews, K. A. (2009). Optimism, cynical hostility, and incident coronary heart disease and mortality in the Women's Health Initiative. *Circulation, 120*(8), 656–662. https://doi.org/10.1161/CIRCULATIONAHA.108.827642

Chapter 18 - Anxiety

Abel, E. L., & Kruger, M. L. (2010). Smile intensity in photographs predicts longevity. *Psychological Science, 21*(4), 542-544.

American Psychological Association (APA), (February 2, 2021). *APA: U.S. adults report highest stress level since early days of the COVID-19 pandemic*. APA, Washington, D.C.

Arnett, J. J. (2022). Joy: An integrative theory. *The Journal of Positive Psychology*, 1-14.

Bahrami, F., & Yousefi, N. (2011). Females are more anxious than males: a metacognitive perspective. *Iranian journal of psychiatry and behavioral sciences, 5*(2), 83.

Baron-Cohen, S., Johnson, D., Asher, J., Wheelwright, S., Fisher, S. E., Gregersen, P. K., & Allison, C. (2013). Is synaesthesia more common in autism?. *Molecular autism, 4*, 1-6.

Cahill, L. (2006). Why sex matters for neuroscience. *Nature reviews neuroscience, 7*(6), 477-484.

Cannon, W.B., (1930). *The wisdom of the body*. W.W. Norton & Company.

Centers for Disease Control and Prevention (CDC), (October 24, 2022). *Facts about suicide*. Centers for Disease Control and Prevention, National Center for Injury Prevention and Control. Retrieved: https://www.cdc.gov/suicide/facts/index.html

Dimberg, U., & Söderkvist, S. (2011). The voluntary facial action technique: A method to test the facial feedback hypothesis. *Journal of nonverbal behavior, 35*(1), 17-33.

Kaiser Health News, (September 30, 2022). *Suicide rates rise, spotlighting pandemic's mental health toll*. KHN Morning Briefing. Retrieved: https://khn.org/morning-breakout/suicide-rates-rise-spotlighting-pandemics-mental-health-toll/

Liu, S., Seidlitz, J., Blumenthal, J. D., Clasen, L. S., & Raznahan, A. (2020). Integrative structural, functional, and transcriptomic analyses of sex-biased brain organization in humans. *Proceedings of the National Academy of Sciences, 117*(31), 18788-18798.

Martin, J., Rychlowska, M., Wood, A., & Niedenthal, P. (2017). Smiles as multipurpose social signals. *Trends in cognitive sciences, 21*(11), 864-877.

McLean, C. P., & Anderson, E. R. (2009). Brave men and timid women? A review of the gender differences in fear and anxiety. *Clinical psychology review, 29*(6), 496-505.

Pasquini, G. & Keeter, S. (December 12, 2022). *At least four-in-ten U.S. adults have faced high levels of psychological distress during COVID-19 pandemic.* Pew Research Center.

Weekes, C. (1962). *Self Help for Your Nerves: Learn to Relax and Enjoy Life Again by Overcoming Stress and Fear.* HarperThorsons.

Social

Karasavvas, T. (January 21, 2017). Neolithic Romeo and Juliet? The star-crossed lovers of Valdaro, *Ancient Origins*. Retrieved: https://www.ancient-origins.net/history/neolithic-romeo-and-juliet-star-crossed-lovers-valdaro-007413

Chapter 19 – Social Convoys

Antonucci, T. C., & Akiyama, H. (1987). Social networks in adult life and a preliminary examination of the convoy model. *Journal of Gerontology, 42*(5), 519-527.

Carstensen, L. L., Isaacowitz, D. M., & Charles, S. T. (1999). Taking time seriously: A theory of socioemotional selectivity. *American psychologist, 54*(3), 165.

Löckenhoff, C. E., & Carstensen, L. L. (2004). Socioemotional selectivity theory, aging, and health: The increasingly delicate balance between regulating emotions and making tough choices. *Journal of personality, 72*(6), 1395-1424.

Cox, D. (June 8, 2021). *The state of American friendship: Change, challenges, and loss.* May 2021 American Perspectives Survey conducted by Survey Center on American Life, American Enterprise Institute, Washington. D.C.

De Tocqueville, A. (1956). Democracy in America [1835].

Elder, G. H., & Johnson, M. K. (2018). The life course and aging: Challenges, lessons, and new directions. In *Invitation to the life course: Toward new understandings of later life* (pp. 49-81). Routledge.

Fuller, H. R., Ajrouch, K. J., & Antonucci, T. C. (2020). The convoy model and later-life family relationships. *Journal of Family Theory & Review, 12*(2), 126-146.

Silk, J. B. (2007). Social components of fitness in primate groups. *Science, 317*(5843), 1347-1351.

Snelling, S. (Host). (January 16, 2023). *Financial Wellness Month, Harvard Study & New Book on Living Longer, Hugs for Health,* Season 3, Episode 20 - interview with Marc Schulz, "Caregiving Club On Air," [podcast]. Caregiving Club and Resonate Recordings.

Vaillant, G. E. (2008). *Aging well: Surprising guideposts to a happier life from the landmark study of adult development.* Hachette UK.

Waldinger, R., Schulz, M., (2023). *The good life: lessons from the world's longest scientific study of happiness.* Simon & Schuster.

Chapter 20 - Hugs

Benoit, B., Boerner, K., Campbell-Yeo, M. Chambers, C. (2016) *The power of human touch for babies.* Canadian Association of Paediatric Health Centres.

Clower, T. L., & Neaves, T. T. (2015). *The health care cost savings of pet ownership.* The Human Animal Bond Research Initiative (HABRI) Foundation.

Feldman, R., Rosenthal, Z., & Eidelman, A. I. (2014). Maternal-preterm skin-to-skin contact enhances child physiologic organization and cognitive control across the first 10 years of life. *Biological psychiatry, 75*(1), 56-64.

Harlow, H. F. (1959). Love in infant monkeys. *Scientific American, 200*(6), 68-75.

Janevic, M., Solway, E., Malani, P., Kirch, M., Kullgren, J., Connell, C. (April 3, 2019). National poll on healthy aging: How pets contribute to healthy aging. University of Michigan Health.

Kosfeld, M., Heinrichs, M., Zak, P. J., Fischbacher, U., & Fehr, E. (2005). Oxytocin increases trust in humans. *Nature, 435*(7042), 673-676.

Mehrabian, A. (1968). Some referents and measures of nonverbal behavior. Behavior *Research Methods & Instrumentation, 1*(6), 203-207.

Pinker, S. (2015). *The village effect: How face-to-face contact can make us healthier and happier.* Vintage Books Canada.

Zak, P. (July, 2011) *Trust, morality -- and oxytocin?* TED Talk, Edinburgh, Scotland.

Chapter 21 – Laughter and Loneliness

Anderson, G.O., Thayer, C.E. (2018) *Loneliness and social connections.* AARP Foundation Research and GfK Custom Research, Inc. Washington, D.C.

Bryant, G. A., Fessler, D. M., Fusaroli, R., Clint, E., Aarøe, L., Apicella, C. L., ... & Zhou, Y. (2016). Detecting affiliation in colaughter across 24 societies. *Proceedings of the National Academy of Sciences, 113*(17), 4682-4687.

Flowers, L., et al. (November, 2017) Medicare spends more on socially isolated older adults. American Association of Retired Persons (AARP) Public Policy Institute Report. Washington, D.C.

Gallup, (2022). Gallup *Global Emotions Report.* Gallup, Washington, D.C.

Golaszewski, N. M., LaCroix, A. Z., Godino, J. G., Allison, M. A., Manson, J. E., King, J. J., ... & Bellettiere, J. (2022). Evaluation of social isolation, loneliness, and cardiovascular disease among older women in the US. *JAMA network open, 5*(2), e2146461-e2146461.

Hanc, J. (May 5, 2021). Doctors harness the power of human connections. *New York Times.*

Holt-Lunstad, J., & Smith, T. B. (2016). Loneliness and social isolation as risk factors for CVD: implications for evidence-based patient care and scientific inquiry. *Heart, 102*(13), 987-989.

Mahmood, Z. (January 17, 2018). *UK tackles social isolation with minister for loneliness.* CNN.com.

National Academies of Sciences, Engineering, and Medicine. (2020). *Social isolation and loneliness in older adults: Opportunities for the health care system.* National Academies Press.

Provine, R. R., & Fischer, K. R. (1989). Laughing, smiling, and talking: Relation to sleeping and social context in humans. *Ethology, 83*(4), 295-305.

Shah, S. J., Oreper, S., Jeon, S. Y., Boscardin, W. J., Fang, M. C., & Covinsky, K. E. (2023). Social Frailty Index: Development and validation of an index of social attributes predictive of mortality in older adults. *Proceedings of the National Academy of Sciences, 120*(7), e2209414120.

Shen, C., Rolls, E., Cheng, W., Kang, J., Dong, G., Xie, C., Zhao, X. M., Sahakian, B., & Feng, J. (2022). Associations of Social Isolation and Loneliness With Later Dementia. *Neurology,* 10.1212/WNL.0000000000200583.

Snelling, S. (April 30, 2020). How comedy can help caregivers cope with coronavirus. *Thrive Global.*

Sutin, A. R., Stephan, Y., Luchetti, M., & Terracciano, A. (2020). Loneliness and risk of dementia. *The Journals of Gerontology: Series B, 75*(7), 1414-1422.

U.S. Surgeon General's Office (May, 2023) *Our Epidemic of Loneliness and Isolation: The U.S. Surgeon General's Advisory on the Healing Effects of Social Connection and Community.* Washington, DC.

Chapter 22 – Finding Your Tribe

Chapman, S. N., Pettay, J. E., Lummaa, V., & Lahdenperä, M. (2019). Limits to fitness benefits of prolonged post-reproductive lifespan in women. *Current Biology, 29*(4), 645-650.

Epatko, L. (July 13, 2018). *How Nelson Mandela survived his years in isolated South African jail.* PBS Newshour.

McGroarty, B. (March, 2023). Presentation of highlights from the Global Wellness Institute 2023 Trends Report.

Intellectual

Chapter 23 - Brain Training

Alzheimer's Association (March, 2023). *2023 facts and figures report.* Alzheimer's Association, Chicago, IL.

Balbag, M. A., Pedersen, N. L., & Gatz, M. (2014). Playing a musical instrument as a protective factor against dementia and cognitive impairment: A population-based twin study. *International journal of Alzheimer's disease, 2014.*

Brady. T. (2017) *The TB12 method.* Simon & Schuster, New York, NY.

Buckley, R. F., Mormino, E. C., Rabin, J. S., Hohman, T. J., Landau, S., Hanseeuw, B. J., ... & Sperling, R. A. (2019). Sex differences in the association of global amyloid and regional tau deposition measured by positron emission tomography in clinically normal older adults. *JAMA neurology, 76*(5), 542-551.

Calandra, C. (January 30, 2023). *Gen Z has found a new way to improve their mental and emotional health: intentional brain development.* Insights, Wunderman Thompson.

Dai, H., Milkman, K.L., & Riis, J. (2013). The fresh start effect: Temporal landmarks motivate aspirational behavior. *Management Science, 60*, 1-20.

Davis, S. (December 7, 2022). *50% of Gen Z cite this health improvement as a top New Year's resolution for 2023.* Forbes.com.

De la Monte, S. M., & Wands, J. R. (2008). Alzheimer's disease is type 3 diabetes—evidence reviewed. *Journal of diabetes science and technology, 2*(6), 1101-1113.

Eldadah, B. A., Fazio, E. M., & McLinden, K. A. (2019). Lucidity in dementia: A perspective from the NIA. *Alzheimer's & Dementia, 15*(8), 1104-1106.

Eliot, L., Ahmed, A., Khan, H., & Patel, J. (2021). Dump the "dimorphism": Comprehensive synthesis of human brain studies reveals few male-female differences beyond size. *Neuroscience & Biobehavioral Reviews, 125*, 667-697.

Federal Trade Commission (FTC), (January 5, 2016). [Press release] *Lumosity to pay $2 million to settle FTC deceptive advertising charges for its "brain training" program.*

Franklin, J. (March 31, 2022). *Understanding aphasia, the condition impacting Bruce Willis' acting career.* National Public Radio (NPR) online.

Fuchs, E., & Flügge, G. (2014). Adult neuroplasticity: more than 40 years of research. *Neural plasticity, 2014*, 541870. https://doi.org/10.1155/2014/541870

Goldman, B. (May 22, 2017). Two minds: The cognitive differences between men and women. *Stanford Medicine Magazine - Neurobiology*, Spring 2017.

Grant, I.M. (2014). *Battle of the brain: Men versus women.* Northwestern Medical Group, Neurology

Kidd, D. C., & Castano, E. (2013). Reading literary fiction improves theory of mind. *Science, 342*(6156), 377-380.

Koronyo, Y., Rentsendorj, A., Mirzaei, N., Regis, G. C., Sheyn, J., Shi, H., ... & Koronyo-Hamaoui, M. (2023). Retinal pathological features and proteome signatures of Alzheimer's disease. *Acta Neuropathologica*, 1-30.

Limb, C. D. (2008). This is your brain on jazz: Researchers use MRI to study spontaneity, creativity. *Johns Hopkins Medicine*.

Livingston, G., Huntley, J., Sommerlad, A., Ames, D., Ballard, C., Banerjee, S., ... & Mukadam, N. (2020). Dementia prevention, intervention, and care: 2020 report of the Lancet Commission. *The Lancet, 396*(10248), 413-446.

Mack, J., (2022). *Up close and all in: Life lessons from a Wall Street warrior.* Simon & Schuster, New York.

Nedelec, T., Couvy-Duchesne, B., Monnet, F., Daly, T., Ansart, M., Gantzer, L., ... & Durrleman, S. (2022). Identifying health conditions associated with Alzheimer's disease up to 15 years before diagnosis: an agnostic study of French and British health records. *The Lancet Digital Health, 4*(3), e169-e178.

Park, J. E., Gunasekaran, T. I., Cho, Y. H., Choi, S. M., Song, M. K., Cho, S. H., Kim, J., Song, H. C., Choi, K. Y., Lee, J. J., Park, Z. Y., Song, W. K., Jeong, H. S., Lee, K. H., Lee, J. S., & Kim, B. C. (2022). Diagnostic Blood Biomarkers in Alzheimer's Disease. *Biomedicines, 10*(1), 169. https://doi.org/10.3390/biomedicines10010169

Restak, R. (February 2, 2023). *An 81-year-old brain doctor's 7 'hard rules' for keeping your memory 'sharp as a whip.'* CNBC.com

Snelling, S. (August 4, 2017). USC 'rock stars' of Alzheimer's research share latest developments. *USC News*.

Snelling, S., (Host), (September, 2022). *Healthy aging month, train your brain and body, world gratitude day, ageless fashion, fall prevention.* "Caregiving Club On Air" Season 2, Episode 14 – interview with Henry Mahncke of Posit Science. [audio podcast]. Caregiving Club and Resonate Recordings.

Stern Y. (2012). Cognitive reserve in ageing and Alzheimer's disease. *The Lancet. Neurology, 11*(11), 1006–1012. https://doi.org/10.1016/S1474-4422(12)70191-6

Alzheimer's

Alzheimer's Association (2023). Facts and figures report – 2023. Alzheimer's Association, Chicago, Il.

Goyal, M. S., Blazey, T. M., Su, Y., Couture, L. E., Durbin, T. J., Bateman, R. J., ... & Vlassenko, A. G. (2019). Persistent metabolic youth in the aging female brain. *Proceedings of the National Academy of Sciences, 116*(8), 3251-3255.

Sienski, G., Narayan, P., Bonner, J. M., Kory, N., Boland, S., Arczewska, A. A., ... & Lindquist, S. (2021). APOE4 disrupts intracellular lipid homeostasis in human iPSC-derived glia. *Science translational medicine, 13*(583), eaaz4564.

Chapter 24 - Daydreams

Mlodinow, L. (2018). *Elastic: Flexible thinking in a time of change.* Pantheon.

Mlodinow, L. (2022). *Emotional: How feelings shape our thinking.* Pantheon Books, New York. p. 23

Westgate, E. C., Wilson, T. D., Buttrick, N. R., Furrer, R. A., & Gilbert, D. T. (2021). What makes thinking for pleasure pleasurable?. *Emotion.*

Chapter 25 – Life-Work Balance

American Association of Retired Persons (AARP), (January, 2023). *Understanding a changing older workforce: An examination of workers ages 40-Plus.* AARP Research, Washington, D.C.

American Psychological Association, (May, 2022). *2022 Work and well-being survey.* The Harris Poll.

Autor, D., Mindell, D., Reynolds, E. (Fall, 2019). *The work of the future: Shaping technology and institutions.* MIT Work of the Future Task Force Report, Massachusetts Institute of Technology Sloan School of Management, Boston, Mass.

Baicker, K., Cutler, D., & Song, Z. (2010). Workplace wellness programs can generate savings. *Health affairs,* 29(2), 304-311.

Bradbury, T. (June 21, 2016). Why Women Are Smarter Than Men. *Forbes.com.*

Centers for Disease Control and Prevention. Workplace health in America 2017. Atlanta, GA: *Centers for Disease Control and Prevention, U.S. Department of Health and Human Services,* 2018. Washington, D.C.

Clausen, T., Meng, A., & Borg, V. (2019). Does social capital in the workplace predict job performance, work engagement, and psychological well-being? A prospective analysis. *Journal of occupational and environmental medicine,* 61(10), 800-805.

Clifton, J. (2022). *Blind spot: The global rise of unhappiness and how leaders missed it.* Gallup Press.

Conway, L.T., (2022). 2022 *Alight international workforce and wellbeing mindset report.* Business Group on Health.

Dahlstrom, L. (October 9, 2018). *New Starbucks benefit offers backup child and adult care.* Starbucks Stories & News, news blog on Starbucks.com.

Davis, S. & Lester, J. (July 12, 2022). *59% of U.S. adults find it harder to form relationships since COVID- 19, survey reveals — here's how that can harm your health.* Forbes Health Survey, Forbes.com, New York, NY.

Dravigne, A., Waliczek, T. M., Lineberger, R. D., & Zajicek, J. M. (2008). The effect of live plants and window views of green spaces on employee perceptions of job satisfaction. *HortScience,* 43(1), 183-187.

Ducharme, J. (November 1, 2022). The online therapy bubble is bursting. *TIME,* New York.

Fuller, J. B., & Raman, M. (2019). The caring company. *Harvard Business School, 17.*

Grim, B. J., & Grim, M. E. (2016). The Socio-economic Contribution of Religion to American Society: An Empirical Analysis. *Interdisciplinary Journal of Research on Religion, 12.*

Grim, B.J. & Grim, M.E. (2023) *REDI Index 2023 – 4th Annual Report.* Religious Freedom and Business Foundation, Annapolis, MD.

Harter, J. (April 14, 2021). *Thriving employees create a thriving business.* Gallup research, Washington, D.C.

Hatfield, S., Silvergate, P., Fisher, J. (June 22, 2022). *The C-suite's role in well-being.* Deloitte Insights. London, England.

Henderson, J.M., (December 16, 2014). Why the open-concept office trend needs to die. *Forbes.*

Hustwit, G., Producer and Director, (2016). [Film] *Workplace.* Film First Productions, New York.

Hwang, D. *Creating 'age-friendly' businesses.* AARP online.

Ingraham, C. (October 7, 2019). Nine days on the road: Commute time reached a record last year. *Washington Post.*

International WELL-Building Institute (January, 2023). *2023 State of Workforce Well-Being Poll*. IWBI and The Harris Poll, New York, NY.

Kochan, T., & Dyer, L. (2020). *Shaping the future of work: A handbook for action and a new social contract*. Routledge.

Koenig H. G. (2012). Religion, spirituality, and health: the research and clinical implications. *ISRN psychiatry, 2012*, 278730. https://doi.org/10.5402/2012/278730

Mark, G., Gudith, D., & Klocke, U. (2008, April). The cost of interrupted work: more speed and stress. In *Proceedings of the SIGCHI conference on Human Factors in Computing Systems* (pp. 107-110).

Musser, G. (August 17, 2009). The origin of cubicles and the open-plan office. *Scientific American*.

National Alliance for Caregiving, (October, 2021). *Lessons from the workplace: Caregiving during COVID-19*. NAC, Washington, D.C.

Oommen, V. G., Knowles, M., & Zhao, I. (2008). Should health service managers embrace open plan work environments?: A review. *Asia Pacific Journal of Health Management, 3*(2), 37-43.

Otterbring, T., Pareigis, J., Wästlund, E., Makrygiannis, A., & Lindström, A. (2018). The relationship between office type and job satisfaction: Testing a multiple mediation model through ease of interaction and well-being. *Scandinavian journal of work, environment & health, 44*(3), 330-334.

Patel, A. & Plowman, S. (August 17, 2022). *The increasing importance of a best friend at work*. Gallup American Workplace Report 2023, Washington, D.C.

Smith, B. W., Ortiz, J. A., Wiggins, K. T., Bernard, J. F., & Dalen, J. (2012). Spirituality, resilience, and positive emotions. *The Oxford Handbook on Psychology and Spirituality*, U.K.

Snelling. S. (April 8, 2019). Employer wake-up call: It's time to become "caring companies." *Stria*.

Sohal, G. (June 2, 2022). *The 6 Twitter employee benefits & perks keeping the company competitive*. Perk Up.

Strawbridge, W. J., Cohen, R. D., Shema, S. J., & Kaplan, G. A. (1997). Frequent attendance at religious services and mortality over 28 years. *American journal of public health, 87*(6), 957–961 https://doi.org/10.2105/ajph.87.6.957

Terry, P. E. (2022). Do Faith Friendly Workplaces Increase Well-Being?. *American Journal of Health Promotion, 36*(6), 909-912.

Vickburg, S., Langsett, M., Christfort, K., (June, 2019). *The practical magic of 'thank you' – How your people want to be recognized, for what, and by whom*. Deloitte Greenhouse.

Environmental

Levine, L. (July 30, 2020). 'The lungs of the city': Frederick Law Olmsted, public health and the creation of Central Park. *The Gotham Center for New York City History*.

Rosenzweig, R., & Blackmar, E. (1992). *The park and the people: a history of Central Park*. Cornell University Press.

Chapter 26 – Biophilic Design

Agadoni, L. (June 12, 2018). Why does waterfront property cost more? *SF Gate.com*.

Albrecht, G., Sartore, G. M., Connor, L., Higginbotham, N., Freeman, S., Kelly, B., Stain, H., Tonna, A., & Pollard, G. (2007). Solastalgia: the distress caused by environmental change. *Australasian psychiatry : bulletin of Royal Australian and New Zealand College of Psychiatrists, 15 Suppl 1*, S95–S98. https://doi.org/10.1080/10398560701701288

Arvay, C. G. (2018). *The biophilia effect: A scientific and spiritual exploration of the healing bond between humans and nature.* Sounds True.

Baker, B. (November 25, 2022). How dipping into the cold has become a hot trend. *Boston Globe.*

Banay, R. F., James, P., Hart, J. E., Kubzansky, L. D., Spiegelman, D., Okereke, O. I., ... & Laden, F. (2019). Greenness and depression incidence among older women. *Environmental health perspectives, 127*(2), 027001.

Bratman, G. N., Daily, G. C., Levy, B. J., & Gross, J. J. (2015). The benefits of nature experience: Improved affect and cognition. *Landscape and Urban Planning, 138,* 41-50.

Coburn, A., Vartanian, O., & Chatterjee, A. (2017). Buildings, beauty, and the brain: A neuroscience of architectural experience. *Journal of Cognitive Neuroscience, 29*(9), 1521-1531.

Dzhambov, A. M., Lercher, P., Browning, M. H., Stoyanov, D., Petrova, N., Novakov, S., & Dimitrova, D. D. (2021). Does greenery experienced indoors and outdoors provide an escape and support mental health during the COVID-19 quarantine?. *Environmental Research, 196,* 110420.

Ellard, C. (2015). *Places of the heart: The psychogeography of everyday life.* Bellevue literary press.

Elsadek, M., Sun, M., & Fujii, E. (2017). Psycho-physiological responses to plant variegation as measured through eye movement, self-reported emotion and cerebral activity. *Indoor and Built Environment, 26*(6), 758-770.

Felly, R., & Susanto, D. (2020, April). The changing effects through biophilic design in increasing elderly memory capacity. Case study: Sasana Tresna Werdha Yayasan Karya Bakti Ria Pembangunan, Cibubur. *In IOP Conference Series: Earth and Environmental Science Vol. 452,* No. 1, p. 012110. IOP Publishing.

Golden, R., & Holm, S. (2017). Indoor air quality and asthma: has unrecognized exposure to acrolein confounded results of previous studies?. *Dose-Response, 15*(1), 1559325817691159.

Gómez-Puerto, G., Munar, E., & Nadal, M. (2016). Preference for curvature: A historical and conceptual framework. *Frontiers in human neuroscience, 9,* 712.

Han, K. T., & Ruan, L. W. (2019). Effects of indoor plants on self-reported perceptions: a systemic review. *Sustainability, 11*(16), 4506.

Just, M. G., Nichols, L. M., & Dunn, R. R. (2019). Human indoor climate preferences approximate specific geographies. *Royal Society open science, 6*(3), 180695.

Kellert, S. R., Heerwagen, J., & Mador, M. (2011). *Biophilic design: the theory, science and practice of bringing buildings to life. John Wiley & Sons.*

Lange, E., & Schaeffer, P. V. (2001). A comment on the market value of a room with a view. *Landscape and Urban Planning, 55*(2), 113-120.

Li, Q. (2010). Effect of forest bathing trips on human immune function. *Environmental health and preventive medicine, 15,* 9-17.

Li, Q. (2018). *Into the forest: How trees can help you find health and happiness.* Penguin.

Li, Q., Morimoto, K., Nakadai, A., Inagaki, H., Katsumata, M., Shimizu, T., ... & Kawada, T. (2007). Forest bathing enhances human natural killer activity and expression of anti-cancer proteins. *International journal of immunopathology and pharmacology, 20*(2_suppl), 3-8.

Liao, W. C., Landis, C. A., Lentz, M. J., & Chiu, M. J. (2005). Effect of foot bathing on distal- proximal skin temperature gradient in elders. *International journal of nursing studies, 42*(7), 717-722.

Louv, R. (2012). *The nature principle: Reconnecting with life in a virtual age.* Algonquin Books.

MacKerron, G., & Mourato, S. (2013). Happiness is greater in natural environments. *Global environmental change, 23*(5), 992-1000.

National Air Duct Cleaners Association (2016). Report on dust accumulation and health hazards.

Nichols, W. J. (2014). *Blue mind: The surprising science that shows how being near, in, on, or under water can make you happier, healthier, more connected, and better at what you do.* Little, Brown.

Qin, J., Sun, C., Zhou, X., Leng, H., & Lian, Z. (2014). The effect of indoor plants on human comfort. *Indoor and Built Environment, 23*(5), 709-723.

Reggio, G. (April 27, 1982). *Koyaanisqatsi.* [Film]. Institute for Regional Education, American Zoetrope.

Reggio, G. (May 28, 2017). *Koyaanisqatsi explained in two minutes.*

Ruggles, D. (2017). *Beauty, neuroscience & architecture.* Fibonacci Publishing, Denver, Colo.

Snelling. S. (June 27, 2022). New trends in retirement living. *PBS Next Avenue.*

Snelling. S. (November 9, 2022). A new study reveals a link between Alzheimer's disease & environmental risks. *PBS Next Avenue.*

Snelling, S., (Host), (September, 2022*).* Sandwich Generation Month & Self Care Day, Serenbe Wellness Living & Summer Travel From Staycations to Wellcations. "Caregiving Club On Air" Season 2, Episode 11 – interview with Steve Nygren of Serenbe. [audio podcast]. Caregiving Club and Resonate Recordings.

Squillacioti, G., Carsin, A. E., Bellisario, V., Bono, R., & Garcia-Aymerich, J. (2022). Multisite greenness exposure and oxidative stress in children. The potential mediating role of physical activity. *Environmental Research, 209*, 112857.

Stevens, J. A., Haas, E. N., & Haileyesus, T. (2011). Nonfatal bathroom injuries among persons aged≥ 15 years—United States, 2008. *Journal of safety research, 42*(4), 311-315.

Tinkelman, D. G., Price, D. B., Nordyke, R. J., & Halbert, R. J. (2006). Misdiagnosis of COPD and asthma in primary care patients 40 years of age and over. *The Journal of asthma : official journal of the Association for the Care of Asthma, 43*(1), 75–80.

Ulrich, R. S. (1984). View through a window may influence recovery from surgery. *Science, 224*(4647), 420-421.

U.S. Energy Information Administration (EIA), (June 2022). *Highlights for air conditioning in U.S. homes by state, 2020.* U.S. EIA Office of Energy Demand and Integrated Statistics, Form EIA-457A of the 2020 Residential Energy Consumption Survey.0

Van den Berg, A. E., Maas, J., Verheij, R. A., & Groenewegen, P. P. (2010). Green space as a buffer between stressful life events and health. *Social science & medicine, 70*(8), 1203-1210.

Wallace, L. A., Pellizzari, E. D., Hartwell, T. D., Whitmore, R., Sparacino, C., & Zelon, H. (1986). Total Exposure Assessment Methodology (TEAM) Study: personal exposures, indoor-outdoor relationships, and breath levels of volatile organic compounds in New Jersey. *Environment International, 12*(1-4), 369-387.

Weinstein, N., Przybylski, A. K., & Ryan, R. M. (2009). Can nature make us more caring? Effects of immersion in nature on intrinsic aspirations and generosity. *Personality and social psychology bulletin, 35*(10), 1315-1329.

Wheeler, B. W., White, M., Stahl-Timmins, W., & Depledge, M. H. (2012). Does living by the coast improve health and wellbeing?. *Health & place, 18*(5), 1198–1201. https://doi.org/10.1016/j.healthplace.2012.06.015

White, M. P., Alcock, I., Grellier, J., Wheeler, B. W., Hartig, T., Warber, S. L., ... & Fleming, L. E. (2019). Spending at least 120 minutes a week in nature is associated with good health and wellbeing. *Scientific reports, 9*(1), 1-11.

White, M., Smith, A., Humphryes, K., Pahl, S., Snelling, D., & Depledge, M. (2010). Blue space: The importance of water for preference, affect, and restorativeness ratings of natural and built scenes. *Journal of environmental psychology, 30*(4), 482-493.

Wilson, E. O. (1984). Biophilia. In *Biophilia*. Harvard University Press.

Wolverton, B.C., Johnson, A., Bounds, K. (September 15, 1989). *Interior landscape plants for indoor air pollution abatement*. (The NASA Clean Air Study). National Aeronautics and Space Administration (NASA), Associated Landscape Contractors of America (ALCA).

Wolverton, B.C. (April 1, 1997). *How to grow fresh air: 50 house plants that purify your home or office*. Penguin Books, New York, NY.

Chapter 27 – Color Psychology

Alter, A. (2014). *Drunk tank pink: And other unexpected forces that shape how we think, feel, and behave*. Penguin.

Baron-Cohen, S., Johnson, D., Asher, J., Wheelwright, S., Fisher, S. E., Gregersen, P. K., & Allison, C. (2013). Is synaesthesia more common in autism?. *Molecular autism, 4*, 1-6.

Berryman, J. (2016). The Colour Treatment: A Convergence of Art and Medicine at the Red Cross Russell Lea Nerve Home. *Health and History, 18*(1), 5-21.

Breuning, L.G. (June 21, 2017). Why flowers make us happy. *Psychology Today*.

Buechner, V. L., Maier, M. A., Lichtenfeld, S., & Schwarz, S. (2014). Red-take a closer look. *PLoS One, 9*(9), e108111.

Dunne, T. E., Neargarder, S. A., Cipolloni, P. B., & Cronin-Golomb, A. (2004). Visual contrast enhances food and liquid intake in advanced Alzheimer's disease. *Clinical nutrition (Edinburgh, Scotland), 23*(4), 533–538.

Emanuel, D. (June 30, 2017). "How yellow affects your state of mind." CNN online.

Genschow, O., Noll, T., Wänke, M., & Gersbach, R. (2015). Does Baker-Miller pink reduce aggression in prison detention cells? A critical empirical examination. *Psychology, Crime & Law, 21*(5), 482-489.

Goldstein, K. (1942). Some experimental observations concerning the influence of colors on the function of the organism. *Occupational Therapy*.

Gruber, N. (2018). Green for hope and red for fear? Testing the color effect on the implicit achievement motive. *Romanian Journal of Psychology, 20*(1).

Jonauskaite, D., Abu-Akel, A., Dael, N., Oberfeld, D., Abdel-Khalek, A. M., Al-Rasheed A. S., ... & Mohr, C. (2020). Universal patterns in color-emotion associations are further shaped by linguistic and geographic proximity. *Psychological Science, 31*(10), 1245-1260.

Mammarella, N., Di Domenico, A., Palumbo, R., & Fairfield, B. (2016). When green is positive and red is negative: Aging and the influence of color on emotional memories. *Psychology and aging, 31*(8), 914.

Moan, J., Grigalavicius, M., Dahlback, A., Baturaite, Z., & Juzeniene, A. (2014).Ultraviolet- radiation and health: optimal time for sun exposure. *Advances in experimental medicine and biology, 810*, 423–428.

Schauss, A. G. (1979). Tranquilizing effect of color reduces aggressive behavior and potential violence. *Journal of Orthomolecular Psychiatry, 8*(4), 218-221.

Science Daily (June 6, 2009). University of Toronto. "People who wear rose-colored glasses see more, study shows." Science Daily.

Weil, R. S., Schrag, A. E., Warren, J. D., Crutch, S. J., Lees, A. J., & Morris, H. R. (2016). Visual dysfunction in Parkinson's disease. *Brain, 139*(11), 2827-2843.

Chapter 28 - Digital Detox

Hanley, A. W., Warner, A. R., Dehili, V. M., Canto, A. I., & Garland, E. L. (2015). Washing dishes to wash the dishes: brief instruction in an informal mindfulness practice. *Mindfulness, 6*(5), 1095-1103.

Kaspar, K. (2013). Washing one's hands after failure enhances optimism but hampers future performance. *Social Psychological and Personality Science, 4*(1), 69-73.

Konclus, J. (January 26, 2023). Marie Kondo's life is messier now — and she's fine with it. *Washington Post.*

Nielsen, (Q1, 2018). *Time flies: U.S. adults now spend nearly half a day interacting with media.* Nielsen Total
Audience Report, New York, NY.

Oka, N., Ankel, S. (January 1, 2020). Why you should opt for the Dutch de-stressing method 'niksen' over 'hygge,' according to a health expert. *Business Insider Deutschland.*

O'Sullivan, J., (March 8, 2023). *The new Luddites: The inevitable backlash against the all-encompassing role of technology in our lives has begun.* Wunderman Thompson.

Financial

Trueheart, C (August 5, 1997). Champion of longevity ends her reign at 122. *The Washington Post*, Washington, D.C.

Whitney, C. (August 5, 1997). Jeanne Calment, world's elder, dies at 122. *New York Times*, New York, NY.

Chapter 29 – Healthspan/Wealthspan

American Association of Retired People, (2015). *Family financial caregiving rewards, stresses and responsibilities.* AARP, Washington, D.C.

Administration of Community Living. *How much care will you need?* Longtermcare.gov database.

American Community Survey (2021). United States Census Bureau, Washington, D.C.

Bruno, J. (March 23, 2023). *Federal Trade Commission warns AI voice cloning is enhancing 'grandparent scam.'* WPTV (NBC), West Palm Beach, FL.

Deevy, M., & Vernon, S. (October, 2022). *Disconnected: Reality vs. perception in retirement planning.* Stanford University Center on Longevity.

Dychtwald, K. (2017). *The journey of caregiving: honor, responsibility and financial complexity.* Merrill Lynch and Kantar TNS. San Francisco, CA.

Embracing Carers (2020). *The global carer well-being index: who cares for the carers? Perspectives on COVID-19 pressures and lack of support.* EMD Serono, Rockland, MD.

Genworth Financial. *Cost of Care Survey Annual Calculator.* Genworth Financial, Richmond, VA.

Harris Interactive Poll Online Panel, (2014). *Financial experience and behaviors among women.* The Prudential Insurance Company of America and its affiliates Newark, NJ.

Horowitz, J.M. (April 8, 2022). *More than half of Americans in their 40s are 'sandwiched' between an aging parent and their own children.* Pew Research Center, Washington, D.C.

Kemper, P., Komisar, H. L., & Alecxih, L. (2005). Long-term care over an uncertain future: what can current retirees expect?. *Inquiry : a journal of medical care organization, provision and financing, 42*(4), 335–350. https://doi.org/10.5034/inquiryjrnl_42.4.335

Killingsworth, M. A., Kahneman, D., & Mellers, B. (2023). Income and emotional well-being: A conflict resolved. *Proceedings of the National Academy of Sciences, 120*(10), e2208661120.

National Academies of Sciences, Engineering, and Medicine. (2016). *Families caring for an aging America*. National Academies Press.

National Alliance for Caregiving. AARP. (May, 2020). *Caregiving in the U.S. 2020*.

O'Hara, C. (January 27, 2015). How much money do I need to retire? *AARP Magazine*, Washington, D.C.

Parker, K. & Patten, E. (January 30, 2013). *The Sandwich Generation Rising Financial Burdens for Middle-Aged Americans*. Pew Research Center, Washington, D.C.

Pew Research Center, (December 11, 2013). *On pay gap, millennial women near parity—for now*.

Ryu, S., & Fan, L. (2023). The relationship between financial worries and psychological distress among US adults. *Journal of Family and Economic Issues, 44*(1), 16-33.

Snelling, S., (Host), (January, 2022). *Live Colorfully: A Year of Happy, Healthy and Wealthy*. "Caregiving Club On Air" Season 2, Episode 1 – interview with Cindy Housell - WISER. [audio podcast]. Caregiving Club and Resonate Recordings.

Snelling, S., (Host), (January, 2022). *Coastal Grandmother & GrandMillennial Trends, Grandparent Scams, Never Forget Sept 11th and Family Emergency Plans*. "Caregiving Club On Air" Season 2, Episode 13 – interview with Liz Loewy- Eversafe. [audio podcast]. Caregiving Club and Resonate Recordings.

United States Attorney's Office, Southern District of California, (November 17, 2022). [Press release]. Two defendants sentenced for participating in nationwide grandparent scam.

Wettstein, G., & Zulkarnain, A. (2017). How much long-term care do adult children provide? *Issue in Brief*, 17-11.

Wilson, T. D., & Gilbert, D. T. (2005). Affective forecasting: Knowing what to want. *Current directions in psychological science, 14*(3), 131-134.

Chapter 30 - Peter Pan Homes

Accessible Living (September 15, 2022). *Werner House showcases aging-in-place design, open for Airbnb guests*. Inform Publishing Group.

Binette, J. and Vasold, K. (August, 2018). *Home and community preferences: A national survey of adults age 18 plus*. Washington, DC: AARP Research.

Carnemolla, P., & Bridge, C. (2019). Housing design and community care: How home modifications reduce care needs of older people and people with disability. *International journal of environmental research and public health, 16*(11), 1951. https://doi.org/10.3390/ijerph16111951

Cusato, M. (2017) *Aging in place report*. University of Notre Dame School of Architecture and Home Advisor.

Joint Center for Housing Studies at Harvard University. (2018). *Housing America's older adults*. Harvard University, Cambridge, MA.

Joint Center for Housing Studies at Harvard University. (2018). *Projections and implications of housing a growing population: Older households 2015-2035*. Harvard University, Cambridge, MA.

Pynoos, J., & Sanford, J. (2002). New tools for better home modifications. *The Case Manager, 13*(1), 67-70.

Snelling. S. (November 4, 2022). How big brands and younger generations are embracing boomers, - Coastal Grandmother style is trending, Pottery Barn and Lowe's go accessible, and Jane Fonda is the face of H&M's new 'movement' clothing line. *PBS Next Avenue.*

Snelling, S. (December 8, 2021). Creating dementia-friendly home design. *USA Today – Future of Personal Health* supplement produced by Media Planet.

Chapter 31 - Wellcations

Baratti, L. (March 17, 2023). Kimpton Hotels launches 'Plant Pals' program ahead of Earth Day. TravelPulse.com.

Bedini, L. A., & Phoenix, T. L. (1999). Addressing leisure barriers for caregivers of older adults: A model leisure wellness program. *Therapeutic Recreation Journal, 33*, 222-240.

Gump, B. B., & Matthews, K. A. (2000). Are vacations good for your health? The 9-year mortality experience after the multiple risk factor intervention trial. *Psychosomatic medicine, 62*(5), 608–612. https://doi.org/10.1097/00006842-200009000-00003

Hilbrecht, M., & Smale, B. (2016). The contribution of paid vacation time to wellbeing among employed Canadians. *Leisure/Loisir, 40* (1), 31-54.

Joudrey, A. D., & Wallace, J. E. (2009). Leisure as a coping resource: A test of the job demand- control-support model. *Human Relations, 62* (2), 195-217.

Melore, C. (January 14, 2023). *Office on the beach! 4 in 5 would work on vacation if it meant having a longer trip.* Study Finds.

Morgan, K. (January 19, 2023). Forget Google maps: Why paper map sales are booming. *Wall Street Journal.*

Schulte, Brigid (March 3, 2015). *Overwhelmed: How to work, love, and play when no one has the time.* Picador, Pan Macmillan, United Kingdom.

Wen, J., Zheng, D., Hou, H., Phau, I., & Wang, W. (2022). Tourism as a dementia treatment based on positive psychology. *Tourism Management, 92*, 104556.

Spiritual
Chapter 32 – Gratitude and the God Code

Albom, M. (1997). *Tuesdays with Morrie.* Bantam Doubleday Dell, New York, NY.

Armenta, C., Fritz, M., & Lyubomirsky, S. (2017). Functions of Positive Emotions: Gratitude as a Motivator of Self-Improvement and Positive Change. *Emotion Review, 9*(3), 183–190. https://doi.org/10.1177/1754073916669596

Babbitt, E. D. (1881). *Religion as revealed by the material and spiritual universe.* Babbitt & Company.

Baltes, P. B., & Baltes, M. M. (1990). Psychological perspectives on successful aging: The model of selective optimization with compensation.

Braden, G. (January 30, 2004). *The God code: The secret of our past, the promise of our future.* Hay House.

Brooks, A. (July 2, 2014). *A formula for happiness.* Aspen Ideas Conference. The Aspen Institute.

Burgess, B. (August, 2013). *We will see our pets again in heaven: The afterlife of animals from a Biblical perspective.* Outskirts Press, Parker, CO.

Chang,. C. (June, 2012). *Before I die . . .* TED Talk, Edinburgh, Scotland.

Clyne-Rekhy, E. (February, 1994). *Rainbow bridge.*

Digdon, N., & Koble, A. (2011). Effects of constructive worry, imagery distraction, and gratitude interventions on sleep quality: A pilot trial. *Applied Psychology: Health and Well-Being, 3*(2), 193-206.

Dosa, D. (February 2, 2010). *Making the rounds with Oscar.* Hyperion, Westport, CT.

Fahmy, D. (April 25, 2018). *Key findings about Americans' belief in God.* Pew Research Center.

Fox, G. R., Kaplan, J., Damasio, H., & Damasio, A. (2015). Neural correlates of gratitude. *Frontiers in psychology,* 1491.

Hill, P. L., Allemand, M., & Roberts, B. W. (2013). Examining the pathways between gratitude and self-rated physical health across adulthood. *Personality and individual differences, 54*(1), 92-96.

Jones, J. (June 17, 2022). *Belief in God in U.S. dips to 81%, a new low.* Gallup Values and Beliefs poll 2022, Washington, D.C.

Kessler, D. (2019). *Finding meaning: The sixth stage of grief.* Simon and Schuster.

Kübler-Ross, E. (1969). *On death and dying* (Vol. 1). New York: Macmillan.

Kubler-Ross, E., & Kessler, D. (2005). *On grief and grieving: Finding the meaning of grief through the five stages of loss.* Simon and Schuster.

Meier, E. A., Gallegos, J. V., Thomas, L. P., Depp, C. A., Irwin, S. A., & Jeste, D. V. (2016). Defining a Good Death (Successful Dying): Literature Review and a Call for Research and Public Dialogue. The American journal of geriatric psychiatry: official journal of the American Association for *Geriatric Psychiatry, 24*(4), 261–271. https://doi.org/10.1016/j.jagp.2016.01.135

Nuwer, R. (February 22, 2023). The 'Rainbow Bridge' has comforted millions of pet parents. Who wrote it? *National Geographic.*

Seligman, M. E. (2006). *Learned optimism: How to change your mind and your life.* Vintage.

Smith, G. (December 14, 2021). About three-in-ten U.S. adults are now religiously unaffiliated. *Pew Research Center.*

SpiritShack, (January 26, 2022). *What Britons really think about the afterlife.* United Kingdom.

Stefan, D. R., Lefdahl-Davis, E. M., HSPP, A., Alayan, A. J., Decker, M., Wittwer, J. L., & Parsell, J. S. (2021). The impact of gratitude letters and visits on relationships, happiness, well-being, and meaning of graduate students. *Journal of Positive School Psychology, 5*(2), 110-126.

Wong, Y. J., Owen, J., Gabana, N. T., Brown, J. W., McInnis, S., Toth, P., & Gilman, L. (2018). Does gratitude writing improve the mental health of psychotherapy clients? Evidence from a randomized controlled trial. *Psychotherapy Research, 28*(2), 192-202.

Chapter 33 – Sonic Seasoning

Al'Absi, M., Nakajima, M., Hooker, S., Wittmers, L., & Cragin, T. (2012). Exposure to acute stress is associated with attenuated sweet taste. *Psychophysiology, 49*(1), 96-103.

Baltes, P. B., & Baltes, M. M. (Eds.). (1993). *Successful aging: Perspectives from the behavioral sciences (Vol. 4).* Cambridge University Press.

Biswas, D., Lund, K., & Szocs, C. (2019). Sounds like a healthy retail atmospheric strategy: effects of ambient music and background noise on food sales. *Journal of the Academy of Marketing Science, 47,* 37-55.

Cho H. K. (2018). The Effects of Music Therapy-Singing Group on Quality of Life and Affect of Persons With Dementia: A Randomized Controlled Trial. *Frontiers in medicine, 5,* 279. https://doi.org/10.3389/fmed.2018.00279

Eerola, T., & Peltola, H. R. (2016). Memorable experiences with sad music—reasons, reactions and mechanisms of three types of experiences. *PLoS One, 11*(6), e0157444.

Feldman, R., Magori-Cohen, R., Galili, G., Singer, M., & Louzoun, Y. (2011). Mother and infant coordinate heart rhythms through episodes of interaction synchrony. *Infant Behavior and Development, 34*(4), 569-577.

Hur, K., Choi, J. S., Zheng, M., Shen, J., & Wrobel, B. (2018). Association of alterations in smell and taste with depression in older adults. *Laryngoscope investigative otolaryngology, 3*(2), 94-99.

Ivanov, P. C., Ma, Q. D., & Bartsch, R. P. (2009). Maternal–fetal heartbeat phase synchronization. *Proceedings of the National Academy of Sciences, 106*(33), 13641-13642.

Johnson, J. E. (2003). The use of music to promote sleep in older women. *Journal of Community Health Nursing, 20*(1), 27-35.

Kraemer, D. J., Macrae, C. N., Green, A. E., & Kelley, W. M. (2005). Sound of silence activates auditory cortex. *Nature, 434*(7030), 158-158.

Lai, H. L., & Good, M. (2006). Music improves sleep quality in older adults. *Journal of advanced nursing, 53*(1), 134-144.

Lesiuk, T. (2005). The effect of music listening on work performance. *Psychology of Music, 33*(2), 173– 191.

Linnemann, A., Ditzen, B., Strahler, J., Doerr, J. M., & Nater, U. M. (2015). Music listening as a means of stress reduction in daily life. *Psychoneuroendocrinology, 60*, 82-90.

Palmer, A. (2003). Violent song lyrics may lead to violent behavior. *Monitor on Psychology, 34*(7), 25.

Quinci, M. A., Belden, A., Goutama, V., Gong, D., Hanser, S., Donovan, N. J., Geddes, M., & Loui, P. (2022). Longitudinal changes in auditory and reward systems following receptive music-based intervention in older adults. *Scientific reports, 12*(1), 11517. https://doi.org/10.1038/s41598-022-15687-5

Rossoto-Bennett, M., McDouglad, A., Scully, R. & Rossoto-Bennett, M. (2014) *Alive inside*. U.S.: Projector Media.

Roth, E. A., & Smith, K. H. (2008). The Mozart effect: evidence for the arousal hypothesis. *Perceptual and motor skills, 107*(2), 396–402.

Rubenstein, A. (April 16, 2020). *My many years.* Renaissance Literary & Talent.

Sachs, M. E., Damasio, A., & Habibi, A. (2015). The pleasures of sad music: a systematic review. *Frontiers in human neuroscience, 9*, 404.

Sacks, O. (2008). *Musicophilia: tales of music and the brain.* New York, Alfred A. Knopf.

Snelling, S. (April 11, 2023). Cue up the Johnny Cash for that low-sodium diet 'sonic seasoning' can actually make food taste better. *Wall Street Journal MarketWatch.*

Snelling, S., (Host), (November 21, 2022). *Thanksgiving Episode: Musical Menus with Professor Charles Spence, More National Family Caregiver Month, Gratitude Gravy Recipe.* "Caregiving Club On Air" Season 2, Episode 18 – interview with Charles Spence, University of Oxford. [audio podcast]. Caregiving Club and Resonate Recordings.

Spence, C., & Youssef, J. (2021). Aging and the (Chemical) Senses: Implications for Food Behaviour Amongst Elderly Consumers. *Foods, 10*(1), 168.

Spence, C. (June 20, 2017). *Gastrophysics: The new science of eating.* Viking. New York, New York.

Taruffi, L., & Koelsch, S. (2014). The paradox of music-evoked sadness: An online survey. *PLoS One, 9*(10), e110490.

Chapter 34 - Post Traumatic Growth

Dweck, C. (2014). "The power of believing you can improve." TED Talk, Norrkoping, Sweden.

Erikson, E. H. (1966). Eight ages of man. *International Journal of Psychiatry, 2*(3), 281–300.

Kritsky, G., & Cherry, R. H. (2000). *Insect mythology*. iUniverse.

Li, J., Sun, Y., Maccallum, F., & Chow, A. Y. (2021). Depression, anxiety and post-traumatic growth among bereaved adults: A latent class analysis. *Frontiers in Psychology, 11*, 575311.

Stallard, P., Pereira, A. I., & Barros, L. (2021). Post-traumatic growth during the COVID-19 pandemic in carers of children in Portugal and the UK: cross-sectional online survey. *BJPsych Open, 7*(1), e37.

Tedeschi, R. G., & Calhoun, L. G. (1996). The Posttraumatic Growth Inventory: Measuring the positive legacy of trauma. *Journal of traumatic stress, 9*, 455-471.

Tornstam, L. (2005). *Gerotranscendence: A developmental theory of positive aging*. Springer Publishing Company, New York.

Chapter 35 - Awe

Bai, Y., Ocampo, J., Jin, G., Chen, S., Benet-Martinez, V., Monroy, M., ... & Keltner, D. (2021). Awe, daily stress, and elevated life satisfaction. *Journal of personality and social psychology, 120*(4), 837.

Buchanan, A., & Flouri, E. (2008). Involved grandparenting and child well-being. Full Research Report ESRC End of Award Report, RES-000-22-2283.

Griggs, J., Tan, J. P., Buchanan, A., Attar-Schwartz, S., & Flouri, E. (2010). 'They've always been there for me': Grandparental involvement and child well-being. *Children & Society, 24*(3), 200-214.

Moorman, S. M., & Stokes, J. E. (2016). Solidarity in the grandparent–adult grandchild relationship and trajectories of depressive symptoms. *The Gerontologist, 56*(3), 408-420.

index

Symbols

"60 Minutes" 6, 49, 127, 203, 227, 374
"988" – national mental health hotline 146

A

AARP 184, 230, 287, 290, 293, 301, 334, 367, 378, 381, 386, 387
ADHD 99, 113, 168, 182, 372
affective forecasting 137, 138, 284, 375, 387
aging paradox 139
agrihoods 249, 250
Airbnb 298, 387
air care, air quality 233, 246, 383
Albrecht, Glenn 262
Alice in Wonderland Syndrome (AIWS) 215
allostasis, allostatic overload 43, 44
Altman, Joseph 27
Alzheimer's disease (AD) 208, 209, 211, 213, 214, 272, 370, 373, 379, 380, 384, 385
Americans with Disabilities Act (ADA) 242, 295
ancient brain 30, 31, 43, 67, 77, 81, 94, 97, 98, 149, 199, 232, 235, 243, 245, 247, 297, 301, 309, 311
anthocyanins 273
anticipatory anxiety (see also: Sunday Scaries) 72
anxiety 6, 27, 31, 41, 43, 72, 73, 75, 88, 97, 99, 113, 118, 129, 140, 145, 146, 148, 156, 159, 166, 167, 168, 169, 179, 180, 187, 210, 219, 232, 235, 241, 245, 254, 262, 276, 288, 309, 329, 336, 342, 370, 372, 376, 377, 391
Apple 106, 222, 265, 363
Archangels 41, 147
Aristotle 14, 27, 33, 135, 158, 329
artificial intelligence (AI) 35, 207, 291, 299, 386
Atkins Diet 102
auras 150
autism 168, 182, 210, 266, 329, 376, 385
Automobile Club of America (AAA) 301
autonomic nervous system 30, 97
Avicenna 272, 363
Ayurveda 14, 363

B

Babbitt, Edwin 273, 310, 363
baby boomer, boomer 9, 21, 222, 301, 388
behavioral plasticity 318
behavioral science 71, 104, 376, 389
Big Five Personality Theory: Five Factor Model (see also: OCEAN: Openness, Conscientiousness, Extraversion, Agreeableness and Neuroticism) 158
biohacking 258, 259
biology 25, 26, 28, 52, 86, 172, 192, 259, 371, 379, 385
biophilia 122, 232, 240, 241, 248, 252, 263, 347, 367, 383, 385
   biophilia hypothesis 241
   biophilic design 231, 232, 238, 239, 240, 241, 242, 243, 244, 245, 246, 247, 249, 250, 288, 296, 383

biopsychosocial framework (BPS) x, 25, 26, 28, 48, 52, 172, 363
bipolar disorder 145, 146
black swan event 40
blue light emission 92, 93, 94, 95
blue wellness 15, 117, 141, 255, 277
blursdays 73, 229
Brady, Tom 196, 197, 361, 365
Brain Health Kitchen 110, 111, 372
brainHQ 197, 201, 202, 203
brain plasticity 27, 168, 201, 202, 328, 334
brain training, brain exercises 124, 197, 202, 204, 214, 355
Brooks, Arthur 77, 143, 309
brown noise 99
Brubeck, Dave 319, 321
Buddhism 14, 51, 344
Bürolandschaft 234

C

Calhoun, Lawrence 336
Calment, Jeanne 280, 282, 365, 386
cancer 16, 86, 101, 102, 114, 146, 179, 182, 186, 208, 209, 302, 303, 314, 383
car cuisine 113
care economy 50
Caregiver Walkabout 339
"Caregiving Club On Air" podcast 113
Carer Well-Being Index 41, 366, 386
Carroll, Lewis 215, 216
Carstensen, Laura 138, 164, 175
Carter, Rosalynn 10
cat 181, 182, 217, 228, 317, 320, 330
cave syndrome 47, 164, 248
Center for Retirement Research at Boston College 290
Centers for Disease Control and Prevention (CDC) 88, 146, 370, 376, 381, 399
Centers for Medicare and Medicaid (CMS) 17, 399
Central Park 238, 239, 253, 363, 365, 382
cerebral gymnastics 204
Chang, Candy 313, 321
chromatherapy 264, 272, 273, 274, 295, 296
Churchill, Winston 157, 159
circadian rhythms 28, 94, 95, 96, 146, 152, 234, 273, 274, 295, 370
Clifton, Jon 222

cognitive arousal 95
cognitive maps 77
cognitive reserve, cognitive reserve compensation 213, 318
cold water therapy 259, 347
color psychology 53, 106, 231, 247, 264, 265, 266, 267, 274, 385
color therapy 272
Conway, Bevil 264
coronavirus pandemic, COVID-19 40, 41, 88, 108, 322, 366, 370, 371, 376, 377, 383, 391
Cost of Care Survey 287, 386
cryotherapy 259
crystallized intelligence 199, 200
cubicle farms 234, 235
cuddling cafes 181
cumulative advantage 120
Curie, Madame Marie 220
cyber curfew 96

D

death, dying 40, 214, 314, 315, 389
dementia 16, 27, 42, 98, 110, 111, 117, 122, 123, 186, 188, 206, 208, 209, 210, 211, 212, 214, 288, 291, 304, 324, 328, 329, 370, 372, 373, 378, 379, 380, 388, 389
dementia-friendly design 288
Denmark, Danes, Danish 141, 258, 276
diabetes 15, 16, 38, 61, 90, 103, 104, 110, 114, 116, 117, 184, 207, 211, 214, 323, 371, 379
  diabesity 103, 114, 214
  Diabetes Prevention Program 104
  Type 2 diabetes 15, 38, 90, 110, 184, 323
  Type 3 diabetes 214
digital detox 275, 276, 297, 356, 386
Discover Live 304, 305
Disney, Walt 220, 298
dog 27, 64, 76, 96, 123, 181, 182, 276, 316, 317, 320, 362, 363, 374
doomscrolling ix, 129, 276, 278
dopamine 68, 76, 77, 79, 104, 129, 143, 155, 156, 186, 312, 321, 369, 375
dragonflies 331, 332
Dunne, Halbert 49, 363, 384
Dutch 19, 37, 38, 151, 276, 278, 367, 386
Dweck, Carol 334

E

Ebbinghaus Forgetting Curve 80
    Ebbinghaus, Herman 27, 80
ecotherapy 253
elastic thinking 219, 220, 257, 276
elder abuse 290, 291
Emerson, Ralph Waldo 50, 253, 340
emotional sponges 154
employers, employees ix, 222, 223, 224, 225, 226, 227, 228, 229, 230, 231, 232, 236
endorphins 67, 68, 143, 155, 156, 181, 187, 321
energy medicine (see also: vibrational medicine) 150
energy vibrations 154, 198
entrainment 151, 152, 154, 326, 345, 375
epigenetic effect 37, 38
Erikson, Erik 335
eudemonic 139, 223, 237
Eversafe 291, 387

F

FBI Cyber Crimes Unit 290
Fenn, Dr. Annie 110, 361, 372
Ferri, Alessandra 130, 131
fight or flight 32, 44
fixed mindset 334, 337, 358
Fletcherism 101
flex and control model 230
Flexner Report 16, 363
flourish, flourishing 135, 164, 165
flow theory 60, 128, 197, 344
fluid intelligence 200
FOMO (fear of missing out) 50, 128, 129, 130, 132, 374
Fonda, Jane 123, 388
food deserts 282
forest bathing 250, 253, 254, 255, 383
forest medicine 254
Forgetting Curve Theory. *See also* Ebbinghaus Forgetting Curve
fractals 244, 245
Francine, Rachel 328, 361
free-moving 219, 220
French Paradox 111, 112, 372
Freud, Sigmund 27
friendship deserts 184
functional medicine 16, 27

G

Gabrielle, John 79
Gallup 72, 140, 141, 185, 222, 224, 229, 258, 308, 368, 374, 378, 381, 382, 389
gastrophysics 322, 390
Gen C Continuum 10, 11, 285, 363
generalized anxiety disorder (GAD) 168
generativity 335
Gen X 21, 72, 125
Gen Z 21, 41, 72, 207, 255, 277, 301, 379
gerontology, gerontologists 3, 14, 25, 76, 149, 218, 281, 315, 335, 340
gerotranscendence 334, 335, 391
Gilbert, Dan 138, 284
Glenn, John 221
Global Wellness Institute (GWI) 36, 47, 50, 192, 193, 236, 249, 254, 297, 369, 379
God, god 75, 143, 189, 231, 255, 308, 309, 310, 311, 316, 330, 370, 388, 389
Goop 13, 20, 22, 193, 363
grandmother hypothesis 193
grandparent scams 290, 386, 387
gratitude 63, 64, 308, 310, 311, 312, 315, 316, 346, 358, 380, 388, 389, 390
gray matter 186, 198, 209
green exercise 122
Greensward Plan 239
grief 41, 135, 149, 299, 313, 315, 316, 317, 329, 353, 389
growth mindset 333, 334, 338, 358
Grube, Kathryn 265, 361
gut microbiome 15, 371, 372

H

habit-stacking 12, 65, 66, 67, 68, 77, 80, 81, 200, 350
Harvard University 28, 172, 240, 367, 385, 387
    Harvard Joint Center for Housing Studies 293
    Study of Adult Development 172
Healing Holidays 299
Healthspan x, 3, 50, 120, 282, 319, 360, 386
hedonia, hedonic adaptation 137, 223
heliotherapy 272
Hepburn, Katherine 259

higher level wellness 368
hippocampus 30, 77, 89, 123, 206, 212, 322, 373
Hippocrates xi, 15, 26, 363
homeopathy 15, 16, 363
homeostasis 31, 32, 43, 44, 136, 380
Homes Renewed Purple Tag 295
Hongerwinter 37, 38
Hopkins Circle 16
hormones 19, 20, 42, 44, 64, 69, 92, 95, 96, 101, 102, 154, 155, 156, 181, 364
hot springs 256, 299
Hounsell, Cindy 288, 361
hugs, hugging 156, 179, 180
hydrotherapy 243, 256, 296, 298, 363
hygge 275, 276, 356, 386

I

ice bathing 259
Iceland 141, 258
iGuard 288
ikigai 12, 55, 64, 80, 349, 350
intermittent fasting 100, 108, 259
iShips 177

J

JOMO (joy of missing out) 128, 132
Joyconomy 47, 49, 50, 282, 297
Judaism 51, 308

K

Kaplan, Bonnie 113, 361, 372
Kohler 295
Kondo, Marie 47, 275, 278, 386
koyaanisqatsi 260, 384

L

Lacks, Henrietta 16
LaLanne, Jack 123, 363, 373
languishing 164, 165
Laughter On Call 188
laughter yoga 186
learned helplessness 70, 71, 159
learned optimism 159, 308, 389
life course ix, x, 25, 68, 135, 138, 139, 158, 175, 373, 377
life expectancy 9, 147, 249, 286, 297
life reform 256

lifespan x, 3, 9, 11, 23, 27, 42, 50, 86, 120, 162, 173, 360, 379
light hunger 234
light therapy 155, 234, 272, 273, 274
linguistic distancing 165
linked lives theory 174
Loewy, Liz 291, 361, 387
loneliness, lonely 28, 50, 155, 181, 184, 185, 186, 192, 214, 229, 335, 341, 374, 378
longevity economy 50, 242, 367, 399

M

macros (macronutrients) 115
Mahncke, Henry 201, 361, 380
Mandela, Nelson 190, 379
Maslow's Hierarchy of Needs Theory (Maslow's Pyramid) 59, 364
Mastication Diet (Fletcherism) 100, 101
Matthew Effect 120, 373
McGroarty, Beth 192
Medicare, Medicaid, MedicareAdvantage 17, 286, 399
Mediterranean Diet 100, 110, 112, 371
Merzenich, Michael 201, 202
Meta 88, 222, 366, 367, 372, 375
metaverse, metaneeds, metamotivation 58
microbiome 15, 28, 114, 371, 372
microflow 12, 48, 60, 61, 62, 65, 74, 75, 80, 81, 121, 125, 348, 359
Millennial 10, 21, 41, 72, 125, 255, 296, 301, 387
mind-body connection 35, 43, 70, 166
MIND Diet 110
mindful eating 111, 112
mindfulness 169, 277, 386
Mlodinow, Leonard 219
Modisett, Dani Klein 188, 361
Moen 288
Monday Campaigns x, 73, 74, 369
monkey gland man, Monkey Gland Affair 19
The Mozart Effect 327, 390
Müller, J.P. 121
multisensory 31, 36, 81, 112, 113, 231, 235, 240, 242, 243, 246, 247, 248, 254, 256, 266, 277, 296, 322, 324, 325, 355, 369
   multisensory dining 113, 322, 325
musical menus 64, 318, 321, 323, 390

music therapy 52, 277, 329, 389
Musk, Elon 220, 222
Muslim 51, 308, 326
MyndVR 304
My System 121, 125, 312, 374

N

nanometers 265
narcissism, Narcissist Nation 163
NASA 151, 221, 246, 261, 299, 332, 385
National Alliance for Caregiving (NAC) 291, 382, 387
National Alliance on Mental Illness (NAMI) 145
National Human Genome Research Institute 87
National Institute on Aging 210, 399
National Wellness Institute 363
Native American tribes 9, 307, 341
Natural Killer (NK) cells 253
nature deficit disorder (NDD) 254
nature effect 231
neocortex 89, 212
neurogenesis 27, 35
neuroplasticity 197, 201, 219, 380
neurotransmitters 155, 213
niksen (also niks) 167, 275, 276, 277, 356, 372, 386
nine-square design 251, 252
Noom 104
nootropics 259
Notre Dame University School of Architecture 295
Nygren, Steve 361, 384

O

OCEAN: Openness, Conscientiousness, Extraversion, Agreeableness and Neuroticism (see also: Big Five Personality Theory: Five Factor Model) 158
office landscaping 234
Olmsted, Frederick Law 239, 382
optimal aging 315
optimism 157, 159, 161, 162, 216, 236, 260, 308, 371, 375, 376, 386, 389
organic food 101
oxytocin 44, 69, 79, 155, 156, 174, 181, 187, 328, 378

P

pajama class 157, 164, 165, 375
Paltrow, Gwyneth 20, 366
parasympathetic nervous system 31, 32, 95, 247
PBS Next Avenue 124, 142, 250, 255, 361, 374, 384, 388
peak experiences 128, 197, 343
Peoplehood 13, 123, 193
Peralta, Ari 36, 254
personality traits 158, 160
pessimism 154, 164, 376
Peter Pan Phenomenon 287
pets 10, 13, 69, 123, 181, 182, 276, 289, 316, 317, 320, 354, 375, 378, 388, 389
phantom phone syndrome 43
photo therapy 272, 273
pink noise 98, 266
podcast 110, 113, 201, 250, 265, 288, 291, 322, 361, 372, 377, 380, 384, 387, 390, 399
Positive Constructive Daydreaming (PCD) 218
positivity psychology 71
Posit Science 201, 380
post traumatic growth (PTG) 331, 334, 335, 336, 337, 365, 390
Pottery Barn Accessible Home 388
primal movement 374
Propst, Robert 235
psychology x, 25, 27, 28, 52, 53, 57, 70, 71, 74, 106, 126, 138, 139, 142, 158, 159, 172, 231, 247, 264, 265, 266, 267, 274, 284, 308, 322, 334, 369, 370, 371, 374, 375, 376, 377, 382, 384, 385, 388, 389, 390, 391
pump room 257
Pythagoras 151, 340

Q

quantum physics 154
Queen Elizabeth II 157
quiet quitting 227, 228

R

Rainbow Bridge 316, 317, 388, 389
Rainbow Diet 104, 106, 364
Red Cardinal Story 306, 365

refuge theory 247
religion 51, 142, 236, 237, 308, 309, 310, 311, 326, 381, 382, 388
reminiscence therapy (RT) 325
REM (rapid eye movement), NREM 90, 91, 92, 93, 94
Rendever 304
resiliency, resilient 69, 71, 75, 78, 132, 147, 150, 163, 192, 198, 217, 218, 236, 254, 310, 315, 335, 336, 337, 338, 342, 353
resolutionary 52, 53, 74, 75
respitality 300
rewards 6, 12, 24, 61, 69, 75, 76, 77, 78, 79, 80, 81, 103, 137, 155, 156, 186, 311, 312, 330, 347, 351, 359, 386, 390
Rubenstein, Arthur 318, 319, 390

S

SAD (seasonal affective disorder) 143, 145, 149, 233, 234, 274, 325, 328, 329, 389, 390
Sandwich Generation 41, 147, 194, 289, 384, 387
Sanitoriums 167
savanna hypothesis 30
savoring 95
SBNR (spiritual but not religious) 236, 308
Scarsdale Diet 102
schizophrenia 19, 38, 146, 210
Schulz, Marc 173, 377
selection, optimization, compensation theory (SOC) 318, 319, 320, 321
self-care ix, x, xi, 3, 4, 5, 6, 10, 11, 12, 47, 52, 53, 55, 57, 63, 132, 176, 186, 229, 260, 275, 276, 298, 299, 307, 321, 333, 346, 347, 349, 350, 351, 357, 360
self-transcendence 58, 343, 344, 369
senescence 86
sensemaking 24, 30, 31, 33, 35, 64, 79, 113, 232, 240, 243, 253, 256
Serenbe 249, 250, 251, 384
serotonin 69, 79, 95, 96, 114, 141, 143, 155, 156, 181, 234, 248, 257, 321
Seventh Generation Principle 9, 342
Sherwin Williams 246
shibboleth 341

shinrin-yoku 253, 254
signal songs 341
SingFit 328
sisu 338
skip-gen travelers 298
sleep debt 88
social contracts at work 221, 225, 226
social convoy model 175, 176, 354
social determinants of health (SDoH) 17
Social Frailty Index 177, 378
social isolation 40, 51, 181, 184, 185, 186, 214, 303, 309, 335, 378
social media 15, 54, 63, 88, 93, 94, 95, 129, 130, 174, 177, 187, 207, 278, 291, 336, 353, 354, 360, 374
social prescribing 17
Social Security 287, 289
socioemotional selectivity theory (SST) 175, 377
sociology 25, 28, 52, 172, 174
solastalgia 260, 262, 382
soliphilia 262
solo agers 185, 294, 305
songlines 326, 339
sonic seasoning 318, 321, 323, 324, 325, 389, 390
Soul Cycle 13, 123, 193
Spence, Charles 33, 322, 361, 390
spirituality 58, 63, 306, 308, 309, 311, 315, 316, 321, 325, 335, 336, 342, 344, 382
stagnation 66, 335
Stanford Center on Longevity 287
Starbucks 62, 222, 227, 322, 381
stress 3, 6, 24, 27, 30, 31, 32, 37, 38, 40, 41, 42, 43, 44, 48, 49, 62, 66, 72, 73, 74, 75, 91, 92, 93, 96, 104, 106, 113, 115, 118, 122, 128, 138, 140, 155, 161, 164, 166, 167, 168, 181, 182, 192, 207, 214, 216, 218, 219, 224, 236, 247, 248, 249, 253, 254, 283, 297, 301, 303, 307, 321, 335, 336, 343, 346, 351, 367, 368, 372, 376, 377, 382, 384, 386, 389, 390, 391
subaru 51
successful aging 315, 388, 389
Sullenberger, Captain Chesley "Sully" 126, 127, 133, 364

Sunday Scaries (see also: anticipatory anxiety) 72, 75, 351, 368
sunset mode 343
Sunshine Diet 100, 104, 108, 364
sympathetic nervous system 30, 31, 164, 167

T

Tedeschi, Richard 336
TED Talk 181, 313, 378, 388, 390
telomeres 42, 44, 364, 368
tend and befriend 44
terminal lucidity 213
theology 16, 51, 308
Theory of Mind (TOM) 206
Thoreau, Henry David 253
Thrive Global 188, 222, 379
time poverty, time affluence 5, 60, 61, 310
Tornstam, Lars 334, 340
toxic positivity 162, 163, 228
toxic productivity 228
Traditional Chinese Medicine (TCM) 14, 150, 363
Travis, Dr. John 49, 363
Tubman, Andy 328, 361
Tuskegee experiments 16

U

U-Curve of Happiness 138, 139, 140
U.N. World Happiness Report 141, 258, 374
U.S. Administration on Community Living (ACL) 286
USC 73, 114, 139, 210, 294, 312, 362, 363, 368, 380, 399
    USC Center for the Digital Future 73
    USC Leonard Davis School of Gerontology 362, 399

V

Viarama 304
vibrational medicine (see also: energy medicine) 150
virtual reality (VR) 303, 304
virtual travel, virtual tourism 303, 304, 357
vision quest 341
vitamin D 108, 248, 372, 373

W

Waldinger, Robert 173
Weekes, Claire 166, 276
Weight Watchers 102
WELL Building Standards® 231, 242
wellcation 297, 303, 305, 357, 384, 388
Well Home Design for Life Plan 242, 266, 288
wellspan x, 3, 319
Werner House 298, 387
white matter 198, 209, 263
white noise 98
Wilson, E.O. 239, 241, 254
Wilson, Timothy 138, 284
Winfrey, Oprah 102, 220
WISER (Women's Institute for a Secure Retirement) 288, 289, 319, 387
Woolley, Hannah 84
workplace (workplace loneliness) 13, 221, 223, 224, 225, 226, 227, 229, 230, 231, 232, 233, 234, 235, 236, 237, 335, 355, 363, 381, 382
Wowzitude 305
wyda 300

Z

Zimman, Jeff 201

about the author

SHERRI SNELLING is a corporate gerontologist, "authorpreneur" and founder/CEO of Caregiving Club, a strategic consulting and educational content creation firm with an expertise in caregiver wellness, well home design and brain health/Alzheimer's. She is the host of the podcast, "Caregiving Club On Air," producer/host of the cable reality TV show, "Handle With Care" and author of *Me Time Monday – The Weekly Wellness Plan to Find Balance and Joy for a Busy Life* and *A Cast of Caregivers – Celebrity Stories to Help You Prepare to Care*. Snelling writes articles for various online news outlets and serves as an on-air aging wellness expert for TV and radio news. She advises Fortune 1000 companies and start-ups in the longevity economy on caregiving and wellness programs as well as on well home and office interior design. She also conducts caregiver wellness educational workshops and webinars for employer groups and other organizations and speaks internationally on topics from her books. Snelling has served on aging and caregiving advisory committees for the White House, the Center for Disease Control & Prevention (CDC), Centers for Medicare and Medicaid Services (CMS), Alzheimer's Association, the National Institute on Aging and Georgetown University. She also is a mentor for the Techstars and Pivotal Ventures longevity start-up incubator program. Snelling has a master's degree in gerontology from USC Leonard Davis School of Gerontology and a master's certification from MIT Sloan School of Management on Shaping the Jobs of the Future. She lives in Newport Beach, California.

www.ingramcontent.com/pod-product-compliance
Lightning Source LLC
Chambersburg PA
CBHW070744060526
44119CB00099B/475/J